Understanding Communication and Aging

This book is dedicated to Jean and Tony Harwood.

Understanding Communication and Aging

Developing Knowledge and Awareness

Jake Harwood
University of Arizona

SAGE Publications
Los Angeles • London • New Delhi • Singapore

For information:

Sage Publications, Inc.
2455 Teller Road
Thousand Oaks, California 91320
E-mail: order@sagepub.com

Sage Publications India Pvt. Ltd.
B-42, Panchsheel Enclave
Post Box 4109
New Delhi 110 017 India

Sage Publications Ltd.
1 Oliver's Yard
55 City Road
London EC1Y 1SP
United Kingdom

Sage Publications Asia-Pacific Ptd. Ltd.
33 Pekin Street #02-01
Far East Square
Singapore 048763

Printed in the United States of America

Library of Congress Cataloging-in-Publication Data

Harwood, Jake.
Understanding communication and aging : Developing knowledge and awareness/Jake Harwood.
     p. cm.
Includes bibliographical references and index.
ISBN 978-1-4129-2609-6 (pbk.)
    1. Aging. 2. Older people—Health and hygiene. 3. Older people—Communication.
4. Interpersonal communication. 5. Intergenerational communication. 6. Old age—Social aspects. I. Title.
RA564.8.H37 2007
613′.0438—dc22   2006101375

Printed on acid-free paper.

07   08   09   10   11   10 9 8 7 6 5 4 3 2 1⁻

Acquiring Editor:	Todd R. Armstrong
Editorial Assistant:	Katie Grim
Production Editor:	Sarah K. Quesenberry
Copy Editor:	Teresa Wilson
Proofreader:	Colleen Brennan
Typesetter:	C&M Digitals (P) Ltd.
Indexer:	Wendy Allex
Cover Designer:	Edgar Abarca
Associate Marketing Manager:	Amberlyn M. Erzinger

Brief Contents

Contents

Acknowledgments

W ork with many mentors, collaborators, and students has contributed immensely to the development of this book. In many cases these are also personal friends, so I trust they'll forgive me for using (hopefully not stealing!) their good ideas. Thanks are due to Howie Giles, Mary Lee Hummert, Nikolas Coupland, Jon Nussbaum, Ellen Ryan, Justine Coupland, Jordan Soliz, Yan Bing Zhang, Karen Anderson, Mei-Chen Lin, Priya Raman, Angie Williams, Miles Hewstone, Tito Roy, Lisa Sparks, Jaye Atkinson, Loretta Pecchioni, Cindy Gallois, Hiroshi Ota, Sik Hung Ng, Richard Clément, Richard Bourhis, and undoubtedly many others. I owe a particular debt to Howie, Jon, Ellen, Mary Lee, Nik, and Justine who as (relatively!) senior scholars were endlessly supportive of my interest in communication and aging when I was very early in my career. I thank those who reviewed chapters from the book: Jaye L. Atkinson (Georgia State University), Jo Anna Grant (California State University, San Bernardino), Sherry J. Holladay (Eastern Illinois University), Judith K. Litterst (St. Cloud State University), Sandra Metts (Illinois State University), Loretta L. Pecchioni (Louisiana State University), Jim L. Query, Jr. (University of Houston), Lisa Sparks (Chapman University), and Janelle D. Voegele (Portland State University). The feedback was uniformly constructive and incredibly useful. Mei-Chen Lin also provided invaluable feedback on Chapter 10. I also thank those who contributed to the book by writing their personal narratives—they're a great addition, and I appreciate the time put into them. I am indebted to the team at Sage, particularly Todd Armstrong who persuaded me to begin the project and then shepherded me through the obstacle course of book writing with a permanently encouraging tone. I thank my colleagues at the University of Arizona who provide a great working environment, as well as my former colleagues at the University of Kansas and the University of California, Santa Barbara, who did likewise. Everyone involved in the National Communication Association's "Communication and Aging Division" also deserves mention: The division has served as a wonderful resource and meeting place for people with an interest in the issues addressed in this book. Finally, thanks are due to Lori, Chloe, and Jonah who help me understand more about family relationships and human development than any book ever could.

*I wonder if age, in fact, may offer the opportunity
to develop values and abilities, for each of us and for society,
that are not visible or fully realized in youth.*

—Betty Friedan, *The Fountain of Age*

PART I

——•◦•——

Introduction to the Study of Aging and Intergenerational Communication

The first part of this book introduces central theories of aging and discusses different disciplinary approaches to aging. The first chapter focuses primarily on aging, the second primarily on communication, but links between the two are drawn where appropriate.

⊰ ONE ⊱

Perspectives on Aging

This chapter presents central theories
of aging from different disciplines
and describes the approach taken in
the current book. By the end of this
chapter you should be able to:

- Describe demographic changes
  that will occur in the next
  50 years
- Describe the variability among
  older people
- Distinguish between
  biological, psychological,
  sociological, and life-span
  approaches to aging, and be
  able to talk about some
  theories of aging
- Understand the difference
  between a longitudinal and a
  cross-sectional design for studying aging
- Understand the difference between qualitative and quantitative
  approaches

SOURCE: © Renee Lee/Istockphoto.com

Simply put I want to grow old,
Dying does not meet my expectation

—Pavement, "We Are Underused"

S o do *you* want to get old? Given the choice, most people do—it is better than the alternative! Benjamin Franklin is thought to have said that the only two things in life that are inevitable are death and taxes. Well, you can add aging to that list. *All* of us are getting older *all* of the time, and while modern medicine, cosmetics, and plastic surgery may mitigate some of the things that come along with aging, they don't change the course of time.

This book is about communication and aging. I am going to be describing how we talk about age and how our communication sometimes betrays our less-than-positive perceptions of aging. I will be exploring some of the pleasures and pitfalls that occur when younger and older people talk to one another. I will also be discussing broader issues of how whole societies communicate about aging (for instance, through mass media). As you read the book, it is important to remember that aging is something that is happening to all of us. If you are 60, you are probably well aware of this; if you are 20, you may not have thought about it so much. On the next page, you'll find an exercise that you should complete before reading any further.

I am going to use the term **aging** to refer to the passing of time for an individual—the inevitable chronological change in our age from year to year. You perhaps use "aging" to refer to other things—a progression of physical decline, a change in family roles (e.g., becoming a grandparent), a change in work status (retirement), or forgetting where you left your keys. While some of these may be *associated* with increasing age, to call them "aging" confuses the issue. Aging is not associated with physical decline for all individuals at all points in time, so we need to separate the two concepts. Likewise, I am going to avoid talking about how we "stay young" on the basis that it is impossible. We may want to stay fit, healthy, socially active, or in touch with the current music scene, but treating those things as equivalent to being "young" only serves to reinforce notions about aging that (as I will argue) are inappropriate. Staying physically fit is an excellent idea; "staying young" is impossible. This book

Exercise 1.1 **Perceptions and Expectations of My Own Aging**

```
|
|
|
|
|
|
|
|
|
|
|
|_____
  [ Birth ]  |————————————————————————————————▶|  [ Death ]
```

1. Draw a line (like a temperature chart) across the page to depict the peaks and troughs that you have experienced and that you expect to experience in your life.

2. Use vertical lines to divide your lifeline up into important life periods, with as many or as few stages as you like.

3. Give each stage a name and indicate the approximate age at which it starts and ends.

4. Above each stage mark ++, +, 0, −, or − −, depending upon how you feel about that stage.

5. Answer the following questions:
    - What is the shape of the line, and what does that tell you about your experiences and expectations? What does a peak indicate? Happiness? Wealth? Control over your life?
    - Are the peaks and troughs major or minor?
    - Is there more volatility (ups and downs) during certain periods of the life span?
    - How could you decrease the troughs, increase the peaks? What changes could you have made in the past (or might you make in the future) to make life better?
    - Might some positive results have emerged from the troughs, or negative results from the peaks?
    - Where are the divisions closest together? Further apart?
    - What are the important events/issues marking boundaries between stages?
    - Why did transitions occur at the time that they did? Are these transitions that lots of other people might experience at about the same time, or are they unique to you?

6. If you are working as a class, consider sharing your (anonymous) responses and discussing some of the differences.

SOURCE: This exercise is derived from Whitbourne and Dannefer (1985) and Harwood and Giles (1994).

focuses on older adults—the group that perhaps you've talked about as "the elderly." However, it is important to remember that older adults don't appear out of nowhere. They used to be younger adults and children, so to understand them, we have to consider the entire life span.

To begin, let's think about why studying human aging is a valuable thing to do.

Why Study Aging?

Recently, the obvious answer to this question has been a **demographic** one. Following the Second World War, there was a worldwide surge in births (the **baby boom**). In part, this was because families had postponed childbirth until the war was over. But it was also a result of increased wealth and availability of devices like washing machines—it's easier to have kids if you have more money and more time-saving devices! The elevated birth rates lasted into the early 1960s, and the baby boom generation is generally defined as those born between 1946 and 1964. Population change is also occurring as a result of **life expectancy**. Currently, individuals turning 65 in the United States can expect to live about another 20 years, and that number is increasing all the time. If we treat age 65 as the start of older adulthood, then the oldest baby boomers will enter older adulthood in 2010. They will continue to be a significant influence on the population well into the middle of the 21st century.

Figure 1.1 shows a **population pyramid** for the United States in the year 2005. Notice that it's shaped something like a house with a pitched roof: Younger generations are roughly equal in size, but above the age of about 50, the size of the population begins to shrink (hence the term "pyramid"). In contrast, Figure 1.2 shows a projection of the U.S. population in 2050. Notice the bulging shape, and the fact that the slimming at the top of the pyramid occurs later (above age 60). In particular, it's interesting to note a very substantial increase between the two figures in the number of individuals 90 years and older. Thus, simply the number of older people in the United States has made studying aging important. Similar trends exist worldwide—indeed the baby boom in East Asia is larger than in the United States. Figure 1.3 shows what the Chinese population will look like in 2050. Compared with Figure 1.2, you can see that the shape for China is even more "top heavy," and that those 60 to 64 years old are the largest single age group in the entire

Figure 1.1   U.S. Population Pyramid: 2005

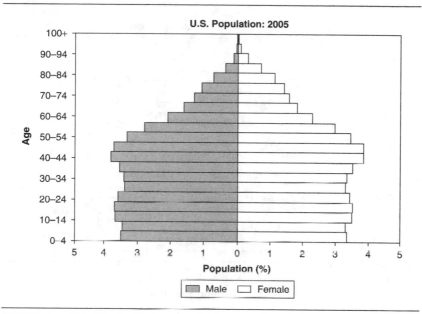

SOURCE: From United Nations Department of Economic and Social Affairs (2005).

Figure 1.2   U.S. Population Pyramid: 2050

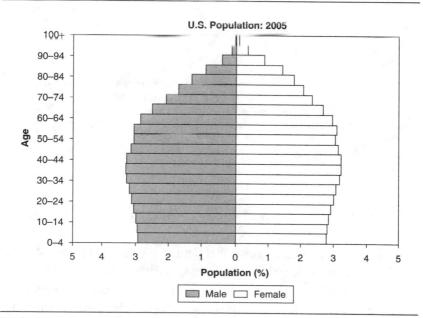

SOURCE: From United Nations Department of Economic and Social Affairs (2005).

Figure 1.3   China Population Pyramid: 2050

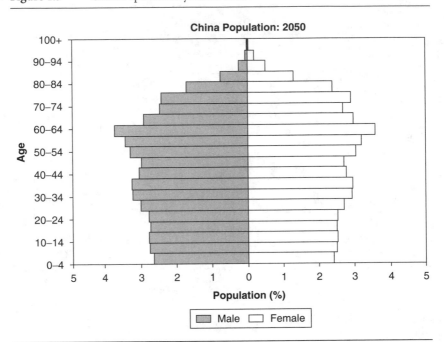

SOURCE: From United Nations Department of Economic and Social Affairs (2005).

Exercise 1.2   **Demographics of Aging**

Pick a country. Go to http://esa.un.org/unpp/ and download population data for that country for the current time and for the year 2050 (you'll need to click on "detailed data" and go to "population by five year age and sex"). If you are working as a class, compare some of the different patterns observed in how populations change over time for different nations. Consider South Africa, Russia, Zimbabwe, Nepal, or Brazil as countries with interestingly different profiles.

---

population. Exercise 1.2 shows you how to create a population pyramid for other countries and times.

Before moving to other issues, it is perhaps worth noting that the "tidal wave" of older people has been the subject of much social discussion in recent years, and this will probably increase as more boomers retire. Some of these discussions have fed the fires of prejudice against older people: "They" are presented as an enormous and greedy mass who are going to strain our health care system, destroy pension funds, and generally disrupt how society functions. Hence, while it is important to describe imminent demographic changes, it is also crucial to exercise caution that such discussions do not reinforce prejudicial myths about the older population (N. Coupland & J. Coupland, 1999).

Demographics aside, there are many other important reasons why we should be interested in studying aging. All humans share the experience of thinking about their past and their experiences when they were younger, as well as contemplating possibilities for the future. Part of the study of aging is trying to make sense of what it means to be the same person inhabiting many different roles, bodies, and age groups with the passing of time. Aging is also interesting for some of the paradoxes it encompasses. For instance, one paradox is that most young people claim to love their grandparents, but in general they are not very fond of older people as a group (see Chapters 3–4). We often discriminate against older people, even though eventually we are going to become one (see Chapter 3). We often claim that old age is associated with great wisdom and knowledge, yet as a society we rarely listen to older people talk (and when we are forced to, we often don't enjoy it very much—see Chapter 5). Hence, we should be interested in studying aging so as to understand these paradoxes, and hopefully improve relations between older and younger people in society.

Finally, old age is also interesting because of the **diversity** in the older adult population. Far from being a homogenous group, over 65s are incredibly diverse (Dannefer & Perlmutter, 1990). Researchers are interested in uncovering the causes for that diversity: Why is it that one 70-year-old can end up as president, while another requires care in a nursing home? The variability among older adults becomes particularly clear with recent increases in longevity. Between ages 65 and 95 there is a huge amount of change in our bodies and minds. P. B. Baltes (1997) calls those 80 and older the "fourth age" and describes that age group as a new frontier for research. This is largely uncharted territory for scientists because people in this age group were extremely rare until fairly recently. When we compare people in the "fourth age" with the "young old" (roughly 65–80 years old) we can see some dramatic differences in physical well-being, social functioning, and the like. In Chapter 2, for example, we'll see the dramatic differences in the prevalence of Alzheimer's disease between 70- versus 90-year-olds. Finally, there are diversity implications related to sex and ethnicity. Chapter 10 will address some of the cultural variability in aging: Getting old is simply not the same experience for people in different cultural groups. Similarly, getting old can be quite different for men versus women. For instance, women are much more likely to lose a spouse as they get older (because men die younger, and women tend to marry slightly older men). All of these examples point to the conclusion that older people are very diverse, and scientists need to understand more about that diversity.

Why I Study Communication and Aging
Jake Harwood (Professor, University of Arizona)

During my teenage years I became increasingly interested in issues of prejudice against people of other nationalities, ethnic groups, religious orientations, and the like. Why are such forms of hatred so widespread, and why do they seem so hard to get rid of? This interest was stoked in my undergraduate classes (I was a Psych major)—there I learned about theories of racism, intergroup relations, and social identity. During this period, I also came to recognize that prejudice against older adults was similarly widespread, and similarly hard to get rid of. And over time I came to understand that this prejudice was just as wrong, and just as interesting from a communication perspective as any of the others. Along with this personal journey, my interest in aging was spurred by all of the great people who study communication and aging issues—you'll see and hear about many of them in this book. These people have inspired and encouraged me. Finally, my own aging has made me more directly aware of the personal stake that we all have in understanding more about aging, and in trying to change ageist attitudes.

Approaches to Aging

It is possible to study aging from biological, psychological, or sociological perspectives (among many others). The way in which you begin thinking about aging will probably influence the conclusions that you draw, so we will consider a few of these perspectives. It should be noted that the field of **gerontology** (the study of aging) is relatively new, and hence most people in the area come from other disciplines (e.g., they are gerontologists who were originally trained as psychologists). Hence, the study of aging tends to be interdisciplinary—it spans a lot of the traditional boundaries established in universities. Below, I consider some of the most common approaches people have taken to studying aging, briefly describing the kind of knowledge that emerges when we take each approach.

Biological/Biomedical Approaches

For many people, studying aging is all about biological changes that are generally negative: illness, decline, and ultimately death. Attempting to understand the biological and biomedical processes that underlie aging can help us understand how to intervene in age-related illnesses, can spur the development of new and more effective medicines, and can improve the quality of life for older people. Biological theories of aging are complex and not central to this book. However, it is important to be aware that scientists remain somewhat uncertain about what causes physical symptoms associated with old age.

Some focus on the process of gene reproduction and mutation. Our genetic material (DNA) is being reproduced constantly, and during the process of reproduction, errors occur. One theory of aging suggests that the accumulation of these errors over time causes problems in the production of proteins (very basic building blocks of life) that make it more likely that crucial organs, like the brain, liver, or heart, will stop functioning properly.

Other biological approaches focus on metabolism rate (the speed with which bodies perform their basic chemical functions). These theories suggest that organisms that live longer have slower metabolism rates. Mice, for example, don't live very long and have exceedingly high metabolism rates (they almost literally burn themselves out very quickly: Flaming mice, Batman!). If physical decline associated with aging is a function of metabolism rate, then we should be able to extend our lives by slowing our metabolism rate, and such effects have been shown in some creatures. For instance, mice that are fed calorie-restricted diets (no Big Macs!) tend to live substantially longer than mice whose food intake is not restricted. Proponents of this theory have advocated seriously calorie-restricted diets for humans to slow the metabolism and thus increase the life span. Experiments on humans in this area are obviously challenging.

The **Free Radical** theory proposes that certain highly reactive agents in the body ("Free Radicals") cause damage to all sorts of parts of our body over time. These free radicals are produced as a natural part of body chemistry. As the damage they cause accumulates, so are serious malfunctions in body functioning more likely (disease, organ failure, etc.).

Finally, cross-linking theories suggest that over time certain proteins in our body start to connect to one another when they shouldn't. This is clearly evident in the skin, which even at relatively young ages begins to lose the smoothness and elasticity it had when we were babies. While skin is fairly superficial (only skin deep!), such processes occurring elsewhere might cause more significant problems. For instance, proponents of this theory explain vision decline with aging as a function of proteins cross-linking in the eye's lens, which reduces the normal flexibility of the lens that allows our eyes to focus.

The common thread across all of these theories is that the body slowly wears itself out, whether as a function of internally produced complications or environmental damage. However, what is also clear from many of these theories is that some of the changes that we view as "inevitable" with aging could actually be addressed with preventative care. If metabolism rate influences our life span, we can eat fewer calories. If it's free radicals, then substances like vitamin C may be very important, because they neutralize free radicals. Indeed, we need only look at the changes in longevity over the past 100 years to understand the impact of lifestyle on age-related processes. In Western nations, life expectancy increased from about 45 years in 1900 to about 75 years in 1995. In the United States, the National Center for Health Statistics (Hoyert, Kung, & Smith, 2005) reports life expectancy of 77.6 years in 2003, up from 77.3 years in 2002—so babies born just a year later are expected to have an average life span about 4 months longer. Such changes are a function of lifestyle developments (better diet, better understanding and treatment of disease, better education, and the like: P. B. Baltes, 1997). Therefore, it is clear that the nature of biological change that occurs with aging is distinctly "plastic"—it can be changed.

Nonetheless, some illnesses and conditions continue to be chronically associated with old age. Evolutionary biologists have discussed why "natural selection" hasn't taken care of such problems. Didn't Darwin say that over time the fittest would survive? So why do people continue to experience negative health consequences in old age (like **Alzheimer's disease**)? Put simply, there is no **evolutionary selection** *against* genes that predispose us to Alzheimer's disease (or other physical problems associated with old age), and there is no evolutionary selection *in favor* of genes that might protect us against the disease. By the time the disease develops, we have already reproduced and passed our genes on to the next generation. Because old age occurs after we've had children, as a population we do not select against predisposing genes, or in favor of protective genes, in the way that we might for a disease that produced symptoms in the teenage or early adult years. Indeed, the evolutionary significance of old age is remarkably complex. Some have suggested that old people are detrimental to a species' success (because they use resources that could be used by younger, reproductively active individuals). These theories have not received a lot of support from researchers (or from those who advocate for older adults!). Other researchers have noted that the presence of older adults in a community has many positive effects. For instance, grandparents can serve a fundamentally important role in caring for grandchildren in societies where parents are involved in farming, hunting, or industry. At least one area of research has suggested that significant strides in human culture are directly traceable to the point in time when people's life spans reached the length that grandparenting was possible (Caspari & Lee, 2004; Hawkes, 2003).

Psychological Approaches

Like biologists, many psychologists focus on decline and deficit in aging. A great deal of attention in this area has focused on memory and the ways in which people forget more when they get old. While evidence has emerged showing that memory deficits can be a problem in old age, some work has also demonstrated that certain elements of memory are largely spared. Short-term memory appears to be more of a concern than long-term memory. So, for instance, as we get older we may have a harder time remembering a 7-digit phone number for long enough to find a pen and write it down. However, we are just as likely to be able to remember the state capital of Kentucky (if you're interested, it's Frankfort).

A second area of decline is that suggested by **disengagement theory**. This theory suggested that older adults disengage from society and their social networks as they approach death. This increasing isolation in older adults was suggested to be functional for older people and those around them (particularly in terms of decreasing stress and bereavement associated with death). This theory has been largely discredited. However, a more recent ewhat similar predictions and has received more support. selectivity theory predicts that older individuals are more 'here and now," and hence will focus on the relationships that with the most significant rewards, while reducing their invest- peripheral relationships. This theory has received support, with evidence at older adults focus their energies on family, for instance, and are less concerned with collecting large numbers of casual acquaintances than younger people (Carstensen, 1992). Hence, while older adults' networks of social relationships do get *smaller*, it is incorrect to view this as a *decline* of any kind. Rather, it reflects focusing and shifting emphasis (see Chapter 5).

Continuity theory is a theory of aging that downplays the changes associated with aging, and instead focuses on what doesn't change. Research emerging from this theory has consistently uncovered patterns of stability in old age. Our personalities, our preferences and tastes, the activities we enjoy and those we don't enjoy all remain relatively stable and predictable in old age. Continuity theory is a useful theoretical framework for those who are terrified of aging. In spite of the notion that everything is going to fall apart at age 65, in fact, things are going to remain much the same!

Activity theory is a psychosocial theory designed to explain successful aging. This theory suggests that those who maintain high levels of activity will be more successful in aging. Extensive support for this theory emerges in studies of older adults who maintain hobbies, develop new ones, and remain socially active. These older people are happier, healthier, and live longer than those who do not maintain their activity level.

A final substantial area of social psychological research has been on issues of attitudes about aging and stereotypes of the elderly. Because of the very direct links between this work and the study of communication, this work is described in considerable detail in Chapter 3. However, for now it is worth noting that psychologists and communication scholars have discovered a lot about why we aren't always very positive about getting old.

Sociological Approaches

One substantial emphasis of sociologists has been on the demographics of aging. While some baby boomers were still in diapers, sociologists were already beginning to consider the impact of this group on the population as they entered older adulthood. Sociologists have been particularly concerned with the ability of social institutions to cope with a large population of older adults. They are also interested in phenomena like the geographic mobility of older adults. For instance, here in Tucson we have a large older adult population that is only here for about half of the year—they very sensibly escape the city during the extreme heat of summer! For a sociologist, this raises interesting questions about the availability of social services for year-round older residents—either services are "stretched" beyond capacity during the winter, or they have excess capacity in the summer. There are also interesting questions here regarding the friendship networks of older people in this sort of context—do they maintain two separate networks of friends in their two cities of residence?

Another important demographic issue is the sex ratio among older people. Among people 65 and older, 58% are women and 42% men. This ratio becomes even more skewed with advancing age: 80-year-olds are only about 35% men. The implications of these disparities for providing services, financial planning, health care decision making, and personal relationships are, as you can imagine, substantial. To the extent that sociologists overlap with those interested in social policy issues, these scholars are concerned with the provision of services to older adults and government policies regarding aging. These are the experts you see on television talking about the Social Security system reform in the United States. Included in this group would be a cadre of people who examine, for instance, the influence of retiring baby boomers on the stock market—if older people sell their stocks to buy more conservative investments, will the market crash?

A few theoretical approaches are worthy of brief mention here. **Modernization theory** examines the ways in which societal changes influence the place of older people. Specifically, theorists in this tradition argue that more "modern" societies (think big cities and suburbs, Wal-Mart, computers) have led to a more peripheral position for older adults in society. Evidence for this can be seen in some traditional cultures where traditionally older adults live with their family members. With a move to city living, there is less space in the children's homes, and the extended family living structure has broken down. However, some question the assumptions underlying this theory, particularly as even in very "modern" societies, children continue to provide extensive support for aging parents, albeit perhaps of a different nature from in the past. Others also question whether there ever really was a time when older people were fully integrated.

Social stratification theory concerns itself with the ways in which age, like gender and race, serves as an organizing principle for social life. Theorists from this perspective would be interested in examining the extent to which societies are segregated by age. For instance, if you look around a university campus, you tend to find a large number of people in their late teens and early 20s, and not many people much older than that (except for the occasional professor, perhaps). In contrast, if you drive through certain neighborhoods, you may find them almost exclusively inhabited by families with young children, or in other cases by retired people. How this happens and its implications for the organization of social behavior would be of interest to stratification theorists. Is this extent of age segregation functional for society, or does it cause problems? Some sociologists advocate higher levels of age integration and experimental concepts like multigenerational living environments and schools.

Sociologists have also been at the forefront of criticizing how we think about aging as a society. In particular, those who focus on the **political economy of aging** are concerned with how social and economic structures maintain negative life circumstances for older people. Estes and Binney (1989) describe what they call the biomedicalization of aging. They discuss how we have come to see aging as an exclusively medical and biological phenomenon—it is something to be treated medically. This occurs because of the focus of the medical community on profit rather than health: For many medical institutions, it is in their interest to encourage older adults' dependence on the medical system, rather than encouraging older people toward health and independence. Thus, ill health and decline in old age can be understood as socially constructed phenomena: As a society we create the conditions in which it is easy for older people to buy into their own decline, and very difficult for them to maintain independence and health. Political economy theorists criticize spiraling health care costs and declining quality of care, and point to the ways in which government and private industry sometimes appear to collaborate to achieve goals that are in their mutual interest, but perhaps not in the interest of older adults.

Life-Span Developmental Approaches

Erik Erikson (e.g., 1968) may be the first social scientist to consider human development as a **life-span** phenomenon. Prior to Erikson's work (in the late 1950s), human development was something that stopped at the end of childhood—"children develop, adults don't" was the philosophy of the day. In contrast, **Erikson's theory** described various developmental "tasks" that we all have to accomplish throughout our lives. For instance, he said that people in middle age are focused on issues of generativity: A successful middle age is one that is focused on creation and production. This might include productivity at work as well as creating and nurturing a family. Erikson argued that those who do not feel that they have been successful in producing something worthwhile during this phase will not "pass" one of the life span's "tests," and may suffer psychological problems (e.g., depression). Erikson's theory is now a little outdated: His work failed to consider the possibility for continued developmental challenges late into old age, and his final stage of development puts too much emphasis on achieving a final resolution and "closure," rather than engaging in a continued challenge. Nonetheless, his work has set the stage for a proliferation of theory and writing that has come in the subsequent years, and he really was revolutionary in drawing attention to developmental tasks and challenges that occur throughout adulthood.

A more recent life-span developmental approach that offers promise for all people interested in aging is the **Selective Optimization with Compensation** (SOC) model (P. B. Baltes & M. M. Baltes, 1990). This approach acknowledges that at all stages of the life span, there are things that we are good at, and things that we are not so good at. At all ages, we resign ourselves to dependence on certain fronts, in order to gain independence on other fronts. When we are very young, we focus on particular developmental tasks (e.g., learning to read, understanding social interaction) and happily delegate others (when did you last see a 3-year-old cooking dinner?). At other points in our life, the balance shifts — in middle age we might invest relatively little in furthering our education, while focusing a lot on our careers ("Show me the money!"). At this stage, we might have limited time or motivation for taking care of our yard, so we pay somebody to do that for us. In other words, we **select** particular areas of our lives, **optimize** our performance in those areas, and **compensate** in those areas where we lack ability or motivation. P. B. Baltes (1997) describes how the 80-year-old concert pianist Arthur Rubenstein accounted for his continued success in spite of his age. Rubenstein reportedly said that he **selected** fewer pieces to play, practiced them a lot (**optimized**), and **compensated** for declines in his own skill with clever strategies. For instance, he couldn't play the fast bits of some pieces quite as quickly as when he was younger. So instead, he would play particularly *slowly* before he got to the fast bits, thus making his performance of the fast bits seem faster!

The SOC model questions our general inclination to view childhood as a time of gain, and old age as a time of loss. It introduces the idea that we experience gains and losses at all points in the life span. Consider, for instance, the ways in which children become more inhibited and less able to engage in imaginary play as they get older, while simultaneously gaining technical and social skills. Successfully negotiating development is often a process of deciding which areas to select and optimize, and where and how to compensate for losses in other areas. The SOC model presents an optimistic view of old age as a time when we are continuing to do what we've done all our lives: Focus our energies on the things that are important to us, and look for help with the things that we don't have the time or ability to do ourselves. Table 1.1 presents a list of assumptions that underlie most "life-span developmental" theories. The SOC is a nice example of such a theory, but all such theory has similar sets of assumptions.

Table 1.1   Principles of a Life-Span Approach to Human Development

Principle	Definition/Example
We develop and grow throughout the life span.	Development doesn't just happen in childhood. It continues, and at any age we can still be learning new things, and adapting to environmental changes and challenges.
Development involves gains and losses on different dimensions.	Development is not just about getting physically stronger and intellectually smarter. It is about coping with what life throws at you. A time of physical decline may be a time of great intellectual accomplishment, or great social rewards.
Age constrains but does not control development.	The life-span approach does not deny that age influences development—it is unlikely that a 90-year-old will ever win the 100-meter dash at the Olympics. However, humans are immensely adaptable; there are almost infinite options available to us at almost all points in our lives, and successful development is a function of how we deal with those options.
Environment and history constrain but do not control development.	The specifics of our social and physical environment, and the period during which we live, shape our development, but do not control us. Some challenges kill us; others make us stronger. Social and cultural forces interact with the biological in profound ways.

SOURCE: Derived from P. B. Baltes (1987).

Of course, old age presents some unique challenges, in part because it is such a new phase of life in our culture. The numbers of older adults in society are unprecedented. Aging beyond age 70 was not something that society had to take seriously a hundred years ago. Now it is expected, and we will soon have almost a quarter of the world's population in that age range. We have not had time to culturally adjust to that change in our demographic profile, but it is interesting to ponder how society might change in the future to fully realize the potential of this group of people.

ACHIEVEMENTS IN OLD AGE

Lillien Jane Martin

Lillien Jane Martin was born in 1851. She defied the odds for women of the time and graduated from college, going on to teach high school for a number of years. She became increasingly interested in the field of psychology and quit her teaching job to study for a Ph.D. in Germany. In 1909 (aged 58), she was appointed as a Professor of Psychology at Stanford University and went on to be department head—the first woman to head any department at Stanford. After she retired (involuntarily!) at age 65, Dr. Martin went on to write some of the key works that founded the modern study of gerontology, as well as found a clinic for older people at age 78. In 1913, when Martin was 62, the University of Bonn awarded her with an honorary Ph.D.: As part of the award, the university noted that she was "the most distinguished, most illustrious woman . . . worthy both by name and reputation, philosophical, strenuous, strong, successful, most esteemed in experimental psychology and aesthetics." Martin continued working and published books into her 80s, providing some key grounding for today's study of old age. Foreshadowing some of the perspectives presented in this book, she once said, "Age is an accident and nothing to pride oneself on. The important thing is to adapt oneself to the requirements of each successive age class and to function in each as an active participant in life, a fully adjusted human being." Martin lived her own philosophy well: According to the official memorial resolution published by Stanford when she died, she learned to drive a car at the age of 78, and subsequently drove across the country twice. Learning new skills and contributing new ideas are clearly things that are possible even into advanced old age.

Methods for Studying Aging

All research methods that are applied to social phenomena can be used for studying aging. Researchers interested in aging processes use interviews and questionnaires to ask people about their experiences of aging, feelings about older adulthood, and the like. They also use experiments to manipulate various aspects of the environment to see if they have effects on our opinions about aging, or the actual experience of aging. In addition, a multitude of observational methods are used, such as visiting retirement communities and nursing homes to observe how they function, or asking young and old people to have conversations while they are videotaped. With aging, though, some additional considerations come into play—we become interested in how people are changing as they get older, and to understand that, we need some rather specific methods.

Some researchers employ **cross-sectional designs.** These are designs in which people from different age groups are examined at one point in time (e.g., by recruiting a group of 20-year-olds and a group of 70-year-olds, and comparing their scores on a memory test). These are relatively low-cost designs—all of the data can be gathered at a single point in time. However, we can't always interpret the findings. If the 20-year-olds do better on the memory test, is that because memory gets worse with age? If so, you have discovered a **developmental effect**—some fundamental change that occurs as we get older. However, it could be because people born 70 years ago ate less fish (fish is brain food, you know!), and so their memories are worse because of their diet. That would be a **cohort effect**—an effect that is the result of being born at a particular point in time. A cohort is any group of people born at roughly the same point in time, so a cohort effect is any difference between two groups of people that occurs because of *when* they were born, rather than because of how old they are. With cross-sectional designs, it is impossible to distinguish between developmental and cohort effects.

One partial solution to this problem can be found in **longitudinal** studies. These studies take a single group of people and track them over time. So, you start with a group of 20-year-olds and examine them every 10 years. After 50 years (at which point they will be 70) you will be able to see whether their memory has declined with age. If their memory is worse, you know it is *not* a cohort effect, because this is a single cohort. However, it is still possible that events specific to this cohort have caused the changes (for instance, air pollution during the intervening 50 years might have caused memory problems, rather than anything inherent to the process of aging). So we are still not sure that what we have observed is a developmental effect that would apply to all cohorts. After spending 50 years on the study, you can imagine that it is rather disappointing to discover that you can't draw any firm conclusions!!

To fully disentangle cohort effects and developmental effects, researchers have come up with various complex designs, generally known as **cross-sequential** methods. One type is illustrated in Table 1.2. In this design, groups of people of different ages (in this case, 20, 40, 60, and 80) are recruited at a particular point in time (in this case, the year 2000). Whatever variables are central to the study are measured (e.g., memory). Then, at some fixed interval (in this case, 20 years) the people are contacted again, and the variables of interest are measured again. In addition, every 20 years a new cohort of 20-year-olds is recruited. Essentially, this is the equivalent of running multiple longitudinal designs side by side. The arrows in the diagram indicate the direction of each longitudinal wave.

By using the type of design illustrated in the table, it is possible to understand whether effects are caused by cohort or life-span developmental factors. Differences across rows indicate cohort effects. Consider, for instance, all of the different 80-year-olds studied (shown in the ellipse). If we find that 80-year-olds in 2040 have better memories than 80-year-olds in 2000, that difference would clearly be a function of when they were born. Both groups are 80, so the memory difference between them can't have anything to do with their age, and hence it is not a developmental difference.

Table 1.2   A Cross-Sequential Research Design

		Year				
		2000	2020	2040	2060	2080
People studied	20-year-olds	20	20	20		
	40-year-olds	40	40	40	40	
	60-year-olds	60	60	60	60	60
	80-year-olds	80	80	80	80	80

NOTE: Numbers in the cells of the table indicate age of subjects at the time of measurement.

In contrast, if you observe consistent patterns of differences between two age groups no matter when they were born, then those differences are probably reflective of stable life-span developmental patterns. For instance, consider the various 20- and 40-year-olds that we can compare (shown in the grey boxes on diagonals). If 40-year-olds always have worse memories than 20-year-olds across all of those time periods, then we can be fairly confident that this is a life-span developmental trend. It seems to happen no matter which cohort people are from. Clearly the time and energy required to carry out these designs is considerable, and hence they get used fairly infrequently. In contrast, cross-sectional designs are cheap and easy to perform, and they are used a lot, despite their limitations. Possibly the most valuable thing that considering these designs does for us is draw attention to the many different interpretations of a difference we might observe between two age groups. Properly interpreting "age differences" is a very complicated task! Box 1.1 describes a more in-depth and context-rich approach to aging research.

Box 1.1   Qualitative and Interpretive Approaches to Aging:
The Example of Reminiscence

While a traditional "scientific" approach to aging encompasses some of the designs described in the text, it is also possible to examine aging through a more "qualitative" lens. Qualitative researchers try to understand aging by listening carefully to what people say about aging, and by examining older people's "real lives" (as opposed to their responses to questionnaires!). For instance, Buchanan and Middleton (1993) were interested in reminiscence activities in senior centers. In these activities, a facilitator (generally a nurse or social worker) works with groups of older people and encourages them to talk about their life experiences, ostensibly with the idea that this is psychologically functional for older people (e.g., it helps them achieve a sense of personal integrity). These researchers interviewed some facilitators and asked them how they felt about the groups. The goal of the research wasn't to find out whether reminiscing is good or bad for older people. Rather, the researchers wanted to understand how everyday communication about reminiscence shapes our understanding of getting old, older people, and elder care. For instance, one of the facilitators indicates that she is actually quite skeptical about the use of reminiscence, suggesting that it encourages older people to live in the past ("you gotta keep 'em up to date"). Another facilitator, on the other hand, strongly supports the idea that it's useful for the older adults ("you've got to remember your past 'cos that's a part of you"). A third person notes that it can be enlightening for those listening to hear reminiscence, thus focusing on the hearer rather than the speaker ("I feel very honored that I can learn so much about the past"). Thus, the care providers give different "versions" of what reminiscing is good for, and how it functions both for older speakers and the listener. These different versions are, in a sense, "theories" of reminiscence, and are used by the care providers to justify what they do or don't do in working with older people. This kind of research is valuable in giving life to the real voices of older adults and people who have contact with older adults. It also challenges us to think about how people "construct" views of aging in everyday talk: It forces us to recognize that some of what we take for granted about aging simply reflects our conventional patterns of talking about old age.

Summary

As with most aspects of human social life, the study of aging is complicated. It involves contributions from the biological and medical sciences as well as from across the social sciences. Different disciplines have quite different theories to understand aging, and to fully understand old age we must consider all disciplinary perspectives. Increasingly, we will also rely on the insights of gerontologists—people specifically trained to examine aging. As the final portion of the chapter showed, some of the methods we use to study aging are different, and in some ways more complicated, than methods used in other areas. As we face the demographic realities of the 21st century, understanding the why, how, and who of studying older adulthood will become more important. For people making career decisions, understanding aging can be particularly important: The Bureau of Labor Statistics estimates that the number of jobs related to aging will grow by almost 40% by the time we reach 2012, and will continue growing after that point. People who understand more about human aging will have a huge advantage in the labor market over the next 20–30 years. The next chapter will expand on a communication perspective on aging, discussing the kinds of insights that communication scholars can bring to this fascinating part of human life.

Keywords and Theories

Activity theory
Aging
Baby boom
Cohort effect
Continuity theory
Cross-sectional design
Cross-sequential design
Demographic
Developmental effect
Disengagement theory
Erikson's life-span theory
Evolutionary theory

Free Radical
Gerontology
Life expectancy
Life span
Longitudinal design
Modernization theory
Political economy of aging theory
Population pyramid
Selective optimization with
  compensation
Social stratification theory
Socioemotional selectivity theory

Discussion Questions

- How do changing population demographics influence individual lives? How might the aging of the baby boomers influence **your** life?
- What economic opportunities might arise as a result of the aging of the baby boomers?
- What are some ways in which you are currently facing issues of selection, optimization, and compensation in your own life?
- Why has "natural selection" not eliminated Alzheimer's disease?
- What does it mean to say that genes (or anything else) constrain, but do not control, development?

Annotated Bibliography

Estes, C. (Ed.). (2001). *Social policy and aging: A critical perspective.* Thousand Oaks, CA: Sage. A great example of a critical sociological approach to age and aging. Estes and colleagues criticize the way in which we approach and think about aging as a society, and present some radical alternatives.

Hawkes, K. (2003). Grandmothers and the evolution of human longevity. *American Journal of Human Biology, 15,* 380–400. A fascinating article discussing a variety of approaches to aging from an evolutionary perspective. Written in an accessible style, it's a great way to understand a "Darwinian" perspective on getting old.

Rowe, J. W., & Kahn, R. L. (1998). *Successful aging.* New York: Random House. A very readable examination of myths about aging, and a great personal guide for how to maximize your own older adulthood. Buy it for yourself, your aging parent, or grandparent.

TWO

A Communication Approach to Aging

This chapter presents the basics of
a communication approach to
aging. It describes some of the
basic changes that occur in
communication as people
get old, and outlines the approach
taken in rest of the book. By the
end of this chapter you should be
able to:

SOURCE: © Istockphoto.com

- Understand the difference
  between normal and pathological aging
- Understand how communication changes with normal aging
- Understand some of the communication changes that accompany
  Alzheimer's disease
- Express the core elements of an "intergroup" approach to aging
- Describe how communication might shape our understanding
  of getting old

For age is opportunity no less
Than youth, though in another dress,
And as the evening twilight fades away
The sky is filled with stars, invisible by day.

—H. W. Longfellow, *Morituri Salutamus*

Research in communication and aging has increased dramatically over the past 20 years. From an almost completely neglected topic of research, the study of aging has emerged as a theoretically important and widely studied area. There is a 600-page *Handbook of Communication and Aging Research* (now in its second edition, Nussbaum & Coupland, 2004), a division of the National Communication Association dedicated to the study of aging and communication issues, and numerous courses in communication and aging are taught around the United States. It has also become an increasingly international area of study, with scholars from Hong Kong, Taiwan, Australia, Wales, Canada, Japan, and many other countries taking their place along with the U.S. researchers.

This chapter presents some of the key elements that define a communication approach to older adulthood. I begin by discussing some research on decline and decrement (loss) in communication abilities during older adulthood. This work considers both "normal" decline and decline due to disease. Then, I outline what it might mean to have a positive research agenda for communication and aging—as a counterpoint to the research on decline. This part of the chapter also presents the key subfields of communication research that are central to this book, and presents some propositions that guide a positive communication research approach to older adulthood.

Decline in Communication

In this section, I briefly outline some of the key ways in which communication declines with age. The first section deals with **normal aging**—the sorts of changes that anybody might expect to experience as they get older. The second section deals with **pathological aging**—changes that might be experienced as part of an age-related illness or disease such as Alzheimer's disease.

Normal Aging

The term "normal aging" is a somewhat contentious one. Our understanding of what is "normal" as we get old is constantly changing, and things that we took for granted 20 years ago in terms of loss of function are no longer considered that way. As noted in the previous chapter, our expected life spans have grown so dramatically in the past 100 years that the study of 70- and 80-year-olds is a very new scientific enterprise. Hence, as we discuss normal aging in this section, it is only with regard to what we know now. In 20 years, the things that we now think are "normal" may seem bizarre.

Certain areas of **language comprehension** present problems in aging, a fact that has been explained in terms of changes in **short-term memory** capacity (see Chapter 1 for discussion of different types of memory). Age is associated with problems in understanding complex sentence structures— particularly sentences that involve **embedded clauses**. So, for instance, while older and younger adults are equally good at understanding a sentence like "The brown dog sat on the rug," older adults will have more problems with a sentence like "The brown dog, that I saw running away from the car yesterday, sat on the rug." These problems are most severe for older people who have more problems with short-term memory (Norman, Kemper, Kynette, Cheung, & Anagnopoulos, 1991). This makes some sense. In the second sentence above, to understand *what* is sitting on the rug you need to hold "the brown dog" in your head for a long period of time. Consider the following:

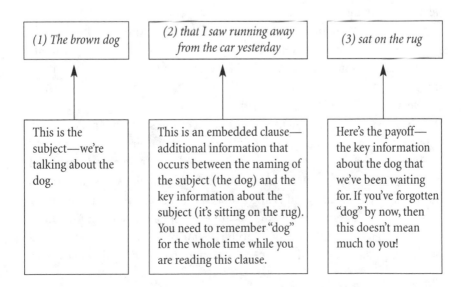

Similar patterns are apparent in **language production**. Older adults *produce* less complex grammatical structures, especially older people who have less short-term memory capacity (Kemper, Kynette, & Norman, 1992). Fast speech rate also results in decreased comprehension for older adults more than for younger adults (Stine & Wingfield, 1987). Interestingly, a number of the changes that can be seen in older people's language begin very early in life. For instance, the declines in memory capacity are seen as early as the 20s, and proceed in a fairly gradual and steady pattern through the life span: There is no sudden "cliff" in memory scores in older adulthood, although there are suggestions of a somewhat more rapid decline once people reach their 80s (Park et al., 2002).

Older adults also tend to have more problems in **recalling people's names** (Cohen, 1994). Indeed, when older people keep diaries of their memory problems, names come up repeatedly as a problem area. While forgetting a name might seem a trivial issue, it can clearly be embarrassing, and repeated instances of forgetting other people's names may result in discomfort in social situations that might have serious consequences for quality of life. Names present a somewhat unique challenge for all of us, given their arbitrary nature—unlike other words there are not many ways to "find" a name in your brain. When people forget other words they can replace them with pronouns (it, that), or with synonyms (if you forget the word for a car's "turn signal," you can say "flasher" or "blinker"). But pronouns are generally rude when dealing with other people ("Hello, you!"), and there are no synonyms for someone's name (Nussbaum, Hummert, Williams, & Harwood, 1996). Recent work suggests that the problems in recalling names are in retrieval: That is, it is not that older people have forgotten the names, but rather that they have a harder time retrieving them from their memory. For instance, it is very common for an older person to have a "tip of my tongue" experience when trying to recall the name of a famous person. They know that they know it, but just can't quite think of the correct name (James, 2006). It's also important to remember that young people also have trouble remembering names. It's only once people get older that they start attributing their forgetting to age—so some of what's going on here has to do with how people explain their forgetting (Erber & Prager, 2000).

More generally, though, there is quite a bit of evidence that verbal knowledge (e.g., vocabulary) increases steadily through the life span, into at least the 70s and perhaps beyond (Park et al., 2002). Hence, while impairment is apparent on certain fronts, other areas are fairly stable, or even improving.

Considerable communication problems for older adults are also caused by the normal age-related decline in hearing ability—called **presbycusis**.

Presbycusis is not a generalized "going deaf." Rather, it is a specific loss of high-frequency hearing ability (think birds chirping). When listening to speech, this can mean that certain sounds ("s," "th") are difficult to hear and distinguish, and thus the speech in general sounds unclear. Background noise exacerbates this problem. This means that an older adult may understand you just fine in a quiet context, but have considerable problems when other people are talking to each other in the same room. Again, of course, this can influence older people's willingness to engage in certain social activities in which noise is prevalent (cocktail parties, for instance). There are suggestions that presbycusis may contribute to some of the problems observed in other research—for instance, some of the declines we see in older people's ability to understand complex sentences might be because they are not hearing the sentences clearly (Schneider, Pichora-Fuller, Kowalchuk, & Lamb, 1994). The most prevalent cause of presbycusis is lifetime exposure to noise—it will be interesting to see the degree of hearing loss in old age for the iPod generation!

A final area is the study of older adults' cognitive inhibition abilities. Being able to think and communicate clearly has as much to do with what you *don't* think about as what you *do* think about. If you've ever tried to study with the television on, you know what I mean. We rely heavily on certain areas of our brain to help us inhibit thoughts that are irrelevant to what we are doing right now. This **inhibitory capacity** resides in the brain's frontal lobe (the bit right behind your forehead). If this ability declines, it can have dramatic effects on certain forms of communication. For instance, Gold and colleagues (e.g., Gold & Arbuckle, 1995; Gold, Arbuckle, & Andres, 1994) have studied **"off-target verbosity"**—the tendency of some older adults to engage in lengthy narratives that tend to drift far from their starting point in ways that may make sense to the speaker, but are very difficult for the listener to follow (e.g., see Box 2.1). A decline in inhibitory capacity would account for such communication. Irrelevant thoughts intrude during the telling of a story and cause the story to diverge from its original path. A decline in inhibitory capacity means that the person is not able to suppress those irrelevant thoughts and stay "on task." So, in Box 2.1, once she begins talking about her daughter and the trip, she is reminded of other issues concerning booking the flight and a party. These issues are not relevant to answering the question, but the ability to inhibit such irrelevant information appears to be absent. Some scholars say that these lapses result from a general decline in frontal lobe functioning that is part of normal aging (e.g., Hasher & Zacks, 1988). Others, however, attribute the association between inhibitory capacity and language use to pathological conditions. For instance, Gold and Arbuckle (1995) note that "off target verbosity" does not occur among all older people, and hence is probably a result of specific impairments or frontal lobe damage among those individuals rather than a shared deficit among all older people. The debate on whether off-target verbosity is "normal" or "pathological" is still ongoing. There is, however, increasing discussion among neuropsychologists concerning the role of the frontal lobes in many aspects of aging and cognitive processing, and this research makes clear that *some* decline in frontal lobe function is a normal part of aging (Phillips, MacPherson, & Sala, 2002). We turn next to some communication problems that are very clearly pathological rather than "normal."

Box 2.1   An Example of Off-Target Verbosity

Interviewer: How often do you see your daughter?

Respondent: I've gone down there twice, she's only been there three years. It's only an hour and 23 minutes by plane, but she said, "What the poop are you coming down for?" Because it was the Royal Commonwealth Conference and since they were preparing for Prince Edward and so she said, "Are you coming?" And so I phoned up Air Canada and I said I wanted a ticket. So I went the next day and it was my birthday and since it was my birthday and I had 12 little roses from my garden in a water vase. And I went back and I said "Don't us poor senior citizens get a break?" and she said "Why yes, dear," she said and took $90.00 off my bill, but I wasn't a delegate to the conference so I couldn't go to that, so my daughter phones Judge __ and the judge said "No, it's only for delegates" and I said "You mean I came all this way for nothing?" Anyway, we went to a dance and my daughter was clapping and snapping with all these people from Newfoundland, Oh my God, and she told all these people that it was her mother's birthday and she made them all sing Happy Birthday and they gave me a long-playing record . . .

[The authors report that this person continued to speak extensively for quite a while longer.]

SOURCE: From Gold et al., 1994.

Pathological Aging: The Case of Alzheimer's Disease

Probably the most discussed pathology of aging is **Alzheimer's disease** (AD). Like many issues associated with aging, AD is relatively rare among the younger old—only about 3% of 65- to 75-year-olds suffer from the disease (interestingly, a small percentage of even younger people have so-called early onset AD, which can strike people in their 30s). However, the disease becomes increasingly common with increasing age, and estimates indicate that up to 50% of people over 85 suffer from the disease (P. B. Baltes, 1997). This is a complex brain illness that causes minor confusion in its early stages and severe **dementia** (mental malfunction) in its later stages. It is ultimately fatal. Given its progressive nature, the communicative issues associated with AD vary considerably as it gets more severe. Be aware that AD is only definitively identified after death (by an examination of the brain): There is no simple test to determine whether a living person has AD. Hence, you hear a lot of references to "probable" Alzheimer's.

Alzheimer's is a complex disease, and it can follow very different pathways among different people. It is a disease that progresses through stages, typically over a period of years, with early stages of the disease being characterized by mild confusion and memory problems, and later stages featuring much more significant and obvious mental and behavioral problems. The most common finding regarding AD patients' *communication* is that **syntax** (grammar) tends to be preserved, while semantic (meaning) and lexical (word) processes become progressively more impaired. What does that mean? Well, it means that people with AD can produce grammatical sentences and notice when sentences are not grammatical. However, they have increasing trouble coming up with the right word for things (lexical problems), and they have broader problems with the *meaning* of language. So, for example, someone with moderate to advanced AD might have trouble distinguishing a meaningful sentence from one that is *grammatically correct* but ridiculous. A sentence like "Sally gazed that the house was drunk" might be seen as acceptable by someone with AD because all of the verbs and nouns and articles are in their grammatically appropriate places. Lexical (word) problems often result in overuse of pronouns (e.g., "Hand me that *thing* from *there*"); this can make understanding someone with AD quite challenging. The overuse of pronouns is an early signal that lexical impairment is occurring. Eventually, most language production ceases and people with advanced AD may be virtually mute, although brief "flashes" of clear communication occur even in the late stages of the disease.

There are different theories about the underlying origins of these deficits. Currently, it seems likely that people with AD still have complete semantic knowledge and lexical structures in their brains. However, they have increasing trouble getting access to those structures. All of us struggle to find a word for something at times even when we *know* that we *know* it (it's on the "tip of our tongue"). AD patients encounter such struggles to "access" what is still in their mind much more frequently. Some of the best demonstrations that people with AD do retain linguistic knowledge occur during moments of **lucidity**, when a severely impaired and otherwise mute AD patient suddenly talks coherently and sensibly, only to then lapse back into silence or incoherence. These episodes illustrate that the underlying person is still *there* in Alzheimer's disease, and that the person probably knows more than is apparent a lot of the time.

One study has provided additional insight into the relationship between AD and communication. Snowdon et al. (1996) studied a group of nuns aged 75–95. The researchers examined biographies written by the nuns at the age of 20 and found that certain aspects of language use at that young age predicted development of AD decades later. Nuns who used more complex grammar in their language at age 20 were significantly less likely to develop AD later in life. The same was true of idea density: a measure of how many different thoughts are packed into a given number of words. Nuns who wrote with higher levels of idea density early in life were less likely to develop AD in their later years.

Others' communication can play a significant role in maximizing quality of life and communication abilities for Alzheimer's patients. Supportive communication can often serve to bring out the potential of AD victims. Box 2.2 illustrates a conversation between a researcher and a patient with probable Alzheimer's disease. The patient illustrates disorientation about which city she is in, and where she taught. However, given some prompting from the researcher, she engages in coherent interaction and is able to display lexical knowledge. While at first she struggles to retrieve the word "needle," she is able to. Notice the way the researcher uses the woman's own words to help her move forward with her narrative (e.g., clumsy). Also notice that at one point the researcher reinforces the patient's *inaccurate* response as to where she worked ("Oh yes, you worked in Y City") in order to provide support that might ultimately lead to more coherent responding. As noted by Dreher (2001), effective communication with an AD patient may often involve not arguing about the truth of a particular statement: Truth may well not be relevant in the circumstances. Rather, accepting the statement as a legitimate communicative act is more likely to result in a positive exchange. Dreher also notes that sensitive communicators will notice particular times and particular topics that elicit more productive and useful responses from an AD patient. Paying attention, listening and observing carefully, and being accepting of the other person's communication are crucial skills for individuals who work with older adults suffering from AD. Sabat (1999) describes the process of **"indirect repair"** in conversations with people who have Alzheimer's disease. This technique involves "correcting" what is said by asking questions, clarifying, and restating in order to confirm understanding. Again, the practice of careful listening and strategic communication to maximize the partner's effectiveness comes to the fore.

Box 2.2   Supportive Communication and Alzheimer's Disease

Hans Normann and his coworkers interviewed a woman with probable Alzheimer's disease over a long period of time. The researchers describe the woman as "being cared for in a nursing home. She had severe dementia and language problems. She showed reduced cognitive capacity and disorientation and was hospitalized permanently . . . she was not orientated regarding time or place and showed rigidity and tremor . . . the woman needed the support of a nurse to walk and help with all daily activities. She spent the day either sitting in a chair or lying on her bed."

The patient was a handicraft teacher in "X City," which was also the city where this conversation took place. "Y city" is the place where the patient was born and grew up. She never taught there, although she believed that was where the conversation was occurring. The researcher knew which city she had worked in before the following conversation took place:

Researcher: Which school did you work in when you worked as a handicraft teacher?

Patient: Where did I work? I taught in "Y city."

Researcher: Oh yes, you worked in "Y city."

Patient: Yes, that's right.

Researcher: Didn't you teach in "X city"?

Patient: No, not in "X city."

(Continued)

(Continued)

Researcher:	I see (4).
Patient:	No, here, here in "Y city."
Researcher:	I see (4).
Patient:	and teaching, and teaching. No, where have I been teaching? (She laughs.)
Researcher:	Did you like being a handicraft teacher? Was it fun?
Patient:	Yes, I found, I found it fun. Yes. They were so clumsy they, many times.
Researcher:	Were they very clumsy?
Patient:	Clumsy in many ways, oh, my God. They weren't able to . . . not able to . . .
Researcher:	Able to sew (5)?
Patient:	To sew. They were not able to, not able to, with, yes, they, they were quite incapable, I mean. Because they did not manage to, to . . . I taught them how to use . . . how to use the needle. They could not do that from before.

SOURCE: Normann, H. K., Norberg, A., & Asplund, K. (2002). Confirmation and lucidity during conversations with a woman with severe dementia. *Journal of Advanced Nursing, 39,* 370–376, with permission from Blackwell.

It is important to note that other diseases and conditions such as stroke and Parkinson's disease can also cause dementia: Alzheimer's disease is just one cause of dementia. There are, of course, other age-related pathologies that have considerable implications for communication, and a good introduction to those can be found in Kemper and Mitzner (2001).

Counterpoint: A Positive Research Agenda on Aging

The research described in the previous sections reveals some elements of decline in old age. As noted in Chapter 1, for some people studying aging is all about decline. And I should be clear: The work that many of these people do is absolutely essential for older people and has resulted in amazing scientific advances. However, focusing almost exclusively on decline is a somewhat pessimistic approach. It may lead some to believe that communication in older adulthood becomes virtually impossible due to grammar, hearing, memory, and inhibition issues. Of course, that is not the case: As noted in the introduction, a life-span approach reminds us that there are gains and losses throughout life. Below are some of the key arguments for why focusing on decline alone is inappropriate, and why you can look forward to positive and vibrant communication in your old age.

First, the findings from the work above on normative aging generally reveal relatively **small effects**. For instance, while older adults are generally less good at processing complex grammar, the fact is that complex grammar does not play a large role in most of our daily conversations. With typical, everyday language, the effects described above are rarely noticeable (Ryan, 1991). Considerable evidence indicates that differences found in laboratory experiments are much less noticeable in "real life" (Pasupathi & Lockenhoff, 2002).

Second, older adults compensate for specific deficits in multiple and creative ways. Many older adults become effective at lip-reading to compensate for any decline in hearing, they rely more heavily on prosody (the *tone* of what is being said), and they process what is being said at a more global level (focusing on the *big picture*: Stine & Wingfield, 1987; Stine Morrow, Loveless, & Soederberg, 1996). Of course, the most obvious form of compensation is to get a hearing aid. These devices are increasingly effective and unobtrusive.

Third, many of the negative issues described above only kick in above age 80 for many people (P. B. Baltes & Smith, 2003). So, as noted earlier, it is crucial that we remember the *diversity* in the aging population—what is true for an 87-year-old is probably not true for a 67-year-old. And what is true for one 75-year-old is not necessarily true for others. There are older adults who experience none of the declines described earlier, and others who experience all of them in fairly severe fashion. Note, for instance, that very few 65- to 75-year-olds have Alzheimer's, whereas a very significant portion of those 85 and older have the disease. A more general message here: Averages across groups actually tell us very little about individuals within those groups! This issue of diversity was also addressed in Chapter 1.

Fourth, and maybe most crucially, relatively little research has paid attention to what might *improve* or remain unchanged with age. Again, it seems that researchers have been influenced by our stereotypes of old age and have forgotten that development and growth are possible throughout the life span. We have little systematic knowledge of older adults' abilities in group decision making, public speaking, or emotional expression, yet each of these seems open to improvement into late old age (Colonia-Willner, 1998). The creative writing skills of older people might also merit investigation as a potential area of improvement in language (Sternberg & Lubart, 2001; see Box 2.3). Other areas of creativity can also prosper in old age: Grandma Moses (Anna Mary Robertson Moses) was in her 70s when she began painting and became an international phenomenon as an artist. When Henri Matisse became physically unable to continue his normal style of painting (in his 70s), he responded by creating an entirely new style of visual art (*gouaches découpés*), and these later works are now among his most admired.

The few positive things we do know: Normal aging has no effect on our long-term memory—our basic knowledge of the world and understanding of life does not decline (Kemper & Mitzner, 2001). Age also does not appear to influence our ability to attend to partners in conversation (Vandeputte et al., 1999). Our vocabulary *increases* into old age (Salthouse, 1988), as does the ability to correctly pronounce words and our ability to use diverse words in our speech (Kemper & Sumner, 2001), and storytelling abilities improve with age (Kemper, Kynette, Rash, O'Brien, & Sprott, 1989). Beyond that, there is a massive gap in our knowledge about the ways in which growth and development continue in older adulthood.

Fifth, most of this research fails to consider how some of the problems uncovered may themselves be caused by negative attitudes about older adulthood. Work by Levy (1996) has shown that negative beliefs about aging have dramatic consequences for older adults: Figure 2.1 illustrates the effects on older people's memory; other studies have shown effects on health. This tells us that some portion of the "decline" that is documented in studies of older adults' language and communication may be *created* by the beliefs about aging that they are exposed to. A recent study at UCLA demonstrates that older people with more negative expectations about aging are substantially less likely to exercise and more likely to lead sedentary lifestyles: Thus, negative expectations about aging become a self-fulfilling prophecy (Sarkisian, Prohaska, Wong, Hirsch, & Mangione, 2005).

As a result of these issues, recent years have seen broader attention to communication phenomena in old age that moves away from studying older

Box 2.3   Creative Writing in Old Age

Crossing the Bar

Alfred Lord Tennyson

Sunset and evening star,
And one clear call for me!
And may there be no moaning
of the bar,
When I put out to sea,

But such a tide as moving seems
asleep,
Too full for sound and foam,
When that which drew from
out the boundless deep
Turns again home.

Twilight and evening bell,
And after that the dark!
And may there be no sadness of
farewell,
When I embark;

For tho' from out our bourne of
Time and Place
The flood may bear me far,
I hope to see my Pilot face to
face
When I have crossed the bar.

How Beautiful the Queen of Night

William Wordsworth

How beautiful the Queen of Night,
on high
Her way pursuing among scattered
clouds,
Where, ever and anon, her head
she shrouds
Hidden from view in dense
obscurity.
But look, and to the watchful eye
A brightening edge will indicate
that soon
We shall behold the struggling
Moon
Break forth,—again to walk the
clear blue sky.

NOTE: The Tennyson poem was written when he was 80 years old. He is clearly concerned with issues of aging and dying at this point in his career, and the poem addresses those themes. Wordsworth, on the other hand, has more traditional "poetic" concerns with images of nature and the sensory experience of the world. The Wordsworth poem was written when he was 76. To whatever extent old age may lead to changes in linguistic abilities, these two poems illustrate that there is no evidence of age negatively influencing creativity in thought or expression. It is also interesting to note that old age provides material for beautiful artistic expression (as in the Tennyson poem). However, contrary to what is sometimes thought, older people are not obsessed with their age, and older artists' work is not solely centered on their age (as illustrated by the Wordsworth).

Figure 2.1   Effects of Stereotyping on Memory Function

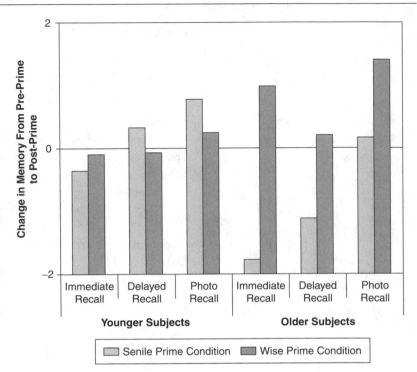

Younger and older people's memory was tested, and then they were exposed to a "prime" (a word shown so quickly on a computer screen that people can't even see it) that suggested either positive or negative stereotypes of old age (*wise vs. senile* prime conditions). Then their memory was tested again. Three types of memory were tested. For instance, for the "photo recall" condition, subjects were shown photographs and told an activity the person did ("This person watches TV most of the time"). They were then shown the photos again and had to recall the activity the person did. The chart shows the *change* in memory from before the prime to after the prime on three different measures of memory. Younger people's memory performance didn't change much as a result of the prime. Older people's, however, was better after the *wise* prime, and generally worse after the *senile* prime (values below zero indicate that memory ability actually declined). Thus, for older people, merely being exposed to positive or negative ideas about aging is enough to change their performance on "objective" tests of their memory.

SOURCE: From "Improving Memory in Old-Age Through Implicit Self-Stereotyping," by B. R. Levy, 1996, *Journal of Personality and Social Psychology, 71,* 1092–1107.

people's "problems." Instead, communication scholars have attempted to understand how communication involving older adults differs from that involving younger people, what the root causes of those differences are, and how communication processes provide unique insight into the nature of growing old in today's society.

Approaches to Communication and Aging

In what remains of this chapter, I will talk about three areas of communication research that guide the remainder of the book, and I will present some propositions that frame this book's approach to communication and aging.

Interpersonal Communication

Most older people continue to have interpersonal conversations, marriages, families, friendships, and even romantic liaisons, right up until they die. A lot of research now exists telling us what goes on in these relationships as people get older. Some elements of interpersonal communication are crucial to the continued growth of older adults, and to maintaining a high quality of life into old age. Other aspects of interpersonal communication may become increasingly difficult, either because of specific age-related problems (as described above), or because of the attitudes of those to whom older people are talking (see "Intergroup Communication" below). Throughout this book, I will be describing some of these changes. Chapters 3–6 focus particularly on this area.

Mass Communication

The discipline of communication is not only concerned with interpersonal relationships, of course. Scholars in our field also examine the nature of mass communication. Our mass media are perhaps the most potent transmitters and reflectors of our culture—television, newspapers, magazines, and the Internet convey messages about what we value, who is important, and where our priorities are placed. Hence, we need to examine what we know about how older adults use the media, how they may be affected by mass communication, as well as the messages that the media send about the aging process. This is the focus of Chapters 7–8, but issues of media representations also appear in a number of other places in this book.

Why I Study Communication and Aging
Jon Nussbaum (Professor, Penn State University)

I began my graduate student career in the Department of Psychology at West Virginia University studying Life Span Developmental Psychology. My "assignment" was to collect data for the "follow through" program in numerous grade schools throughout rural West Virginia. This program followed Head Start kids to determine if Head Start was worth the federal investment. My experience with those wonderful children was not good! The children saw my fear and exploited my lack of patience! I made the decision to investigate the other end of the life span. Working with the Communication faculty at West Virginia and later on with the Communication faculty at Purdue (Mark Knapp, Bob Norton, Don Ellis, Tom Porter to name a few) and Victor Cicirelli in the Department of Psychological Sciences, I was able to combine the theories and methods within Life Span Developmental Psychology and Communication to create for me this area of Communication and Aging. As a research assistant for Prof. Cicirelli, I had the opportunity to interview hundreds of older adults and became passionate about the social world of older adults. I could also see the importance of studying communication as a developmental process that is key to understanding our ability to adapt and cope with the many challenges we encounter throughout the entirety of our lives.

Reprinted with permission of Jon Nussbaum.

Intergroup Communication

This book takes the perspective that older people are a substantial, recognizable, and psychologically important group in society. All of us (including older adults) have ideas about what growing old is all about, and we have feelings (positive and negative) about aging and old people. In a sense, therefore, age groups work in a similar way to other groups in society (cultural groups, gender groups, and the like). So, when we examine communication between people of different ages and messages about aging in the media, it is useful to think of that communication in terms of the group memberships involved. A conversation between a younger and an older person is not always simply a conversation between two individuals ("interpersonal communication"). At times, the respective group memberships of the individuals involved may become important to one or both of the people involved. At that point, we would say that they are engaging in "intergroup communication." When communication scholars consider the role of broad social group memberships in communication, they are studying intergroup communication. We are also studying intergroup communication when we consider how older and younger people are portrayed in the media. A grumpy old man in a television show isn't simply an individual character; he is a character who may be understood by viewers in terms of his age, and his grumpiness may be related to his age in various ways by the viewing public. So, to understand him fully, we must factor his age into our understanding. Throughout this book, we will be adopting this intergroup perspective and applying it to individual and societal communication concerning aging.

Key Propositions Guiding the Book: A Communication Approach

When many people think about aging, they think about improving hospital care for geriatric patients, helping older people get social security benefits, developing social services for older people, or perhaps trying to cure Alzheimer's disease. Communication is rarely treated as central to understanding human aging. So what does a communication approach to aging look like, and why might it be useful? I see the following propositions as key to comprehending why communication is central to figuring out the role of older people in our society.

1. Communication reflects and shapes our understanding of aging. As was shown in Figure 2.1 (and also discussed in Chapter 1), many people are now convinced that some of the negative changes that we observe in older adults are a product of the ways in which we understand aging as a society. Communication is the fundamental process by which we transmit and recreate these understandings. Therefore, throughout this book I will be pointing out the ways in which our talk to one another and the mass media perpetuate and construct negative images of aging. These images serve to reinforce attitudes about decline and ill health in aging, which in turn cause such ill-health to exist. For example, imagine the different approach of a physician who expects older patients to be sick and ill, as compared to one who expects health and vitality in late life. Who is more likely to prescribe an effective medication? Likewise, imagine how an older person who expects pain and depression in old age will react to experiencing pain, as compared to one who does not view pain as an inevitable accompaniment to aging. Our expectations will shape how we respond to the experience of aging and communicate it to others, which in turn will shape the realities of our experiences. Communication is fundamental to this process, because the messages we hear and send shape our expectations of aging, as well as reveal our biases. Even the words we use to label older people can have important implications (see Table 2.1).

2. Communication shapes people's experience of aging. Given that communication reflects our understanding of aging, we can assume that messages about aging influence and construct our *experience* of aging. Older adults receive communication that sends them messages about other people's perceptions of their competence. When an older woman is called "sweetie" in the same manner that one might address a child, it conveys something to her about how her age is seen by those around her. This communicative act constructs the very meaning of old age for that woman. As we move forward in the book, we will describe more about the ways in which our communication changes the experience of aging for older people. Indeed, these phenomena extend much earlier than our traditional ideas of "old age." Giles (1999) notes the ways in which birthday cards and interpersonal exchanges contain age-related teasing that orients us to our own aging much earlier than age 65. Remember, of course, that it is human beings who create all this communication. Hence, we are not simply passive *recipients* of messages that influence us. Rather, we are active *participants* in the message system, continuously creating and receiving messages that construct and reflect our understandings of aging.

Table 2.1   So What Do I Call These People?

Biddies, Cronies, Wrinklies, Gerries, etc.: All of these kinds of terms are pejorative (demeaning, negative) and should be avoided. They are almost universally used in speech that is simultaneously describing older people negatively in other ways. Avoid!

Geriatrics: Again, this is not the best choice. The field of geriatrics is the area of medicine that is particularly focused on old people. Hence, when older people are called "geriatrics," associations with the medical and health issues associated with aging are immediately brought to mind. The mental image raised by this word does not encompass all of the aspects of getting older, and tends to focus thought on the more negative. The term is also dehumanizing, emphasizing a dependent role rather than a human being. Avoid!

The Elderly: Describing any group of people using a definite article ("The Blacks," "The Gays") tends to be overly homogenizing—it makes it sound like you are talking about a group of items that are all identical. As noted elsewhere, older people are very diverse, so this phrase is probably not appropriate. "The elderly enjoy bingo" suggests that every single older person enjoys bingo, which is not the case. Generally avoid!

Elders: This is a respectful term and one that probably has a place in our talk about aging. However, it should be remembered that in many societies "elders" are a specific group of wise and trusted community leaders. Often, the "elders" in those societies are not defined by age, but rather by status, tradition, or skills (e.g., among Australian aborigines). More generally, the term can sometimes have overly deferential connotations—"elders" are not people you kid around with or have a light and casual conversation with. In the same way that we don't want aging to become associated with negative feelings of ill health and decrepitude, we also don't want to end up so intimidated by older people that we are scared to talk to them! Use sparingly!

Oldsters: Too cute. While not offensive, the term is not respectful and seems to invoke a playful childishness that is probably not appropriate.

Seniors/Senior Citizens: This is a reasonable label in certain circumstances. The single word "seniors" can be a little ambiguous at times (e.g., in the United States, "seniors" includes people in their final year of high school or college). And "senior citizens" may have too much of a legal tone for some (e.g., it's associated with getting discounts at movie theaters, a free bus pass, and the like). So this phrase may be appropriate at times, but probably shouldn't be overused. Use sparingly!

Elderly People: Getting better. This phrase acknowledges that we are talking about people, and the use of the plural "people" gives a clear understanding that there may be diversity within the group. The word "elderly" is somewhat associated with ideas of frailty and dependence, and

(Continued)

(Continued)

from this perspective it's a word that is often avoided by scholars in the field, but this phrase is acceptable. Use sparingly!

Older Adults: Now this is about as vanilla as you can get! It's a nice neutral way of describing a group of people. I like the use of the word "adults" in the label, as it emphasizes a shared status with all other adults. Older people are sometimes treated as if they were reverting to childhood, so a reminder that they are adults isn't out of place! Use!

3. *Age-group memberships are fundamentally important to our sense of self.* While we are all, of course, unique individuals, we also gain a substantial sense of who we are and what we value from our social groups. Being an American/Iraqi/Scot, an African American/Chicano(a)/Caucasian, or a woman/man, contributes to our sense of *identity.* Identity is your sense of self, and the groups that you belong to make up your **social identity.** According to Tajfel's social identity theory (Tajfel & Turner, 1986), we are motivated to think well of the groups that we belong to, we often act in terms of those group memberships, and we sometimes may be motivated to discriminate against members of other (perhaps perceived to be competing) groups. People care about being of a particular age, and tensions exist between age groups. Hence, we can consider age groups to be social groups of some importance, we can consider the ways in which individuals' age group memberships drive their behavior, and we can understand relations between age groups as *intergroup* relations. The next two chapters illustrate the ways in which such identities are established and expressed in communication.

4. *Age-group memberships influence communication phenomena.* When we talk to other people, their group memberships (relative to our own) influence what styles and topics of communication we feel are appropriate, and how we interpret their communication. The same statement from an older person might be interpreted totally differently from a younger person (e.g., imagine hearing "I forgot where I was going" from a confused looking person standing on a street corner—would their age affect how you interpreted the comment?). So, if we are interested in human communication processes, it is essential that we understand the ages and age identifications of the individuals who are engaged in that process.

Summary

A communication approach to aging focuses on the ways in which communication shapes our understandings and expectations of aging. It emphasizes that we learn about aging from the messages that we send and receive, and that the details of those messages change depending on the age group of the sender and receiver. For some people, the study of communication and aging is focused on decline in communication with increased age. This book, however, makes the argument that a focus on decline is too narrow and ignores the continuing possibilities for growth and development into old age.

Keywords and Theories

Alzheimer's disease
Embedded clauses
Indirect repair
Inhibitory capacity
Language production versus
    comprehension
Memory for names

Normal aging
Off-target verbosity
Presbycusis
Short- and long-term memory
Small effects
Social identity theory
Syntax

Discussion Questions

- What things that are now thought of as "normal" aging might be viewed as "pathological" in 25 years?
- What are the areas in which you see the most growth in older adulthood? From your contact with older people, what might older adults be better at than younger people?
- If you have taken other Communication classes, discuss what you have learned about old age in those classes. If you have learned nothing about old age, discuss why that might be.
- What are some good ways to talk with someone who is suffering from dementia?
- In what way might a conversation between a grandparent and a grandchild be an "intergroup" conversation?

Annotated Bibliography

Kemper, S., & Mitzner, T. L. (2001). Language production and comprehension. In J. E. Birren & K. W. Schaie (Eds.), *Handbook of the psychology of aging* (5th ed., pp. 378–398). San Diego: Academic Press. Provides excellent coverage of some of the key changes in linguistic ability with increasing age, both in normal and pathological aging. It does focus largely on decline in linguistic ability.

Nussbaum, J. F., & Coupland, J. (Eds.). (2004). *Handbook of communication and aging research* (2nd ed.). Mahwah, NJ: Lawrence Erlbaum. Pretty much the most comprehensive reference work on communication and aging issues. At 600 pages, most people won't have time to read the whole thing, but it has individual chapters on all of the key topics so you can pick and choose.

Williams, A., & Nussbaum, J. F. (2001). *Intergenerational communication across the lifespan.* Mahwah, NJ: Erlbaum. A textbook with a particular focus on interpersonal communication between people of different ages. This book doesn't cover the breadth of areas of study that are included in the book you are reading, but it provides more depth in areas of personal relationships and interpersonal communication.

PART II

Attitudes About Aging and Interpersonal Communication

The second part of this book introduces key facts about our attitudes concerning old age and the aging process. Chapter 3 describes some of the ways in which we *think* about aging, focusing on ageist attitudes, stereotypes of old people, and age group identities. Chapter 4 describes how ageist attitudes, age stereotypes, and age identities influence communication between older and younger people, and communication about old age. Chapters 5 and 6 address issues of interpersonal communication in close relationships involving older adults; the first looks at intragenerational relationships and the second at intergenerational relationships. Finally, Chapter 7 discusses the ways in which interpersonal communication might contribute to a more positive older adulthood.

THREE

Stereotypes and Attitudes About Aging and Intergenerational Communication

In this chapter, we'll examine what people think about aging—their feelings about getting old and their attitudes concerning communicating with people of different ages. By the end of this chapter you should be able to:

- Distinguish between an attitude and a stereotype
- Describe positive and negative elements of attitudes about aging
- Discuss evidence that we "identify" with our age groups
- Express arguments *disputing* common myths of aging
- Describe some ways in which people might cope with belonging to an age group that is not respected

SOURCE: © Alex Hinds/Istockphoto.com

The great thing about getting older is that you don't lose all the other ages you've been.

—Madeleine L'Engle (novelist),
New York Times, 1985

B efore reading further, please look at the questionnaire in Table 3.1, and answer the questions. Think a little about why you answered the way you did. Now answer the questions in Table 3.2. Do your answers differ? The two questionnaires illustrate one of the unique and interesting phenomena concerning attitudes about aging and old people. When we think about older adults, we are thinking about what we will be at some point in our life. This is very different from examining, say, men's attitudes about women. With the rare exception of those who seek sex-change surgery, men will never be women during their lives. Similarly, when we examine attitudes about other cultures, we are considering how people feel about some group to which they will never belong. This is, of course, not true for aging. So did your responses differ to the two sets of questions? Why? This chapter describes the extensive research on attitudes and stereotypes of aging. It describes the possible origins of negative attitudes about aging, as well as attitudes about communication between younger and older people. The last part of the chapter considers age identification: the way in which we affiliate and identify ourselves as "members" of particular age groups.

Distinguishing Stereotypes and Attitudes

At the outset, it is worth distinguishing between stereotypes and attitudes. A **stereotype** is a cognitive representation of a group. Stereotypes are often framed in terms of **traits**—specific characteristics that we expect members of certain groups to possess. For instance, an expectation that women be nurturing or Asians be studious is a stereotype. While some stereotypes may have a kernel of truth to them, they often have negative consequences both because they are often inaccurate and because they often get applied to an individual group member regardless of that person's individual

Table 3.1   Example of Measuring Attitudes Toward Aging

Please respond to each of the following statements by circling a number. Circling "1" indicates that you strongly agree with the statement, and circling "6" indicates that you strongly disagree. Numbers in the middle indicate weaker levels of agreement or disagreement.

1. Older people are quite capable of performing tasks that require effort and stamina.

1	2	3	4	5	6
Strongly disagree					Strongly agree

2. Older people are as capable as ever of concentrating on any given task.

1	2	3	4	5	6
Strongly disagree					Strongly agree

3. Once people get to a certain age, life inevitably goes downhill.

1	2	3	4	5	6
Strongly disagree					Strongly agree

4. Old age brings satisfactions that are just not available to the young.

1	2	3	4	5	6
Strongly disagree					Strongly agree

5. Old age is the most enjoyable time of life.

1	2	3	4	5	6
Strongly disagree					Strongly agree

Calculating your score: First, you need to "flip" your score for question 3—give yourself a 6 if you circled 1, a 5 if you circled 2, a 4 if you circled 3, a 3 if you circled 4, a 2 if you circled 5, and a 1 if you circled 6. Then add your scores on the remaining questions to your flipped score on question 3. The resulting score is how you feel about the aging process: The minimum is a 5 and the maximum is a 30. Higher numbers mean that you are more positive about old age and old people.

SOURCE: Adapted from "An Empirical Study of Ageism: From Polemics to Scientific Utility," by V. Braithwaite, R. Lynd-Stevenson, and D. Pigram, 1993, *Australian Psychologist, 28,* pp. 9–15.

Table 3.2   Example of Measuring Attitudes Toward Aging

Please respond to each of the following statements by circling a number. Circling "1" indicates that you strongly agree with the statement, and circling "6" indicates that you strongly disagree. Numbers in the middle indicate weaker levels of agreement or disagreement.

1. When I am old, I will be capable of performing tasks that require stamina.

1	2	3	4	5	6
Strongly disagree					Strongly agree

2. When I am old, I will be as capable as ever of concentrating on any given task.

1	2	3	4	5	6
Strongly disagree					Strongly agree

3. Once I get to a certain age, life will inevitably go downhill.

1	2	3	4	5	6
Strongly disagree					Strongly agree

4. Old age will bring me satisfactions that are just not available to the young.

1	2	3	4	5	6
Strongly disagree					Strongly agree

5. Old age for me will be the most enjoyable time of life.

1	2	3	4	5	6
Strongly disagree					Strongly agree

Calculating your score: Calculate exactly as you did in Table 3.1. The resulting score is how you feel about your **own** aging process: The minimum is a 5 and the maximum is a 30. Higher numbers mean that you are more positive about your own aging.

SOURCE: Adapted from "An Empirical Study of Ageism: From Polemics to Scientific Utility," by V. Braithwaite, R. Lynd-Stevenson, and D. Pigram, 1993, *Australian Psychologist, 28,* pp. 9–15.

characteristics. So, whether or not Asian people are more studious than any other group, if you expect every single Asian person you meet to be incredibly studious, you're going to be wrong a lot of the time! It's important to note that this perception (studiousness) is a relatively positive one; so while it's a stereotype, it wouldn't necessarily reflect a negative *attitude*—we turn to attitudes next.

For our purposes, an **attitude** is an overall emotional response to a person or group of people (certainly you also have attitudes toward other things, but this chapter is concerned with attitudes about groups of people). When we talk about having negative ("Gross!") or positive ("Cool!") attitudes about a particular group, we are saying that individuals have a generally negative or positive response to people belonging to that group. Negative attitudes are problematic because they result in dislike or avoidance of members of a group, often with no justification. In the next sections of this chapter we will examine research on attitudes and stereotypes concerning *age* groups. These attitudes and stereotypes are reasons why people may sometimes avoid contact with people of different age groups, as well as why that contact may not always be pleasant.

ACHIEVEMENTS IN OLD AGE

Ronald Reagan

Ronald Reagan was born in 1911 and died in 2004. During his 93 years, he was a lifeguard, a radio sports announcer (for the Chicago Cubs), a movie star, president of the Screen Actor's guild, a television talk show host, governor of California, and president of the United States. He was married twice and had five children (two of whom he outlived). He survived an assassination attempt in 1981 shortly after his election as president, but continued on to become one of the nation's most popular presidents (although certainly not universally loved!). Reagan was 69 when elected and 77 when he left the presidency—the oldest president in U.S. history. He was the first to appoint a woman to the Supreme Court and he overhauled the U.S. tax code—so much for the idea that older people are resistant to change! While many disagreed with his policies, Reagan is a startling example of the opportunities for continued

---

(Continued)

(Continued)

> growth and achievement in old age. Running for election to be president
> when you are almost 70 is a sign that you're not willing to believe what
> other people tell you about getting old! In a debate with Walter Mondale
> when running for his second term as president, then 73-year-old Reagan
> quipped: "I will not make age an issue of this campaign. I am not going to
> exploit, for political purposes, my opponent's youth and inexperience."
> Ultimately, one part of Reagan's legacy will be the question about whether
> he was experiencing early symptoms of Alzheimer's disease while still in
> office. This is impossible to answer definitively, but as mentioned in the
> chapter, it is clear that some indicators of Alzheimer's disease may be appar-
> ent years before the obvious symptoms start to appear.

Attitudes Concerning Aging

A negative attitude about aging—ageism—is widespread. In an analysis of 43
independent studies, Kite and Johnson (1988) found that attitudes toward older
adults are clearly more negative than attitudes toward younger adults (for a
recent update of this classic work, see Kite, Stockdale, Whitley, & Johnson, 2005).
Such negative attitudes emerge very early in life: Children as young as *3 years old*
can distinguish between adults of different ages and show negative *attitudes*
toward older people (Marks, Newman, & Onawola, 1985; Seefeldt & Ahn, 1990).
These negative attitudes appear to improve somewhat in middle childhood
(approximately ages 7–11). However, during middle childhood and into adolescence, some individuals begin to form more permanent negative attitudes that
become fairly well-entrenched for life (Doyle & Aboud, 1995). Kite and Johnson
note that attitudes toward older adults are complex, and that in certain domains
(e.g., physical attractiveness) they are more negative than others (e.g., wisdom).
However, the overall finding of negative attitudes is very consistent—some of
these studies include older people, who also demonstrate negative attitudes
about aging, although they tend to be somewhat less negative than the young.

Recent research has begun to illustrate that these negative attitudes about
aging are held very deeply in our unconscious. Imagine the following scenario. You are sitting in front of a computer. You have to press a blue button if
a young face appears on the screen and a green button if an old face appears
on the screen. At the same time, you have to press the blue button if a "nice"

word appears (e.g., flower), and the green button if a "nasty" word appears (e.g., vomit). Most people find this task pretty easy.

Now switch it around, so the blue button is for old faces and nice words, while the green button is for young faces and nasty words. Most people find this task quite a bit more challenging (i.e., it takes them a longer time to decide which button to press). This shows us that people associate "young" and "nice" together, and they associate "old" and "nasty" together—negative attitudes toward old age. The task is easier when each button represents consistent objects (e.g., young faces, nice words) and harder when each button represents inconsistent objects (e.g., old faces, nice words). Work like this example shows how deeply embedded and "uncontrollable" our negative attitudes about aging are (Hummert, Garstka, O'Brien, Greenwald, & Mellott, 2002).

Understanding the *origins* of such negative attitudes is a more complex issue, and one that has raised some very interesting ideas. One explanation emerges from **social identity theory**. As noted in the previous chapter, people of different ages sometimes deal with each other as "group" members. Younger people look at older people as a separate group in society, and vice versa. If those group memberships become important for some reason, then we start to **identify** with the groups that we see ourselves belonging to. Identifying means that you see your group membership as an important part of your sense of self—who you are is partly defined by your age group. Social identity theory says that once you identify with a particular group, you will want to view that group positively, and as a result you may be inclined to view other groups negatively. Thus, younger people are to some extent motivated to view older people in a negative light—it makes them feel good about being young!

This does a good job of explaining why *younger* people might have a negative attitude toward older adults. It doesn't do such a good job of explaining why older people *also* sometimes have negative attitudes about aging. In part, I suspect that older people's attitudes are the result of a lifetime of TV programs, jokes, and birthday cards that send a negative message about getting old (see Chapter 7). Of course, as noted above, relations between people of different ages are a unique type of intergroup relation. Older people were once young, and therefore they were once in the position of feeling negative about older people and aging as something *different* from what they were. Other possibilities abound, and some of these are probably also a factor in younger people's negative attitudes. One possibility is that older adults are associated with death, and thus they remind us of our own mortality (not something most people enjoy thinking about!). Martens, Greenberg, Schimel, and Landau (2004) showed that when young people are reminded of their own death, they tend to be more negative toward older people. The same may be true for older adults—thinking about their own age may raise issues of mortality that are not comfortable. Older adults are also aware of the realities of aging in today's society. Certain health issues, bereavement, financial challenges, and the experience of belonging to a devalued group may all contribute to a negative feeling about aging among older adults. As will be argued below, some of these "realities" may be the case right now, but these are not things that are inevitable with aging.

Examination of sex differences also tells us something about the origin of negative attitudes about age. It has been repeatedly suggested that older women are subjected to more negative attitudes than older men, and some research supports this. Older men benefit more from positive age stereotypes concerning wisdom and status than older women do. Some scholars (e.g., Kogan & Mills, 1992) provide an evolutionary explanation for this "**double standard**" of aging. Specifically, they note that women have most reproductive value when they are relatively young, and also when they are healthy. Hence, any physical indications of aging or ill health in women would be signs that they are less valuable as reproductive partners. In contrast, men's prime reproductive value comes somewhat later in life: Men are more valuable as mates when they have status and wealth to support their offspring. Hence, men retain reproductive value at least into middle age much better than women. As a result, signs of aging are more strongly associated with negative evaluations for women than men. Clearly such reproductive arguments become less and less sensible in the modern world. However, to the extent that 60,000 years of human evolution have "hard-wired" such preferences into our brains, they might persist beyond a time when they are really useful for our reproductive fitness.

Whatever the cause, these negative attitudes about aging are certainly harmful in terms of older people's expectations and behaviors in old age, and in terms of younger people's behaviors toward them. Rowe and Kahn (1998) have identified a set of "**myths of aging**" that result from our negative attitudes. These are outlined next, along with explanations for *why* they are myths.

To be old is to be sick: While there is no doubt that many older adults experience health problems, and that certain diseases are quite strongly associated with age, it is important to remember that many older adults are healthy and active. As will be expanded on throughout this book, we must also be aware of how much we contribute to ill health in old age with our negative attitudes and discriminatory practices.

You can't teach an old dog new tricks: Older people are just as capable of learning and growing, and sometimes have more motivation and opportunity than younger people. Certainly older adults learn in different ways—something that education institutions and employers need to recognize. Research suggests that if an emphasis is placed on *speed,* then the young will generally prevail. But older adults often demonstrate more commitment to the task and may end up producing higher quality outcomes.

The horse is out of the barn (i.e., whatever bad habits you have aren't worth changing in old age): It is always worth the effort to grow and change. Even into advanced old age, for instance, there are demonstrable benefits to giving up smoking, eating more health foods, and beginning a program of regular physical exercise. The oldest documented human was Jeanne Calment who died at age 122. She reportedly quit smoking when she was over 90!

The secret to successful aging is to choose your parents wisely: Genetics play a significant role in determining longevity, and in influencing predispositions to specific diseases. However, controllable aspects of lifestyle are equally important. Lifestyle choices that are associated with physical and mental health are always valuable and have positive effects regardless of genetic predispositions. Your genes are fairly unimportant in determining your longevity if you choose to smoke a pack of cigarettes a day.

The lights may be on, but the voltage is low: This myth suggests a general decline in function in old age, with perhaps a particular emphasis on sexual activity. While older adults do experience losses in certain areas, I'll argue in this book that they also experience gains—we have paid insufficient attention to the positive aspects of aging. In terms of sexuality in particular, while there are some decreases in sexual activity in old age, many older adults remain sexually active. Moreover, Rowe and Kahn (1998) point out that other aspects of expressing love and affection with physical contact remain intact and even improve throughout the life span.

The elderly don't pull their own weight: Overall, fewer older people than younger people work for pay, and older people tend to work part-time more than the young. However, they do continue to contribute to society in numerous ways. They volunteer, care for spouses and grandchildren, and serve as mentors. Many older people want to work but are excluded from the workplace by outdated and discriminatory practices. As the proportion of older people in the population grows, it is likely that more employers will recognize the wide skillbase, experience, and maturity that these people can bring to the workplace, and will consider the benefits of hiring older workers.

In the next chapter, I will address the ways in which some of these negative attitudes influence communication, but first I want to cover what research has told us about *stereotypes* of aging.

Why I Study Communication and Aging
Howard Giles (Professor, University of California, Santa Barbara, and Reserve Lieutenant, Santa Barbara Police Department)

Having been in British academia for a little while, I felt a need to switch careers and do something more hands-on within the community. Having had cops on both sides of my family and seen the mayhem of what happens when police go on strike, I decided to apply to be a police officer. At a phone interview, having gleaned a lot of my personal information, the recruiter asked me if I'd like to consider working in London. I answered "no," he retorted "you're too old here then!" Backed into the academy after all, I decided I'd now research aging issues given this, frankly, huge shock that so early in my life I was told I was too old to do something I really wanted to do. And so to cut a long story short, after that I moved to the USA. I would love to go back and tell that recruiter that over a quarter of a century later, I was selected and trained as a police officer (and have been one for the last ten years). As a Reserve Lieutenant, I can arrest, fight, pursue, shoot, and all those "good" things with the best of them. Ageisms, pah, bring 'em on!

Reprinted with permission of Howard Giles.

Stereotypes of Aging

Knowing that we have generally negative feelings about aging is interesting, but some of the work on stereotypes of aging has provided more concrete details on how we understand older adults in today's world. In some of my own research, I have looked at two dimensions underlying our mental representations of aging:

1. A dimension that relates to health, activity, and attractiveness, and

2. A dimension that relates to wisdom, kindness, and generosity.

In general (and across many cultures), people perceive health and attractiveness as declining across the life span, but wisdom and generosity as increasing or at least remaining stable. This is also supported by work on the **stereotype content model**. This model aligns stereotypes of various groups along dimensions of competence and warmth. Figure 3.1 shows the results of this model for a wide variety of groups. Groups that are perceived as high in competence and low in warmth (e.g., rich people) are near the bottom right-hand corner. Groups that are rated as statistically similar to one another are included in the same circles. The figure shows that older people are rated relatively low on a *competence* dimension, but relatively high on a *warmth* dimension; they are perceived similarly to people labeled as *retarded* and *disabled* in this area of the model. So, on the warmth dimension, at least, older adults are rated relatively positively. However, they do not end up in an area of the figure that is associated with substantial status or societal respect.

Figure 3.1   American Social Groups Arrayed Along Perceived Competence and Perceived Warmth and Sorted by Cluster Analysis

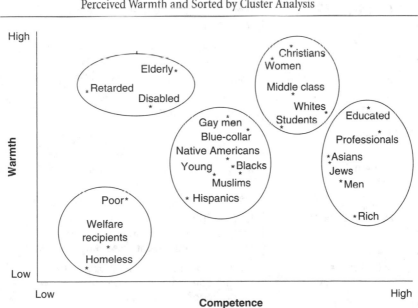

Mary Lee Hummert at the University of Kansas has uncovered a set of positive and negative stereotypes of aging that are held by young and old alike. As can be seen in Table 3.3, she has shown that we have some quite complex representations of aging. These stereotypes are used, in part, to make sense of the realities of older adulthood. A simplistic negative attitude about all older adults in untenable in the face of political leaders, loving grandparents, and renowned movie stars who are over 65. So, we understand some of the complexity of aging by creating mental categories that account for some of these different *types* of older person.

Table 3.3   Stereotypes of Older Adults Held by Young, Middle-Aged, and Older Adults

Stereotype	Selected Traits
NEGATIVE	
Severely Impaired	slow-thinking, incompetent, feeble, incoherent, inarticulate, senile
Despondent	depressed, sad, hopeless, afraid, neglected, lonely
Shrew/Curmudgeon	complaining, bitter, prejudiced, demanding, selfish, stubborn, nosy
Recluse	quiet, timid, naïve
POSITIVE	
Golden Ager	lively, adventurous, sociable, witty, independent, skilled, productive, volunteer, well-traveled, curious, healthy, sexual
Perfect Grandparent	kind, loving, family-oriented, generous, grateful, supportive, understanding, trustworthy, intelligent, wise, knowledgeable
John Wayne Conservative	patriotic, religious, nostalgic, reminiscent, retired, conservative, emotional, mellow, determined, proud

SOURCE: Adapted from Hummert, M. L., Weimann, J. M., Nussbaum, J. F., *Interpersonal Communication in Older Adulthood,* copyright ©1994. Reprinted with permission from Sage Publications, Inc.

Of course, these stereotypes are still simplifications. If you put an older person in the "box" of being a *perfect grandparent* (see Table 3.3), this might be somewhat more positive than the category *despondent,* but it still limits the person to a rather restricted set of roles and behaviors. So, even these more "specific" stereotypes can have negative consequences. Nonetheless, the Hummert approach does illustrate that stereotypes are not as simple as you might think. This approach also illustrates the limitations of the approach shown in Figure 3.1. Certain, more specific stereotypes of older adults (e.g., the *golden ager*) are probably perceived as substantially more competent than Figure 3.1 suggests; likewise, stereotypes such as the *shrew/curmudgeon* would be perceived as substantially less warm.

One key issue is what causes us to use them—when are we inclined to use these labels, and which ones do we use? Figures 3.2 and 3.3 provide some

Figure 3.2   Triggers of Negative Stereotyping of Older People

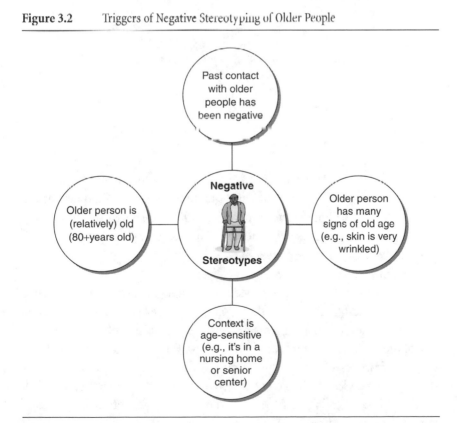

Figure 3.3   Triggers of Positive Stereotyping of Older People

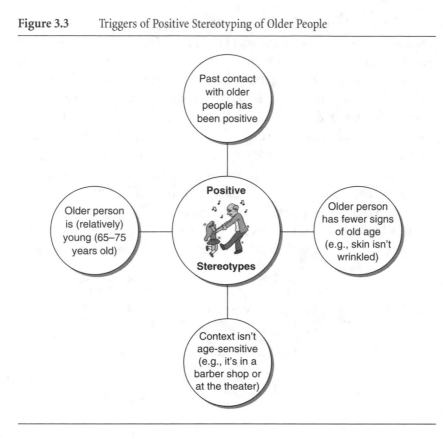

information on this. As you can see, older people who look really old and who are showing signs of ill health are likely to be negatively stereotyped, as are those who are encountered in hospitals or other age-related settings. Young people who have previously had negative contact with older people are also more likely to use negative stereotypes.

In contrast, older people who look younger are likely to be positively stereotyped, as are those who are encountered in non-age-related settings like a library or a restaurant. Interestingly, old people are less likely to negatively stereotype other old people than young people are. So stereotyping is a function of the perceiver, the target, and the context. Clearly we have more to learn about stereotypes of aging. But Hummert's research has given us a very sophisticated understanding of what stereotypes are and when they are used. As you can see from Figure 3.4, stereotypes of aging are common sources of humor in our society.

Figure 3.4 Stereotypes of Memory Loss in Old Age Are Widespread!

THE FAR SIDE® By GARY LARSON

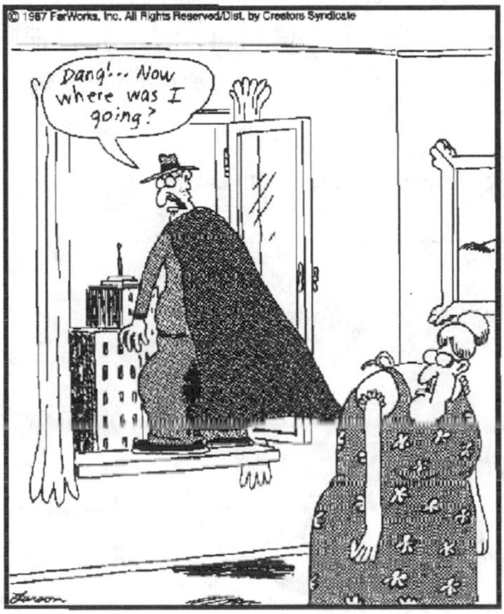

Superman in his later years

Age Identity—Talkin' 'Bout My Generation

As noted at the outset of this chapter, one element of understanding why people feel positive or negative about certain age groups is their feeling of belonging to those groups. Most people reading this book don't have very strong feelings about one type of sea anemone as compared to another, because we don't belong to any group of sea anemones! Our feelings come into play and gain importance once we start feeling like we belong in a particular age group, and hence don't belong in some other age group.

Most people do have a sense that there are distinct and important boundaries between age groups, and people often share a sense of where those boundaries fall. Across multiple cultures, young people tend to perceive young adulthood as beginning in the late teens and ending around 30, middle age as beginning in the 30s and extending to the 50s, and old age as beginning in the 50s. Older people see the boundaries as occurring a little later in life (e.g., old age beginning in the 60s), but there is a fair amount of consensus on these issues (A. Williams & Harwood, 2004).

In addition to agreeing on boundaries between age groups, people tend to also agree that they belong to an age group. Figure 3.5 shows college students' responses to a statement that indicates something about **age identity**. As you can see from the pattern of responses, most see age as important to their sense of self, and very few see it as unimportant. Perhaps more convincing than the evidence from a questionnaire is the evidence from our lives. Think about who

Figure 3.5   College Students' Responses to the Statement "The age group I belong to is an important part of who I am"

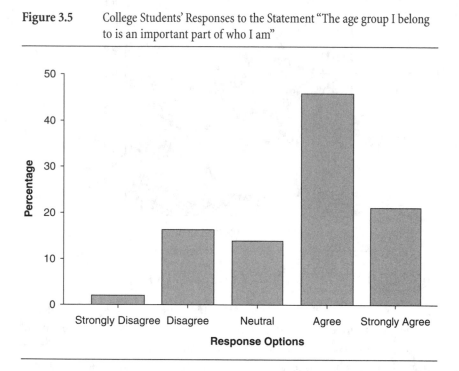

most of your friends are. Friendships are vastly skewed in favor of people our own age. People also tend to marry people of similar age (indeed, there are interesting social judgments made when people marry out of their own age group!). Hobbies, activities, and trends tend to be quite age-specific (for example, consider garage bands vs. bridge clubs). All of these things suggest that individuals perceive shared interests, experiences, and a common fate with those of similar age. And, of course, as we age we also share a cultural history. It is only with friends of a similar age that I can share my great affection for '80s music. Others may know the music, but it is only people of roughly my age who had the same experience of listening to that music as a teen/young adult and therefore have similar sets of associations with that music.

Given this, one important question is how older people "cope" with being a member of an age group about which many people have negative attitudes. Older people surely face some challenges in feeling good about themselves given that they belong to a group that is generally viewed negatively. Social identity theory suggests that people who belong to devalued groups can deal with that identity in three ways.

Social Mobility

Social mobility here means in terms of group memberships. While someone who is old cannot literally become younger, they can choose to identify with and act in accordance with younger groups. Probably the most extreme examples of this involve plastic surgery and botox injections, but other attempts to remove the physical manifestations of aging are more common (dyeing hair, using "age defying" makeup, etc.). Other forms of social mobility might include changing dress style, social activities, or even friends so as to feel engaged with a younger age group. Of course, this option is only available to those who do not particularly value being old—some older adults feel a sense of pride and commitment to their age group and don't want to simply abandon it.

Social Creativity

For older people who are unable or unwilling to engage in social mobility, there is the option of emphasizing the positive aspects of being an older adult. For some of these people, the emphasis may be placed on the positive stereotype dimensions described earlier (e.g., "we may be less healthy, but we have wisdom!"). For others, the emphasis may be placed on positive aspects of their lifestyle (e.g., the leisure time newly available in retirement, finally escaping the rat race). Older people also may choose to adopt a more sophisticated age categorization scheme and distinguish themselves from those who are even older and/or perhaps more impaired. Seventy-somethings may contrast their own health and fitness with the relative decline and deficit of 80-somethings. This, at least, postpones the point at which a given individual falls into the least favored group.

Sometimes, groups of people engage in social creativity together. Perhaps the most "visible" of these groups is the "Red Hat Society," an initially somewhat whimsical organization for women over 50. The group's chapters meet for events and socializing wearing, of course, red hats (and preferably a clashing purple dress). The group symbolizes a desire for freedom in old age—the clashing attire is the most visible example of this, suggesting freedom from rigid fashion conventions to which younger people conform. The group expresses a positive identity for older women: Its Web site explicitly discourages younger women from wearing the red hat attire (younger women are supposed to wear pink hats.). However, there are some indications that the Red Hat Society may be developing a more radical agenda in terms of challenging current views of older women in society. Other, more local older adult groups may also serve social creativity functions (e.g., senior centers, fitness groups, lunch groups, etc.). Simply by existing, these groups provide a sense of belonging and hence a positive age-related social identity.

All of these **social creativity** strategies may be personally effective, but they don't address the essential underlying negativity toward older adults— that is, they may make the individual older people feel better about themselves, but they don't change others' attitudes or provide any solutions to broader societal issues facing older people. That sort of activity is called *social competition*.

Social Competition

There is a long human tradition of social struggle, whereby oppressed groups fight the status quo and try to achieve equality and opportunity. In the United States, this phenomenon is probably best recognized in the Civil Rights Movement of the '50s and '60s. Such social struggles aimed at changing the nature of a group's position in society are called **social competition** in the language of social identity theory, and recent years have seen a growth in such activity among older adults. The key message of these types of action is that change at the level of the individual doesn't really change anything societally. If an individual older adult manages to gain respect and be treated as competent, that doesn't change things for the majority of older people. What is therefore needed are some groups that will attack the status quo "head on" and try to make changes to benefit all older people. While we tend to associate "fighting for your rights" with the historical struggles of African Americans, women, and other oppressed groups, hopefully you can now see that older adults also need such representation.

The most established advocacy group for older people in the United States is the **AARP** (formerly the American Association of Retired Persons: www.aarp.org). AARP was founded in the late 1950s as an organization primarily devoted to helping older people get affordable private health insurance. Since that time, it has emerged as a significant political pressure group acting on behalf of older adults on issues as diverse as campaigning for regulation of quality nursing home care to providing discounts on travel. AARP provides an example of *collective* action, where a group campaigns for better treatment *as a group*. Often this results in better outcomes than when individuals try to go it alone. The AARP currently focuses on three primary domestic areas (AARP, 2005):

Economic issues: Social Security, along with other issues pertaining to pensions, retirement benefits, and continuing to work during older adulthood.

Health care issues: Under health care, the organization is particularly concerned with improving Medicare (the U.S. health insurance program for older people), providing affordable prescription drugs, and more generally improving health care coverage.

Livable community issues: Affordable housing and public transportation.

How do they advance this agenda? Among the most significant activities that AARP engages in are its lobbying activities on Capitol Hill—it hires people to advocate on its behalf with members of the legislative and executive branches of government. This ensures that the agenda of older people is on the

---

Exercise 3.1   **Understanding the AARP's Agenda**

Visit the AARP's web site (www.aarp.org). Pick one of the links along the top of the page (Money and work, Issues and elections, Learning and technology, etc.). Follow each of the major links on the target page, and write a short summary of the issues covered within that link. Then, use the information from the full set of links to write a summary of the AARP's agenda in that area. Which topics does the AARP view as most important in that area, and what is the AARP's position or view on each of those topics? You may want to arrange this in two columns, one headed "Topics," and one headed "Position." If you are doing this exercise as a class, it would be good to distribute the different areas from the Web site among the class (e.g., via groups), and develop an overall picture of the AARP's agenda from the class's analysis of specific areas.

"radar" of congressional representatives. With 35 million members (in 2005), politicians tend to pay attention to the AARP! The organization also uses those 35 million members as citizen advocates, providing them with the information and resources they need to campaign on behalf of all older people. Finally, the organization serves as a clearinghouse for information that it feeds to the media. By providing media outlets with a source for information on aging issues, the AARP controls that information, and hence can shape public debate in interesting ways. That same information is also disseminated to AARP members, who use the organization's publications and Web site for information on important issues pertaining to older adults.

Other groups have emerged to support age groups (and consequently age identity). The Gray Panthers are generally regarded as a more radical organization than AARP, although with similar overall goals. In recent months, their Web site has campaigned for solutions to the Social Security crisis alongside criticisms of the war in Iraq. The 60 Plus Association is a much more conservative group that is focused almost exclusively on policy issues that influence older adults' financial well-being (e.g., the "death" tax). Each of these organizations (and there are many others) serves a different purpose for older people, but each of them demonstrates the value that at least some seniors find in joining together and working for respect, rights, and collective esteem. There is virtually no communication research on such organizations, but they do offer considerable scope for examination of communication issues. In particular, their advocacy strategies exist at an interesting intersection of public relations, social influence, and intergroup relations—all areas in which communication scientists specialize.

Cognitive Representations of Intergenerational Communication

As discussed earlier, stereotypes can be thought of as cognitive representations of old people. They are "pictures in our heads" that describe what older adults are like. Some recent research in the field of communication has begun to look at whether we also have "pictures in our head" that describe how intergenerational conversations proceed. In my research with Jordan McKee and Mei-Chen Lin, we interviewed older and younger people about their conversations with the other age group. By reading through and coding all of their descriptions of intergenerational conversations, we uncovered eight different "types" of such conversations (see Table 3.4). As the table shows, people have quite diverse ideas of what intergenerational conversations can be like, and younger and older people's schemas don't always match up very well. However, these schemas do match up in some interesting ways with the Hummert stereotypes of aging. For instance, what type of older person would

Table 3.4   Intergenerational Communication Schemas (ICSs) in the United States

---

1. *Overwhelmingly positive interaction ICS.* Young person feels warm and connected to the older person. Older person appears friendly, loving, and caring. Young person learns from older adult.

2. *Positive and helping ICS.* Same as #1. In addition, young person wants to help the older person in some way (e.g., keeping him/her company).

3. *Positive and respectful ICS.* Young person is generally positive about the older person and respects him/her. However, young person finds it difficult to find common ground in the conversation and feels an obligation to be polite to the older person (young person "bites his/her tongue").

4. *Neutral and distant ICS.* Young person has ambivalent (mixed positive and negative) feelings about the older person. Same obligation to be polite as in #3, resulting in feeling bored and wanting to leave the conversation.

5. *Sympathy and helping ICS.* This older person is ill, lonely, or disabled. Young person feels sympathetic and wants to help. Young person also feels restrained and unable to be him/herself.

6. *No connection ICS.* Young person has negative feelings about the older person. Older person expresses some hostility or negative attitudes toward the young person in the conversation. Young person still wants to help but does not enjoy the conversation.

7. *No connection and helping ICS.* Young person does not feel any connection with the older person, has some negative feelings about him/her, and really wants to leave the conversation. But young person still wants to help by keeping old person company.

8. *Negative and hostile ICS.* Older person is angry, expresses hostility, and displays negative attitudes toward young person. Older person is prejudiced against young people in general or other groups (e.g., racial or homosexual). Young person really wants to leave the conversation.

SOURCE: Adapted from "Younger and older adults' schematic representations of intergenerational communication," by J. Harwood, J. McKee, and M.-C. Lin, 2000, *Communication Monographs*, 67, pp. 20–41, and *Young adults' intergenerational communication schemas in the Taiwan and the US*, by M.-C. Lin, J. Harwood, and M. L. Hummert, 2006, unpublished manuscript, Kent State University.

you expect to have a "helping" conversation with? For most people, it would probably be the severely impaired type. Recently, Chen and King (2002) have extended this work and demonstrated some of the ways in which these different schemas are connected to satisfaction with communication for older and younger people.

Along with this work on schemas, some of Ellen Ryan's recent work (Ryan, Jin, Anas, & Luh, 2004; Ryan, Kwong See, Meneer, & Trovato, 1994) has examined people's beliefs about changes in communication with increasing age. Her work shows that young and old people tend to rate older adults as worse on expressive communication (e.g., they can't think of the right word to say) and receptive communication (e.g., they forget stuff in a conversation, they have hearing problems). Ryan's work, though, also pinpointed some selected areas in which we have positive expectations for communication with increasing age—storytelling and sincerity. These tie in with traits like wisdom and generosity, characteristic of positive stereotypes. At this point, you might want to refer back to Chapter 2, which discussed some of the realities of communication change with increasing age.

Why Do Negative Attitudes and Stereotypes Matter?

They affect older people's functioning: As described in the previous chapter, Levy's work demonstrates that, for older people, negative self-stereotyping can result in "conforming" to the stereotype—a self-fulfilling prophecy.

They affect younger people's chances of *getting* old! People with negative attitudes about aging live about 7.5 years shorter than those with rosier perceptions of aging (Levy, Slade, Kunkel, & Kasl, 2002). So believing bad things about old age can apparently kill you! How does this happen? One way suggested by Levy et al. is that individuals who "buy into" negative perceptions of aging have relatively little "will to live" when they get to be old. For those individuals, seeking medical care or positive social support in their lives might seem pointless given their negative expectations for their lives.

They affect the quality of intergenerational communication: As will be argued in the next chapter, the nature of communication between younger and older people is dramatically influenced by these kinds of attitudes and stereotypes, generally not in a positive direction!

They lead to discrimination. While discrimination based on race and sex has received more attention in recent years, older adults are also victims of discrimination—they are treated unfairly purely based on their age. Examples of this are found throughout this book. Just to give you one example, an economist recently examined player voting patterns on the television quiz show *The Weakest Link*. On this program, participants answer trivia questions and then have the opportunity to vote for which other contestants should be kicked off the show. In an examination of over 160 episodes of the show, Levitt (2004) showed that older contestants are voted off by the other players in ways that cannot be explained by their performance on the trivia questions. Of course, being voted off a quiz show might seem unimportant, but similar patterns can be seen in job hiring, medical treatment, and other important areas, as you will see as you read further.

Summary

Expectations for aging are largely negative. We expect older adults to experience declines in health and declines in a large number of phenomena closely related to communication. However, in most research, dimensions are identified in which gains are expected—gains in wisdom or storytelling ability for instance. This is a promising sign—having some positive expectations for aging should mean that people are open to broadening their view of the aging process. However, we should resist stereotypical images of aging even when they are positive—stereotypes are always simplifications and may lead to problems even when they are positive. For instance, being perceived as "wise" may be problematic if what you want to do is goof around. In the next chapter, we investigate how these attitudes, stereotypes, and identity phenomena are associated with patterns of interpersonal communication.

Keywords and Theories

AARP	Social creativity
Age identity	Social identity theory
Attitude	Social mobility
Double standard	Stereotype
Myths of aging	Stereotype content model
Social competition	Traits

Discussion Questions

• Why are we so negative about aging? What are some reasons for these attitudes?
• What are some ways in which **younger** people are stereotyped negatively? How might younger people respond (social mobility, social creativity, social competition) to negative stereotyping?
• Can you think of any other "schemas" for intergenerational communication?
• Which of Hummert's stereotypes (Table 3.3) might be associated with which of the schemas for intergenerational communication (Table 3.4)?
• Pick one of the "myths of aging"; why do we call this a myth?

Annotated Bibliography

Harwood, J., Giles, H., & Ryan, E. B. (1995). Aging, communication, and intergroup theory: Social identity and intergenerational communication. In J. F. Nussbaum & J. Coupland (Eds.), *Handbook of communication and aging research* (pp. 133–159). Mahwah, NJ: Lawrence Erlbaum. A chapter that engages the different ways in which older people respond to negative stereotypes and attitudes—it has extensive coverage of social mobility, social creativity, and social competition.

Hummert, M. L., Garstka, T. A., Shaner, J. L., & Strahm, S. (1994). Stereotypes of the elderly held by young, middle-aged and elderly adults. *Journals of Gerontology: Psychological Sciences, 49,* 240–249. A research study showing the multiple stereotypes of aging (perfect grandparent, etc.). The details of the method are very interesting, and it's an impressive study that uses young, middle-aged, and older subjects.

Nelson, T. D. (Ed.). (2004). *Ageism: Stereotyping and prejudice against older persons.* Cambridge, MA: MIT Press. An edited book that covers a lot of different angles concerning negative attitudes toward older people.

FOUR

Aging, Identity, Attitudes, and Intergenerational Communication

This chapter examines the ways in which ageist attitudes, age stereotypes, and age identity affect communication practices. It describes research on how younger people talk to older people, and vice versa By the end of this chapter you should be able to:

SOURCE: © Istockphoto.com

- Describe the communication predicament of aging model
- Describe the age stereotypes in interaction model
- Discuss some of the negative effects of attitudes and stereotypes of aging
- Distinguish between overaccommodation and underaccommodation
- Describe how age identity relates to communication
- Describe the components of patronizing talk
- Describe some of the reasons why older people might (a) tell you about painful things in their lives, or (b) tell you their age

You grew old first not in your own eyes, but in other people's eyes;
then, slowly, you agreed with their opinion of you. It wasn't that
you couldn't walk as far as you used to, it was that other people
didn't expect you to; and if they didn't then it needed vain obsti-
nacy to persist.

—Julian Barnes, *Staring at the Sun*

H ave you ever been in a conversation with an older person who seemed interested in sharing every detail of his or her latest medical complaint? Have you ever overheard a young person talking to an older person and wondered why the young person was using the kind of tone you would use with a child? This chapter will explore some of the phenomena that researchers have observed in intergenerational communication—communication between younger and older people—including understanding how the ideas from the previous chapter concerning stereotypes, attitudes, and identities may influence such communication. To help us on our journey, we are going to begin with a model called the **communication predicament of aging** (CPA) model, and prior to that a theory—**communication accommodation theory**.

Communication Accommodation Theory

Communication accommodation theory (CAT) examines the ways in which people adjust their speech style depending on who they are talking to. For instance, we tend to talk faster when we're talking to someone who talks fast, and we might use more slang when talking to a friend than when talking to a professor. In other words, we converge toward the speech style of someone we believe to be similar to us, someone we like, or someone we believe to have higher status. Alternatively, we might also diverge from someone we do not like or want to be like.

This theory focuses particularly on social group memberships. For example, some CAT researchers examine how conflict between groups changes speech styles. People often exaggerate their accents or even switch into a different language when talking with someone from a cultural group that they dislike (e.g., people from Wales may speak with an extreme Welsh accent, or even speak in Welsh when they are confronted with a disliked English person). The theory also explains why people with a stigmatized speech style (e.g., a heavy Southern accent) might conceal or permanently change their accent in certain contexts (e.g., interviewing for a job with a corporation located outside of the South).

What does this have to do with aging? Well, as noted in the previous chapter, age groups are social groups too. While they don't have accents, per se, it's nevertheless possible to understand some aspects of intergenerational communication using CAT. Drawing on what we know about stereotypes from the previous chapter, recent CAT research has focused on how young people may overaccommodate older people in their communication. **Overaccommodation** means "going too far" in accommodating someone's communication needs, for instance, in talking to an older person as if they were a baby. Here, CAT would argue that the speaker is accommodating not to the older person, but rather to a stereotype of older adults. Specifically, if you are not aware of the specific abilities that someone has, one "short cut" you can take is to rely on a stereotype. If you stereotype an older person as deaf, then you will tend to talk louder to that person. If you hold the stereotype of declining mental speed, you might adopt a slower and simplified speech style. Remember from the previous chapter that our stereotypes of aging are predominantly negative, so those are more likely than positive stereotypes to influence the communication here.

Communication scholars have developed various names for this overaccommodation. It has been called **patronizing talk**, **elderspeak**, and **secondary baby talk**, among others. Some of the key elements of this style are illustrated in Table 4.1. These kinds of adaptations in speech style have been shown in studies where younger people have to, for instance, give instructions to either younger or older targets—they use simpler vocabulary and slower speech style when talking to the older adults. Such speech has been found not only between strangers, but also in service environments like craft clubs (Kemper, 1994) and even in grandchildren talking to their grandparents (Montepare, Steinberg, & Rosenberg, 1992). Extreme versions of such adjustments have also been observed in natural settings such as nursing homes. Consider the following example, addressed to an older woman:

> "That's good. Now I'm going to put your top on before we stand you up. First of all, do a little jump up to release the nightgown. That's a good girl . . ." (Gibb & O'Brien, 1990, p. 1395)

Table 4.1   Common Elements of Patronizing Speech

Element	Definition and example
Simplified grammar	Use of short sentences without multiple clauses. "Here's your food. You can eat it. It is good."
Simplified vocabulary	Use of short words rather than longer equivalents Saying *dog* instead of *Dalmatian,* or *big* instead of *enormous.*
Endearing terms	Calling someone "sweetie" or "love."
Increased volume, reduced rate	Talking LOUDER and s-l-o-w-e-r!
High and variable pitch	Using a slightly squeaky voice style, and exaggerating the pitch variation in speech (a "sing-song" type speech style).
Use of repetition	Saying things over and over again. Repeating. Redundancy. Over and over again. The same thing. Repeated. Again. And again…
Use of baby-ish terms	Using words like *doggie* or *choo-choo* instead of *dog* or *train*: "Oh look at the cute little doggie, isn't he a coochie-coochie-coo!"

Research by Linda Caporael (1981) has demonstrated that people who hear this kind of speech outside of the context in which it originally occurred find it indistinguishable from talk to children in day care.

The Communication Predicament of Aging (CPA) Model

The CPA model (see Figure 4.1) takes the idea of overaccommodation and extends it into a broader picture of the causes and consequences of bad intergenerational communication (Hummert, Garstka, Ryan, & Bonnesen, 2004; Ryan, Giles, Bartolucci, & Henwood, 1986). The CPA model begins with an observation of **age cues**—younger people immediately recognize older people's group membership through visual cues like wrinkled skin and grey hair, and even other cues like tone of voice (top right of Figure 4.1). Even

Figure 4.1   The Communication Predicament of Aging Model

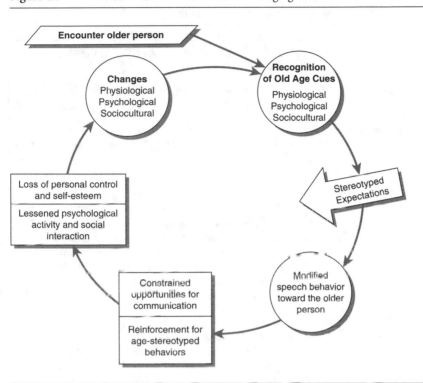

SOURCE: Reprinted from *Language and Communication*, 6, Ryan, E. B., Giles, H,, Bartolucci, G., & Henwood, K., Psycholinguistic and social psychological components of communication by and with the elderly, 1–24, (1986), with permission from Elsevier.

aspects of vocabulary may clue us in to somebody's age—words like "wireless" (meaning radio) or "icebox" (meaning fridge) are strongly indicative of age (see Table 4.2).

The CPA model argues that these cues to age activate stereotypes of aging that influence people's decisions about communication. Of course, when I say "decisions" here, these are processes that are occurring very rapidly and at a largely subconscious level. A typical effect is that the negative stereotypes lead to overaccommodation via the process described above in CAT. This is the area described as "**modified speech behavior** toward the older person" in Figure 4.1.

Table 4.2   Examples of Vocabulary Changes Over Recent Decades (and hence generations). How many of these do you know?

1940s and 1950s	Quonset hut, beehive, Frisbee, ECT, Windsor knot, ICBM, wireless
1970s and 1980s	golden handcuffs, 8-track, headhunter, vermiculture, gimme cap, blaxploitation, Walkman, stoned
1990s and 2000s	iPod, Xbox, bubble (no, not like a soap bubble!), Botox, identity theft, SARS, Da bomb, meth, wireless
Answers	
1940s and 1950s	Quonset hut (a temporary building developed in WWII), beehive (a very high back-combed woman's hairdo), Frisbee (a flying disc toy), ECT (electroconvulsive therapy: an electric shock treatment for schizophrenia and depression), Windsor knot (a type of men's tie knot), ICBM (intercontinental ballistic missile: a long range missile for delivering bombs), wireless (radio)
1970s and 1980s	golden handcuffs (financial incentives that make it difficult for a valued employee to leave a company), 8-track (a music cartridge), headhunter (someone who lures workers from one company to another), vermiculture (composting using worms), gimme cap (a mesh-back, foam front baseball style cap, generally with a product logo on the front), blaxploitation (a controversial genre of movies featuring Black actors), Walkman (portable music player), stoned (high on marijuana).
1990s and 2000s	iPod (portable digital music player), Xbox (video game console), bubble (excessive rise in stock or housing prices), Botox (injectable skin wrinkle reducer), identity theft (stealing personal information to open financial accounts in someone else's name), SARS (severe acute respiratory syndrome: a contagious respiratory ailment), Da bomb (good, as in "you are da bomb!"), meth (methamphetamine: a drug), wireless (generally used to refer to internet access without a physical wire, often in a public place)

SOURCE: From www.Merriam-Webster.com, www.funtrivia.com, and www.wikipedia.org

Whether mild or extreme, this overaccommodative or patronizing style of communication constrains the older adult's options in the conversation. If someone is talking to you as if you are a 4-year-old, it's pretty difficult to display intellectual prowess or sparkling wit! Older adults are also faced with a key dilemma when faced with communication like this. They can either ignore it or "go along with it," which might indicate acceptance, or they can complain or reject it, which might make them look cranky or bitter (remember the *curmudgeon* stereotype?).

The CPA model argues that overaccommodative speech and the resulting constraints on older people's communication can have very negative effects for the older person. Ellen Ryan has demonstrated what she calls the **blame the victim** effect—when people overhear someone being patronized, they automatically assume that person to be cognitively deficient in some way, even when they know nothing about the person (Hummert & Ryan, 2001). Kemper and Harden (1999) showed that *recipients* of patronizing talk also show this effect— that is, when patronized they evaluate *themselves* as less competent. Other research showed the possibility for self-esteem damage as a result of being patronized (O'Connor & Rigby, 1996).

So, in addition to limiting older persons' communicative options, long-term repeated interactions involving being patronized may start to take their toll as older people increasingly believe that they perhaps "deserve" this kind of treatment. Once they buy into this idea, then they may start to behave in ways that are consistent with the stereotype, thus reinforcing the stereotype that started the whole process (see top left of Figure 4.1). This is a complex sequence of events involving many steps. However, the message is relatively simple: Treat someone as if they are impaired and incompetent, and over time they may actually become impaired and incompetent.

Ironically, certain elements of the patronizing style are helpful to some older adults' comprehension. For instance, elaborating on meaning, placing stress in appropriate places (keywords), and reducing grammatical complexity can be helpful in aiding comprehension. However, other elements are actually harmful (e.g., speaking in a high pitch, reducing sentence length) (Cohen & Faulkner, 1986; Kemper & Harden, 1999). In addition, while we might look at this type of speech and see it as disrespectful, in certain contexts it is actually appreciated by older people. In particular, older adults who are suffering from ill health and older adults in institutions like nursing homes tend to see certain elements of patronizing speech as representing caring and **nurturance** from the person who is talking to them. Therefore, while this chapter is presenting the negative side of this style of speech, it should be noted that certain elements of this style may be appropriate at *certain times* with *certain types of older person* (O'Connor & Rigby, 1996; Ryan, Bourhis, & Knops, 1991). The key challenge, therefore, is recognizing the times when such speech might be appropriate, and the specific elements of the speech that might be functional. Chapter 7 addresses some of these issues in more detail.

The Age Stereotypes in Interaction Model

The CPA model has one substantial problem when looked at in the context of the work in Chapter 3. It focuses exclusively on situations in which negative stereotypes are prevalent. Remember, that chapter also discussed positive stereotypes of aging. Mary Lee Hummert's activation of **age stereotypes in interaction** (ASI) model considers situations in which positive stereotypes are salient using a similar structure to that of the predicament model. Some of the key elements of this model were described in the previous chapter—it specifies under what circumstances positive and negative stereotypes are likely to become salient (see Figures 3.2 and 3.3 in Chapter 3).

For this chapter, the important aspect of Hummert's model is its description of how communication is influenced by positive and negative stereotypes (see Figure 4.2). As with the communication predicament model, the ASI model says that negative stereotypes will result in a negative style of speech. Hummert, however, draws attention to the fact that some negative stereotypes may be more likely to elicit a patronizing style than others. A severely impaired elder is quite likely to be patronized. A shrew/curmudgeon type elder (the ornery, bitter, and complaining type) is perhaps unlikely to be addressed in the classic patronizing style. Instead, a young person faced with this type of conversational partner may be more likely to respond in kind (bitter, angry), or simply try to get out of the situation as quickly as possible. Thus, The ASI model uses the term **age adapted speech** to allow for any number of different forms of adaptation (or accommodation).

Hummert also notes that a patronizing style is fairly unlikely with most of the positive stereotypes. Given that the positive stereotypes describe older individuals who are competent and socially engaged, she suggests that they will be addressed with **normal adult speech**. According to Hummert, the negative feedback cycle of the CPA model is "short-circuited" when positive stereotypes are activated. Thus, the model draws attention to the advantages of positive over negative stereotyping.

Figure 4.2   Activation of Age Stereotypes in Interaction Model

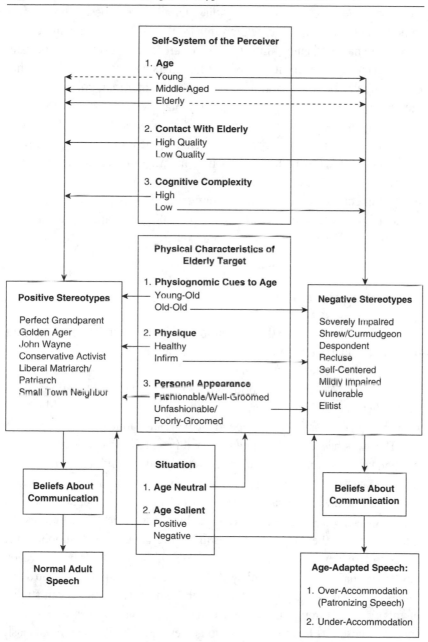

SOURCE: From Hummert, M. L. (1994). Stereotypes of the elderly and patronizing speech. In M. L. Hummert, J. M. Wiemann, & J. F. Nussbaum (Eds.), *Interpersonal communication in older adulthood: Interdisciplinary theory and research* (pp. 162–184). Newbury Park, CA: Sage.

Of course, there might still be some bad consequences from positive stereotypes. Positive stereotypes are still, after all, stereotypes. Nobody wants to be treated like a warm, fuzzy grandma *all* the time, but if you are female, have white hair, and enjoy knitting, chances are that is how you will be categorized. Once this occurs, it is possible that others will restrict the topics they choose to talk about with you (e.g., the weather rather than politics), or they may restrict the tone they use (e.g., they may believe that you would be immensely shocked by even the mildest profanity). As such, while the conversation may be pleasant, it may be restricted in some very meaningful ways.

In Chapter 7, I will talk more about some ways of breaking the negative cycle of the communication predicament model—particularly in terms of the positive effects of contact between younger and older people. Recent versions of Hummert's model (Hummert et al., 2004) also address older adult responses and "breaking the cycle" more explicitly.

Supporting Dependency

One additional area is worthy of mention in this chapter. Rather than focus on an individual's communication (as is the case in the work on patronizing talk), Margaret Baltes focuses on exchanges *between* people (M. M. Baltes & Wahl, 1996). Looking at real-world conversations between older and younger people, her interest is in the ways in which younger people support the independence (or alternatively the dependence) of older adults.

This work has considered a number of different intergenerational communication contexts, from conversations between residents and nurses in nursing homes, to conversations between family members. Across all of these contexts, Baltes has examined what happens when the older person asks for help and what happens when the older person does something independently. In all cases, the question is whether a younger person in the environment supports the **independent/dependent behavior**. Why does this matter? Well, basic psychology tells us that we keep doing things that we are rewarded for, and we stop doing things for which we are punished. You might remember hearing about studies of rats running through mazes and either getting bits of cheese or electric shocks—those rats learn which way to go very quickly! People are obviously more complicated than rats, but nevertheless we respond to rewards and punishments in similar ways. When people support our behaviors, we keep doing them. When they do not support them or contradict them, we tend to stop.

Figure 4.3 illustrates a typical set of findings from one of Baltes's studies—this one involved health care workers visiting the home of an older person. She calls the responses "congruent" (meaning supportive of or consistent with the initial behavior) or "incongruent" (meaning not supporting or inconsistent with the initial behavior). At the top of the figure, you can see that when the older person behaves in a dependent fashion (asking for help, displaying need), younger health care workers responded primarily in a congruent fashion. Only 5% of the time did the older person receive an incongruent response (i.e., a response encouraging independence). In contrast, the bottom of Figure 4.3 shows that when the older person displayed *independence,* incongruent responses that would encourage *dependence* occurred almost half the time (46%). Congruent responses occurred only 20% of the time. The message here is that when older adults behave as if they need help, younger people tend to support that dependence. However, when older people behave in an independent fashion, younger people do not support that independence, and in fact they reject the older adult's independence quite a bit of the time. The consequence is that older people are discouraged from being independent, and hence will move toward reinforcing the stereotype that they are dependent.

Figure 4.3   Home Health Care Workers' Responses to Independent and Dependent Behavior by Older Adult

Older adult behavior	Health care worker response	Frequency of pattern
Dependence "I need help putting on this shirt"	Congruent "OK, I'll help"	58%
	Incongruent "Say, why don't you give it a try today"	5%
Independence "I'll put my own shirt on today"	Congruent "Great—you take care of that"	20%
	Incongruent "Don't be silly, I'll do that for you"	46%

Why does this happen? In contexts like nursing homes, life is often easiest for the staff if older adults are dependent. Encouraging independence may involve waiting for an older adult to complete a task that she or he finds difficult. This can be more time consuming for nurses and other staff than if they just take care of the task themselves. Hence, in some institutional contexts, staff may have a concrete motivation for discouraging independence—their desire to complete the specific task at hand (Grainger, 2004). Stereotypes concerning older adults' general level of competence also factor in. Nurses and other staff in institutional care settings may be particularly vulnerable to stereotypes of older adults' incompetence given that they work in medical care settings and are exposed to unhealthy and dependent older adults more than healthy and independent older people. As such, they may be likely to assume that an older adult cannot accomplish a task, and hence not be concerned about encouraging independence. Older adults may have learned that they get more attention and interaction if they are dependent (Grainger, 2004).

In contexts like family interaction, it's more difficult to see why we would want to support dependence. However, stereotypes probably play a role: We are unlikely to support an older adult's independence if we believe that independence is impossible for older people—and it's certainly not impossible for us to stereotype our own family members. Other factors probably come into play. A younger family member may be concerned about an older adult's safety if they are encouraged to cook their own meals, for instance. Time constraints similar to those in nursing homes may also come into play in families: The younger person might be visiting briefly on the way to work, and getting tasks taken care of efficiently may be a greater priority than encouraging the older person's independence.

The long-term consequences of encouraging dependence and discouraging independence are, of course, clear. The more that our communication rewards dependent behaviors and fails to reward independence, the more dependent older people will become, and hence the more they will come to resemble our stereotype. This is a classic self-fulfilling prophecy, the ultimate result of which is older people who are highly dependent on younger people.

A classic study by Langer and Rodin (1976; Rodin & Langer, 1977) investigated the consequences of a feeling of control for older people in institutions. In their study, they created two groups of nursing home residents. One group were given lots of choices and options for control (e.g., they got to pick which day they would see a movie, they got to decide whether they got a plant in their room and had to care for the plant if they chose to have it). The other group were treated just as nicely, but didn't get the same level of control (e.g., they got told which day they would go see the movie; they received a plant and a staff member cared for it). Over a period of time, these researchers tracked issues such as happiness and health and found that the group who had more control over their lives were not only happier, but also healthier, and more likely to be alive at the end of the study. So a lack of control and independence can have dramatic influences on life satisfaction and physical health.

Other Dimensions of Accommodation

The previous sections have focused extensively on overaccommodation, particularly from younger people to older people. In this next section, we focus on the opposite phenomenon—**underaccommodation**. Where over-accommodation is "going too far" in accommodating another person, under-accommodation occurs when someone does not go far enough in considering a conversational partner's needs. A totally inconsiderate conversationalist is underaccommodative.

The most common form of underaccommodation talked about in intergenerational communication is **painful self-disclosure** (PSD) by older people. J. Coupland and colleagues define PSD as occurring when older people talk about painful events in their lives like illness, bereavement, financial struggles, and the like. Consider the following:

> "You know, yes, mmm . . . I think you see when you're getting older at this age you (pause) there's a lot of things can make us a bit miserable but (breathes) we have a look on the bright side and . . . nobody wants you when you're miserable and moaning . . . and groaning . . . it applies to all ages really doesn't it, you know . . . because I can't breath I've got emphysema and I'm full of osteoarthritis and what have you but erm (breathes) thank goodness the old brain box is still going." (J. Coupland, Coupland, Giles, & Wiemann, 1988, p. 223)

J. Coupland's work shows that PSD occurs quite frequently in older people's talk, and that it occurs to relative strangers. This violates some "rules" of conversation that are generally observed—we tend to reserve intimate information for our close acquaintances and family members, and we tend to disclose such information relatively sparingly. Thus, when older adults engage in PSD, it is often difficult for younger people to cope with. They don't know quite what to say next, they feel embarrassed, and they sometimes feel like the older person must just be totally depressed or totally self-centered. These feelings in the recipient of such talk are what make it underaccommodative (Henwood, Giles, Coupland, & Coupland, 1993). Importantly, J. Coupland et al. (1988) note that the disclosures are not necessarily painful for older people. One of the interesting aspects of this talk is that sometimes it is presented in a very "matter of fact" or even humorous fashion. This disjunct between the apparent emotion of the topic (e.g., bereavement, serious illness) and the tone of the talk may be another reason why it can be disconcerting for younger recipients.

Given that this talk breaks some of our rules for good conversation, and that recipients have a hard time coping with it, one challenge is to figure out *why* it happens. Coupland and his colleagues provide a number of suggestions (see Table 4.3), although we still need more research to understand the origins of this type of talk more fully. The suggestions in Table 4.3 are worth considering, however, because they question a stereotypical assumption that a lot of people might make about this kind of talk. When old people start talking about their problems, a listener might be inclined to think that it is due to depression, loneliness, or just being self-centered and inconsiderate. In contrast, the explanations in the table show that such talk might be a very functional way of operating in the social environment as an older person, and it may even occur as a result of a lifetime of age-related stereotyping. Don't forget: Young people can be underaccommodative too. Discussing topics or using "slang" words that are unfamiliar would be underaccommodative if it occurred repeatedly in interactions with an older person.

Age Identity: Disclosing and Concealing Age in Communication

As Chapter 3 made clear, for many people their age is an important part of who they are. **Age identity** is the sense of shared group membership, and the similarities that come along with that, based on age group. The next section discusses the important role that age identity plays in communication processes. Before we get to these discussions, though, a brief detour is necessary to discuss the social scientific notion of **face**. When social scientists discuss "face," they are talking about a person's self-image or how they present themselves to others in the social environment (Goffman, 1967). You are probably familiar with the idea that someone might "lose face." For instance, you might be afraid that your friends would think less of you if you did something really embarrassing in front of them. Events that might make us

Table 4.3   Coupland et al.'s (1988) Explanations for Painful Self-Disclosure

Therapeutic:	By talking about a problem, older people get it "off their chest," which helps them cope. There is good evidence from other areas that talking about problems contributes to coping.
Life circumstances:	Older adults may experience more negative events in their lives than younger people, both as a function of health issues and age-related discrimination practices. Hence, negative experiences may be the most "newsworthy" things that older people have to talk about. By discussing these things, they are making the conversation as interesting as they can.
Self-handicapping:	We often provide "disclaimers" before doing things (e.g., "I'm not feeling well, but I'll take the exam anyway"—if you flunk the exam, it wasn't your fault; it was because you were ill). By disclosing painful information, older people may be telling their audience that they shouldn't expect "too much." The PSD serves as a disclaimer, making the older adult's current level of functioning more impressive than it otherwise might be.
Self-stereotyping:	Some older people who do PSD may be trying to behave as is socially expected. That is, older people may actually try to conform to how they think they are expected to talk, one aspect of which is talking about health, loneliness, and the like.
Social comparison:	PSD occurs when older people talk to one another. At times, this may serve a function of figuring out how well/poorly you are doing relative to others in your age group. By disclosing when your husband died, you may get a reciprocation, which will let you know whether your husband died earlier or later than your conversational partner's husband. In this sense, disclosure serves as a technique for getting the other person to disclose, and thus finding out information about that person, and hence giving you information to understand your own experiences.

look bad are called face threatening, and actions we engage in to minimize such threats are called face protection. If we are engaged in the process of trying to make ourselves look good to others, we would be engaged in face enhancement (P. Brown & Levinson, 1987). Face is an important concept in discussions of identity because the way we view ourselves and the way others view us are often determined by which identities we claim and which identities others *think* we might claim. As is discussed next, we might also strategically talk about certain identities in order to protect or enhance our face.

One of the most fundamental ways in which we reveal our age identity in conversation is by telling people how old we are. However, telling people our age is something that we don't always do willingly. Indeed, for a large chunk of adulthood, age is something of a taboo topic—traditionally it has been rude to ask people (especially women) their age, and disclosing age is fraught with uncertainty, and even deception ("36. . . . again!!!"). However, in older adulthood, a somewhat different pattern emerges, and we see age being disclosed quite a bit in conversation. N. Coupland, Coupland, and Giles (1989) provide extensive discussion of some of the reasons for this, as well as providing some nice examples from their data. N. Coupland et al. argue that telling other people your age in older adulthood serves two functions for the individual, both of which relate to the idea that there is a relationship between age and health. First, for people who are suffering from illness or disability, telling other people your age can serve an **accounting** function. Consider the following example (from N. Coupland & Coupland, 1995): "[I'm] not on top of the world, but none of us are, are we, no, but when you come to eighty-three years of age you can't expect to be like a spring chicken, can you?"

Acknowledging problems or deficits is never something that people find easy—it tells other people that you are in a sense imperfect. As discussed above, social scientists would refer to this as a face threatening situation. So how do older people protect themselves from such face threat? One way is by telling their age. In the example above, the listing of the age (83) sets into motion a sequence of inferences. This woman is 83, that's old, old people tend to suffer from physical impairments (notice how the stereotype is involved.), and so it's understandable that she's not doing so well. Any potential judgment that this woman is particularly impaired is offset by the underlying assumption that all people of 83 are somewhat impaired. Thus, disclosing age is face *protecting* in this instance: Problems that I have are explained by my age and therefore do not reflect any fundamental flaw with me as a person.

The second function that N. Coupland et al. claim for age disclosures is a disjunctive function. Consider the following example (from N. Coupland et al., 1989): "I lead quite a busy life although I'm eighty-six I'm not young . . . I was eighty-six last May!"

In this case, the speaker is telling us something positive about herself. While leading a busy life might not be remarkable for many people, by disclosing her age (86) she is invoking the stereotypes of decline with age described earlier, and thus she is making her activity level more admirable. This is called "disjunctive" because typical expectations about 86-year-olds are apparently in opposition (disjunction) with the behaviors this person is engaging in. The result is face *enhancement* for this person—she is "beating the odds."

These face-management functions of **age disclosure** are interesting for a couple of reasons. First, they reveal that age is actually a resource (N. Coupland et al. call it a "token") that can be used at any point in a conversation to protect or enhance face. Age is not being disclosed randomly, but rather it is being used strategically when it is needed. The second interesting thing about these two uses of age (disjunctive and accounting) is that both rest on the *same* assumptions about the aging process. That is, they both rely on the hearer understanding and believing in a normative association between age and health. If the receiver of these comments did not believe that old age and ill health go hand-in-hand, then the use of age here would not make sense. One unfortunate implication of this is that for older people, use of this kind of strategy is useful for them as individuals, but it reinforces negative perceptions of old people more generally. When older people say that they are "doing well for their age," they make themselves look good, but simultaneously they make old age look bad.

Why I Study Communication and Aging
Ellen B. Ryan (Professor, McMaster University, Canada)

The physical, psychological, and social changes of old age threaten the identity of aging women and men. Communication predicaments lead them to question whether they have begun to fall over the anticipated precipice. I am seeking ways to empower older adults so that they can find their inner voices and then their social voices to show us the many ways to age successfully.

Reprinted with permission of Ellen B. Ryan.

Summary

Beginning with a description of the communication predicament of aging model, this chapter has covered the key relationships between attitudes and stereotypes of aging, and communication behaviors. I talked about how negative stereotypes may lead to patronizing speech (overaccommodation), as well as the reasons why underaccommodation (e.g., painful self-disclosure) might occur in intergenerational settings. Age identity and categorization emerge as important elements determining how and why people behave in the way they do when talking to people of different age groups. Throughout, one message is that as identities and stereotypes influence communication, negative attitudes and stereotypes tend to get reinforced in a self-fulfilling prophecy.

Keywords and Theories

Age identity

Age stereotypes in interaction model

Age adapted speech

Blame the victim effect

Communication accommodation theory

Communication predicament of aging
    model

Disclosure of chronological age

Elderspeak

Face

Independent/dependent behavior

Modified speech behavior

Normal adult speech

Overaccommodation

Painful self-disclosure

Patronizing speech

Secondary baby talk

Underaccommodation

Discussion Questions

- What might be some ways to break the communication predicament of aging? (Look back at your answers to this question after you've read Chapter 7!)
- What are some other reasons why older people might disclose painful information? Can you think of other things that older people do in conversation that appear unusual to younger people? Why might they do those things?
- How does younger people's communication reflect their age identities? Are there ways that teenagers talk that are a reflection of their age group?
- Are there any aspects of young people's communication that are underaccommodative to older people?
- Do older adults ever patronize young people?

Annotated Bibliography

Coupland, N., & Coupland, J. (2001). Language, ageing and ageism. In W. P. Robinson & H. Giles (Eds.), *The new handbook of language and social psychology* (pp. 451–468). New York: John Wiley. This chapter provides excellent discussion of the ways in which language reinforces ageist attitudes, including coverage of links between health, age identities, and language.

Hummert, M. L., Garstka, T. A., Ryan, E. B., & Bonnesen, J. L. (2004). The role of age stereotypes in interpersonal communication. In J. F. Nussbaum and J. Coupland (Eds.), *Handbook of communication and aging research* (2nd ed., pp. 91–121). Mahwah, NJ: Lawrence Erlbaum. This chapter provides comprehensive coverage of the influence of age stereotypes on communication, including an updated version of the age stereotypes in interaction model.

Ryan, E. B., Giles, H., Bartolucci, G., & Henwood, K. (1986). Psycholinguistic and social psychological components of communication by and with the elderly. *Language and Communication, 6*, 1–24. The classic paper in which the communication predicament model was introduced. This article includes a lot more than just the CPA model and is essential reading for those interested in the history of how communication and aging has been studied.

FIVE

Intragenerational Relationships in Older Adulthood

This chapter describes some of the key intragenerational relational dynamics in older adulthood, focusing particularly on spousal relationships, friendships, and sibling relationships. By the end of this chapter you should be able to:

SOURCE: ©Tomaz Levstek/Istockphoto.com

- Explain why personal relationships can influence physical and psychological health
- Identify life-span changes in marital satisfaction, and understand some reasons for marital satisfaction in old age
- Comment on the role that friends play in older people's lives
- Describe, and explain, life-span changes in sibling relationships
- Describe when sibling relationships tend to be closer in old age

Tell me am I right to think that there could be nothing better
Than making you my bride and slowly growing old together?

—The Postal Service, "Nothing Better"

Interpersonal relationships are essential to our being. For all people, substandard interpersonal relationships generally lead to more depression, poorer health, and the like. We are fundamentally social beings for whom contact with others brings many rewards. One key phenomenon that comes from social contact is **social support**. Everyone has times during which they need help—financial, emotional, practical—and we turn to our friends and our family members for that support. Individuals who do not have strong and reliable sources of support tend to suffer negative consequences. Research now unequivocally demonstrates that quality social relationships contribute to good psychological and physical health, and that poor social relationships contribute directly to negative health outcomes. For instance, Lyyra and Heikkinen (2006) show that older women who receive low levels of social support are *2.5 times more likely to die* in a 10-year period than similar women who receive high levels of social support. Why? Check out the explanations in Table 5.1.

The nature of social relationships is generally pretty stable through the life span. Despite the suggestion of **disengagement theory** (see Chapter 1), most people keep a consistent network of relationships into old age. There are some signs that the network gets smaller in late old age (e.g., among people who are 80+). Of course, this is in part due to bereavement and moving (e.g., relocating for better weather, or to a retirement community). In addition, as described in Chapter 1, smaller social networks are a function of people actively focusing on relationships that are most important to them and "dropping" more peripheral relationships. Similarly, the type of communication that maintains quality relationships tends to stay fairly stable. In addition to social support, quality social relationships feature expressions of affection, agreement about how everyone is going to behave, and regular interaction (whether face-to-face or using the telephone or Internet)

Table 5.1   How Do Good and Bad Social Relationships Influence Physical and
Psychological Health?

Material Support: Need a ride to the doctor? The first person likely to help is a spouse, a close friend, or perhaps an adult child. If those relationships don't offer this kind of material support, you may not get to the physician.

Enhancing Immune Function: Close personal relationships are places where we feel good (e.g., by telling each other jokes and stories, by laughing). Feeling psychologically positive has very direct influence on the body's physiology, particularly in terms of strengthening the immune system and releasing endorphins (Rosenkranz et al., 2003; Segerstrom, Taylor, & Kemeny, 1996). Of course, the flip side here is that relationships that are conflict-ridden and rife with hostility and anger tend to have negative effects on health because they suppress immune system functioning (Uchino, Capioppo, & Kiecolt-Glaser, 1996).

Protecting Against the Effects of Negative Mood: Negative mood states (and particularly stress) can negatively influence health (particularly cardiovascular health—heart disease, etc.). Positive social relationships can reduce the effects of stress on the body (e.g., by offering opportunities for the person to "vent," by encouraging a person to take some time off, or reconceptualize the stressful event as "not so bad after all"). This can buffer the body from some of the negative effects (Rodrigue & Park, 1996).

Encouraging Health-Related Behaviors: Sometimes, relationships can support healthy behaviors. An older couple who take walks together, or who decide to quit smoking together, can be mutually supportive and hence the relationship directly influences their health. Unfortunately, the same reinforcement processes can have negative effects (e.g., for the friends who encourage each other to have one more drink). Hence, social relationships per se are not what helps here!

Encouraging a Sense of Self-Efficacy: "Self-efficacy" is the sense that you are competent to accomplish something (e.g., if you have self-efficacy with regard to quitting smoking, it means that you think you'll be able to quit). Friends and family who provide support can increase older adults' sense of self-efficacy, because they provide the feeling that things can be accomplished. "If I have all these people behind me, I can do X!" That feeling of competence can be crucial in coping with potentially life-threatening situations like illness (e.g., taking medications in the right dose at the right time is more likely if you feel like you are capable of doing it).

(Bengtson & Roberts, 1991). People of all ages are more likely to establish and maintain quality relationships when they have at least a minimal level of social and communicative skills (Hansson & Carpenter, 1994; Segrin & Flora, 2000).

Of course, relationships are not always a positive presence in our lives. Health communication researchers have focused on the ways in which family members can sometimes encourage each other to engage in unhealthy behaviors (e.g., mutually supporting a drug addiction). Intergroup communication scholars have focused on the ways in which people stereotype each other, even in close relationships. Just because someone is your grandma doesn't mean that you forget she's an old person, and you might talk to her in a patronizing fashion because of your stereotypes about old people (see Chapter 4; Montepare et al., 1992). Hence, as you read the positive information in this chapter, try to avoid thinking of close relationships as unequivocally positive—there can be a dark side!

The types of relationships that are important to older people are similar to those that are important at other stages of the life span. Most older adults rate spouses and then other family members as most important. Friends can be very important, but on average they fall behind family members in the hierarchy of importance. This hierarchy appears to be pretty stable across socioeconomic and ethnic groups. In part, family relationships probably achieve priority because the family tie is one that endures over time. Families entail obligations (attending weddings, funerals, remembering birthdays, etc.) that provide scaffolding for relationships to persist, even if they are not tremendously close. In this chapter, I'll focus on three intragenerational relational contexts that we know are important: older adults' relationships with spouses, with friends, and with siblings. The next chapter will focus on intergenerational relationships. Those relationships deserve separate attention, because the age differences inherent in them can lead to processes that are unique as compared to the *intra*generational relationships discussed in the current chapter. Throughout, it's important to remember that specific relationships do not exist in isolation. Your relationship with your grandparents might well be influenced by how well your parents and grandparents get along; your relationship with your spouse might be influenced by your relationship with your children. Hence, while research almost always "isolates" relationships, you should be thinking about how each of these relationships fits into a broader family system.

Marital Relationships in Old Age

When we consider the entire life span of a marriage, most research appears to indicate that marital satisfaction drops after the initial honeymoon period, but then gradually increases through the life span. This results in a commonly cited **U-shaped curve** of satisfaction illustrated in Figure 5.1 (Levenson, Carstensen, & Gottman, 1993, 1994). Thus, older couples appear to have higher levels of satisfaction than younger couples (although perhaps not at the level of newlyweds). Of course, among older couples there is considerable diversity in their levels of satisfaction both currently and in terms of how satisfaction has changed over the years (Weishaus & Field, 1988).

Explanations for these findings vary widely. As is shown in Table 5.2, there are a lot of fairly logical explanations, and it is quite difficult methodologically to distinguish them. In most studies, age of the married partners,

Figure 5.1   U-Shaped Curve of Marital Satisfaction

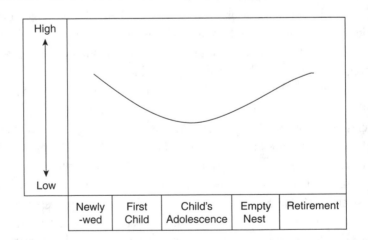

This U-shaped curve of marital satisfaction is supported by considerable research (Glenn, 1990; Rollins & Feldman, 1970), although a few recent studies have questioned its validity (VanLaningham, Johnson, & Amato, 2001). It is important to realize that all marriages are unique, and that while the "launching of children" might lead to increased satisfaction for many couples, there are other marriages for which the empty nest results in stress and dissatisfaction (Segrin & Flora, 2005). Also, it is important to recognize that the curve is relatively "shallow"—there is not a **massive** decline in satisfaction in the middle years.

Table 5.2   Explanations for Decline in Disagreements With Length of Marriage

---

Developmental (length of marriage): The longer people live together, the better they can tolerate each other's idiosyncracies, and the more accustomed they become to each other's strange behaviors. They might even become a little bored of one another, but it's less likely that they will have big fights.

Life course: Many elements of family life change with increasing age, and as the family changes so may the potential for conflict and disagreement. Children have the potential to cause serious disagreements in a marriage. Once children leave, older married couples might display less conflict simply because one source of potential conflict is no longer present.

Aging: Older marriages involve older people. Older people have been shown to be somewhat more passive and less confrontational in conflict management than younger people. Thus, older marriages may show less conflict just because they tend to involve older people.

Cohort: Older marriages at any point in time involve people born and married at a certain point in history. So, observations about older couples right now are observations about a particular cohort of marriages and people (see also Chapter 1). It's possible that people in this cohort have always disagreed less as a function of the historical cohort that they belong to, and that's why we see less conflict in older marriages.

Selective attrition: Over time, not all marriages survive, and it may be that marriages that involve more conflict are less likely to survive. So, marriages in older adulthood may demonstrate less conflict because the high conflict marriages have already ended in divorce.

SOURCE: Adapted from "Does Long Term Marriage Bring Less Frequent Disagreements? Five Explanatory Frameworks," by L. R. Hatch and K. Bulcroft, 2004, *Journal of Family Issues, 25,* pp. 465–495.

the length of time that they have been married, their life experiences, and their cohort are very difficult to disentangle. Couples in their 80s have generally been married longer, had children out of the home longer, and been born at a different time, when compared to couples in their 50s. Initial attempts to distinguish between the explanations seem to favor **cohort** and **selective attrition** explanations for these effects (see Table 5.2 and Hatch & Bulcroft, 2004). It's also important to realize that satisfaction is not the only important issue in a relationship. Issues like security, support, passion, and tension may be equally important in determining the "quality" of the relationship, and may not map in simple ways onto ratings of overall satisfaction.

Sillars and Zietlow (1993) demonstrate that older couples experience fewer conflicts and disagreements than younger couples. They also tend to disclose less to one another, perhaps because they have more common ground established. Recognizing diversity in marriages is crucial here, though. Sillars and Zietlow note that most older couples have a relaxed, compromising, and largely conflict-free pattern of communication. However, among older adults where conflicts do occur, they tend to be long-simmering and unresolved, and communication in such couples is characterized by long strings of confrontational remarks, with apparently little movement toward resolution. So while many older adult marriages reveal highly positive communication styles, when they are negative they can be *really* negative! Dickson, Christian, and Remmo (2004) note that men often become more compromising and emotionally expressive in old age, and that this change in personality may contribute to a more harmonious communication style among older couples.

Other studies suggest that older couples express more affection and positive emotions in their conversations than younger people (Carstensen, Gottman, & Levenson, 1995). Sillars and Zietlow also note that older couples make more comments to one another that confirm joint experience (e.g., "we" statements— "we enjoy Seinfeld"). Such comments are indicative of great comfort and knowledge of the other person, and symbolize a degree of shared experience and "identity" with the relationship. This is revealed also in the thematic analysis undertaken by Sillars, Burggraf, Yost, and Zietlow (1992), who showed that older couples use more **communal themes** in their conversations (see Table 5.3).

Older married individuals receive a number of benefits from their marital status (S. L. Brown, Bulanda, & Lee, 2005). They maintain higher activity levels, are happier and healthier, and live longer than their unmarried peers. People whose spouses have died tend to die younger than those whose spouses are still alive, even controlling for health, age, and sex (Rasulo, Christensen, & Tomassini, 2005). These benefits likely accrue from, among other things, the social support provided by intimate relations, as well as some of the more pragmatic benefits of cohabitation. When people are sick, they often need a little encouragement to get to a doctor, and they may even need a ride. If somebody is drinking too much alcohol or engaging in other unhealthy activities, they may need somebody to notice such behaviors and intervene. That emotional and practical support is more likely to be immediately forthcoming if

Table 5.3   Communal Themes in Marital Communication

---

a. Togetherness

   "We enjoy the same things"

   "We don't take enough time to do things"

   "We enjoy doing chores together"

b. Cooperation

   "We talk out our disagreements so that we don't confuse the children"

   "We work together in paying things"

   "I don't have the right to be irritable with you and vice-versa"

c. Communication

   "We talk all the time"

   "I feel better if I get it off my chest"

d. Romanticism

   "If two people don't show affection, chances are they're not in love"

   "Lack of affection stems from people marrying for the wrong reasons"

e. Interdependence

   "It's hard to be depressed when someone else is not"

   "If you're irritable and I'm feeling irritable, that makes it worse"

SOURCE: From Sillars & Zeitlow in Coupland, N., & Nussbaum, J. F., *Discourse and Lifespan Identity*, copyright © 1993. Reprinted with permission from Sage Publications, Inc.

there is somebody in the same room who cares about you. Men tend to benefit more than women from being married—perhaps because women tend to have more sources of extramarital support than men (Nussbaum, Pecchioni, Robinson, & Thompson, 2000).

A couple of qualifiers are important here (Musick, 2005). First, half of all marriages end in divorce, and therefore we cannot claim that marriage has the same positive effects for everybody. There are marriages that work wonderfully for the people involved, and there are marriages that do not. An *unhappy* marriage is unlikely to provide benefits to anybody! Second, while the legal *institutionalization* of a formal marriage might provide some benefits, most of the positive consequences of marriage probably come from cohabiting with another individual who loves and cares for you. So, in an era in which gay marriage is a contentious issue, we should note that most of the social, psycho-logical, and communicative benefits of marriage are also available to those in long-term cohabiting relationships, even when those relationships occur out-side the legal status of marriage. Marriage *per se* is probably not what provides the psychosocial benefits; rather, it is a stable, loving, and supportive relationship that is the answer (Ross, 1995). Of course, this does not detract from numerous other benefits that are denied to gay couples by actions to ban gay marriage (e.g., legal or financial benefits). Issues specific to gay and lesbian older adult couples are starting to receive research attention (Shenk & Fullmer, 1996).

What are some of the unique challenges faced by older married cou-ples? First, they face the challenge of retirement (Arp & Arp, 1996). With retirement may come the expectation that roles within the household will change—once he's retired, surely the husband will help with the laundry! When such roles remain unchanged and are not discussed, conflicts may arise about issues of equity within the relationship—this is particularly true when the husband is retired and the wife is still working (Rexroat & Shehan, 1987). Second, older couples face the challenge of adjusting to life without children. A marriage that was previously focused on the children (and as noted above, perhaps on work) now has to be focused on the spouse. This can be a rewarding transition, but also a challenging one (Arp & Arp, 1996). Couples also need to adjust to health changes for either partner and potentially to the resulting caregiving responsibilities. Finally, older couples have to maintain a rewarding level of intimacy, including sexual closeness. For some older couples, this may cause problems as a result of a societal taboo on thinking about old people and sex. Older couples may have the sense that being sexual is inappropriate for their age group (which is clearly not the case!) (Dickson et al., 2004).

Spouses are often the first line of defense in situations where an aging individual requires care. Spouses can find caregiving to be both rewarding and stressful (see also discussion in Chapter 6 on children providing care to parents). Edwards and Noller (1998) found that using respectful communica-tion is a key element in maintaining quality relationships during caregiving. Spouses who patronized their partners were viewed negatively by the care recipient, and these couples experienced more conflict. Chapter 11 contains more information on caregiving.

Older couples do experience **divorce**, and the consequences are similar to those among younger couples. Divorce places financial strain on the individuals, and can be damaging to their relationships with their children and grandchildren (particularly for the man). Similarly, the death of a spouse has negative effects for the survivor. Again, men appear to be hurt more by bereavement than women, for reasons outlined elsewhere (Dickson et al., 2004).

Intragenerational Friendships in Old Age

Friendships are crucial to people of all ages. Their importance does not diminish in old age. Of an extensive body of research on friendships among older adults, the most crucial finding is that friends serve similar functions and are similarly beneficial for older people as they are for all other age groups (Blieszner, 2000; Rawlins, 2004). Remember continuity theory from Chapter 1? Here it is again! The **psychosocial benefits** for friendships among older people have been documented repeatedly and are similar to the benefits for people of all ages: Older people with quality friendships are happier, healthier, and more involved in society (Adams, 1986; Rawlins, 2004). Likewise, older adults find similar aspects of friendships appealing to people of other ages. Friends are valued when they are seen to be trustworthy, entertaining, and have similar interests (Blieszner, 2000). Most research assumes that friendships are with people of a similar age, and that is often true. In this chapter we focus on such friendships, but we briefly consider intergenerational friends in the next chapter.

That said, some differences can be observed in the structure and function of friendships in old age. One difference in the nature of friendship networks has already been discussed in Chapter 1. Older adults tend to have fewer friendships, choosing to focus on the most rewarding relationships and shedding peripheral acquaintances (Carstensen, 1992). In terms of how friendships function for older people, one crucial reason why friendships are *particularly* important in old age is the fact that they are voluntary or **nonobligatory** (Antonucci & Akiyama, 1995). Nobody *forces* you to be someone's friend, whereas you have very few choices about who's going to be a family member! For older people, this may be particularly important, because they may be more inclined to view their family's behaviors as motivated by obligation. If you think that your children or grandchildren only come see you because they feel they *have to,* then you are more likely to appreciate friends who come to see you voluntarily (Nussbaum et al., 2000; Roberto & Scott, 1986).

Friendships also offer a context in which exchange is **equitable** for older adults (Nussbaum et al., 2000). Friends often support one another in old age, by running errands, driving, or even with financial support. So long as this exchange is perceived as equal, friendships can be immensely functional. For some older people, relationships with family members lose this sense of equality, and support can be seen as a "one-way street" from the younger family members to the older person.

Friends are also particularly crucial in old age because friends do a better job of connecting older people with society. Contact with family tends to occur in private settings—visits to one another's homes, for instance. In contrast, many activities with friends occur in public, and hence involve the older adult in getting "out." So, friends will go shopping, go to a ball game, or visit a museum, rather than just staying home and talking (Nussbaum, 1983).

The nursing home context provides another setting in which friendships can be crucial in old age. Older adults who are institutionalized are often isolated from their previous social networks, and unable to engage in friendships in as flexible fashion as is possible in the wider community. They may be geographically displaced, and they may be suffering from physical limitations that place constraints on their ability to get out and see old friends. A number of scholars have commented on the restricted social interaction ("**interactional starvation**") that some residents experience (Grainger, 2004). Nursing homes are often arranged in ways that impede social interaction (e.g., televisions are on loud in areas where residents congregate: Gravell, 1988). However, some nursing home residents can and do make significant and meaningful friendships with one another. And for these individuals, their friendships may be particularly crucial in maintaining well-being and happiness, given that other sources of support and companionship may be absent (Nussbaum, 1991).

Finally, friendships are important because they typically provide *intragen-*erational contact—most friends in older adulthood are other older people, generally of a fairly similar age. These friends share similar life experiences, knowledge of cultural/historical events, and the shared worldview that comes from growing up and growing old at similar points in history. Thus, there is identity support and affirmation from these same-generation peers that does not come in the same way from intergenerational contact (Nussbaum, 1983; A. Williams & Nussbaum, 2001). Indeed, it is worth noting that age-peer friendships offer the opportunity for relationships that may last for 80+ years. Siblings are about the only relationship that can last for such a long period. Nussbaum (1983) has suggested that self-disclosure is a particularly beneficial among same-age peers, and others suggest that reminiscence and support of positive age identities is crucial among old age friendships (Rawlins, 2004).

Some unique challenges face older people in their friendships with others. First, when older adults suffer physical problems, friendships can be affected in obvious and nonobvious ways (Matthews, 1996). Obviously, older people are more likely to have friends die, and the resulting loss of social networks can be problematic. The loss of a friend can have further consequences that are equally troublesome: In particular, *other* friendships that were dependent on the deceased may be lost (e.g., mutual friends). There may also be losses in terms of activities: For instance, the death or physical decline of an exercise partner might lead to a reduction in physical activity for an older individual, with the concomitant threat to his or her own health. More generally, older adults who suffer from declines in health tend to lose friends, in large part because they themselves may become less rewarding relational partners (Aartsen, van Tilburg, Smits, & Knipscheer, 2004). It is notable that while friends offer invaluable social and logistical support, it is generally the case that the "buck stops" with family members. When individuals are in need of constant care and support, extensive financial help, or serious medical treatment, it is almost always the family that steps in to deal with the situation (Rawlins, 2004).

There are also unique challenges for older *men* in maintaining friendship networks in old age. Men tend to rely on their wives for support and friendship more than their wives rely on them. So when husbands die, wives often have friendship networks in place. In contrast, when wives die, husbands are often left with very few quality relationships. Earlier in life, men have tended to rely on the workplace for friends and social contact, whereas women relied on places like the neighborhood (this, of course, is particularly true of older generations where women were less likely to work). Hence, with retirement, men lose one principal source of friends. Finally, men simply have fewer other men available in old age due to the fact that men die younger (see Chapter 1). Friendships with women can be problematic for men, both because of a perception that women have different interests, and also because cross-sex friendships can be attributed as romantic, which can cause problems. As a result of all of these issues, friendships provide unique challenges to men in old age (Rawlins, 1982). Women also experience the problem of having cross-sex friendships interpreted as romantic—not to mention that women who *are* seeking a cross-sex romantic relationship suffer from a significant scarcity of likely partners due to the different life-expectancy rates for men and women.

Waldron, Gitelson, and Kelley (2005) report one potential **buffer** to these losses for men. Men in **planned retirement communities**—residential settings for seniors with organized activities—appeared to fare much better in their study than is generally reported for older males. The men in this study had *increased* levels of social support and friendship over the course of 4 years. The authors of this study suggest that men typically make friends through activities—as mentioned above, work is one such activity, but other activities may serve the same function. Outside of a planned community, men may not join in such activities, and hence may not make many new friends after retirement. Within a setting with organized group activities, men may be more likely to participate and will emerge with stronger social networks. More research needs to be done on this phenomenon and indeed on the many social factors involved in large-scale, age-segregated housing. As noted by Waldron et al., a single such community in Florida boasts 36,000 residents!

All of this being said, friendships appear to be a little less *important* for men. More than one study has demonstrated that having close friendships has a significant impact on mortality for women, but not for men. That is, women who lack close friends tend to die younger than women who have close friends, but there is no such effect for men (Rasulo et al., 2005).

ACHIEVEMENTS IN OLD AGE

Ibrahim Ferrer

SOURCE: © Corbis

Ibrahim Ferrer was born in 1927 and died in 2005, aged 77. His professional singing career began in 1941, and over time he became well-respected as one of the leading Afro-Cuban musicians of his time. However, it was only with the popularity of the *Buena Vista Social Club* album in 1997 that Ferrer became known to a broader worldwide audience. The album won a Grammy and sold over 5 million copies. Ferrer then released a solo album, and won the Latin Grammy for best new artist at age 72. His second solo album (*Buenos Hermanos*) also won a Latin Grammy and was described by a BBC reviewer as "eloquent, inventive and utterly life-affirming." You can hear some samples of Ferrer's music at http://www.montuno.com. You can see Ferrer, visit his apartment in Havana, see his wife, see his first visit to New York City, and of course hear him sing in the Wim Wenders film *Buena Vista Social Club*.

Sibling Relationships

A relationship with a sibling has the potential to be the most "lifelong" relationship of all. I remember vividly when my 2-year-old daughter first met my son. He was less than a day old at the time, and it struck me that she might well be alive and an important social presence for his entire life (women do, after all, tend to outlive men.). No other relationship has quite the potential to span the entire life span. And not only do these relationships last a long time, but siblings also share some fundamental experiences that others do not. Siblings tend to be age peers, but they also grow up in the same geographical location, with the same parents and extended family relationships, the same cultural and religious heritage, and many shared childhood experiences (Cicirelli, 1991). Indeed, siblings often look to one another for discussion and confirmation of family experiences—if someone thinks that a parent is doing something crazy, chances are the first person they'll discuss it with is their brother or sister (Goetting, 1986). As time goes on, siblings provide a valuable "sense of continuity" (Nussbaum et al., 2000, p. 206) and coherence to one's life: They are a stable element no matter what other changes may have occurred. Sibling relationships are also interesting because of the variation they exhibit. For some people, their siblings are both their closest family relations and similar to their closest friends. For others, relations with siblings can be strained, or totally indifferent (Mikkelson, 2006). Sibling relationships are also intriguing because they are able to go "dormant" for long periods, and then regain vitality when needed (Allan, 1977). Despite these apparently interesting phenomena, research on sibling relationships, and particularly communication in this relationship, has been rare. Two areas have received enough attention to warrant some discussion here: first, factors associated with closeness in this relationship, and second, the specific role of siblings in older adulthood.

Examinations of factors associated with closeness have found that the following types of sibling relationships tend to be closer (Noller, Feeney, & Peterson, 2001; Walker, Allen, & Connidis, 2005):

Relationships in African American families

Relationships involving at least one sister (although there's some debate on this one!)

Relationships involving siblings who don't have children

Relationships in large families (at least, the more siblings, the more likely that at least one of the sibling relationships will be closer)

Relationships where at least one of the siblings is unmarried, widowed, or divorced

Relationships where the siblings live geographically closer

Relationships in families from lower socioeconomic strata

Relationships that were closer earlier in life

Relationships where the siblings are closer to each other in age (Folwell, Chung, Nussbaum, Bethea, & Grant, 1997)

One fairly consistent finding in the research literature is that older adults tend to be closer to their siblings than younger adults are (Burholt & Wenger, 1998; McKay & Caverly, 2004). According to McKay and Caverly, about 80% of older adults have a living sibling, so this is an important consideration. A number of suggestions have been made as to why the sibling relationship might grow closer in old age. Older people are more likely to have lost spouses, so the sibling may return as a confidant and close partner, in part to "replace" a dead spouse. The relationship also provides a place for aging siblings to share concerns about aging (Nussbaum et al., 2000). Because most siblings are of relatively similar ages, particular age-related problems or concerns might be more easily shared (e.g., both partners might find themselves getting hearing aids or symptoms of arthritis at about the same time). As the life span progresses, more events are likely to occur that bring siblings together. The death or serious illness of a parent, death of a spouse, and other events can be very important in triggering a need and desire for closeness to a sibling. In certain cases (e.g., negotiating how to care for an aging parent: Walker, Manoogian-O'Dell, McGraw, & White, 2001), events may necessitate in-depth sibling communication that hasn't occurred for quite a while. There is also, of course, less pressure from children in older adulthood. Once siblings' children have grown into adulthood, siblings may feel that they have more time and energy to devote to one another—energy that was being devoted to their children during the earlier adult years. It is clear that there are a lot of reasons why older adults might have closer relationships with their siblings, but the research literature hasn't specified which of these are most important.

One particularly interesting form of sibling relationship is the twin relationship—sharing a uterus is an interesting way to begin a relationship! Research has begun on twins, demonstrating that having a close relationship with a twin negatively predicts mortality (i.e., if you are close with a twin, you'll live longer). However, this effect only seems to be really strong among identical twins, where the relationship influences mortality even when health, age, and sex are controlled (Rasulo et al., 2005). Indeed, other research suggests that sibling relationships in general have less of an influence on psychological and physical health than other close relationships (Noller et al., 2001). Nevertheless, siblings are sufficiently interesting that they deserve more attention from researchers, and particularly *communication* researchers, given that we know so little about what goes on communicatively in these relationships. Matthews (2005) makes an unusual and compelling case for why siblings are interesting and important. In a world without siblings, she notes, we would also have no aunts, no uncles, no cousins, and no *intragener-ational* relationships in our biological family. The influence of siblings there-fore extends beyond that individual relationship into broader issues of how families are structured. Future work needs to attend more to sibling relation-ships in non-nuclear families (stepsiblings, half siblings, etc.). These relation-ships are growing in frequency, and present some unique and exciting avenues for enhancing our understanding of family functioning more broadly (Mikkelson, 2006).

Summary

In this chapter I have provided an overview of various intragenerational rela-tionships in old age. The message across all of these relationships is that social contact is crucial to the maintenance of physical and mental health. It is through effective communication that such relationships are developed and maintained. While each relationship has some unique communicative elements, positive communication behaviors such as provision and receipt of social support and mutual exchange of self-disclosure tend to be universally beneficial. In contrast, over- and underaccommodation tend to impede successful relationship devel-opment. These same messages are also true for intergenerational relationships, the subject of the next chapter. Intergenerational relationships, however, have the added challenge of bridging what some may perceive as an intergenera-tional divide.

Keywords and Theories

Buffer	Nonobligatory relationships
Cohort effects	Planned retirement
Communal themes in communication	communities
Continuity theory	Psychosocial benefits
Disengagement theory	Selective attrition
Equitable	Social support
Interactional starvation	U-shaped curve

Discussion Questions

- What unique aspects might be associated with a lifelong friendship (or a sibling relationship)? Try to imagine what it is like to know someone for 80 years, and imagine how communication in that relationship might differ from communication outside of it.
- What characteristics might predict divorce in an older adult couple?
- How do older people cope with widow(er)hood, and how might dating in old age differ from dating among the young?
- Why are friendships in old age more important for women than men (at least in terms of predicting mortality)?
- Why might sibling relationships grow stronger in older adulthood? What other relationships might influence the strength of the sibling relationship in older adulthood?

Annotated Bibliography

Mikkelson, A. C. (2006). Communication among peers: Adult sibling relationships. In K. Floyd & M. T. Mormon (Eds.), *Widening the family circle: New research on family communication* (pp. 21–36). Thousand Oaks, CA: Sage. This chapter focuses on sibling relationships across the life span, but attends to issues in older adulthood better than many such pieces. The author focuses particularly on the absence of real knowledge about communication, while doing his best to tap what we know about phenomena like self-disclosure and social support in sibling relationships.

Noller, P., Feeney, J., & Peterson, C. C. (2001). *Personal relationships across the lifespan.* Philadelphia: Psychology Press. This book examines relationships literally across the life span, with chapters focused on infancy and childhood, adolescence, early adulthood, middle age, and old age. The book covers family and nonfamily relationships in a thorough and efficient fashion—chapters are short and "to-the-point."

Rawlins, W. K. (2004). Friendships in later life. In J. F. Nussbaum & J. Coupland (Eds.), *Handbook of communication and aging research* (2nd ed., pp. 273–299). Mahwah, NJ: Lawrence Erlbaum. This recent chapter describes numerous phenomena surrounding older people's friendships, with interesting sections focusing on retirement and widowhood.

⊰ SIX ⊱

Intergenerational Relationships in Older Adulthood

This chapter describes intergenerational relationships between grandparents and grandchildren and between older adults and their adult children, and friendships between people of dramatically different ages. By the end of this chapter you should be able to:

SOURCE: © Gettyimages

- Understand some key functions of the grandparent– grandchild relationship; state some unique elements of communication in this relationship
- Describe some problems associated with grandparents raising grandchildren
- Understand the role of communication in parent–child relationships in older adulthood
- Describe an important dialectic in intergenerational relations
- Describe some of the effects of having intergenerational friendships

The older we get, the more knowledge we accumulate, and the more we can help our offspring to benefit from our experience. Grandparents . . . have 'been there and done that'—and, crucially, lived to tell the tale.

—Spencer Wells, *The Journey of Man*

The previous chapter considered some of the relationships that older people have with other older people. Those relationships are tremendously important. In the earlier chapters of this book, however, I described some of the interesting processes that occur in intergenerational communication: communication between people from different age groups. While it might seem unlikely that stereotyping, prejudice, or patronizing talk would occur in close relationships, there is some evidence that those "intergroup" processes can occur even among kin. Therefore, the current chapter considers some of the important intergenerational relationships in older adults' lives, including the ways in which the age differences might influence communication processes in those relationships. Such relationships are tremendously important: Numerous studies have documented that while intergenerational contact is typically fairly rare, it is substantially more common in close relationships (Hagestad & Uhlenberg, 2005). Three relationships are the focus of the chapter: grandparenting, adult parent–child relationships, and intergenerational friendships.

Grandparenting

Grandparenting is often what people first think of when they are asked about "intergenerational" relationships. For many younger people, this is where they experience the majority of their communication with older people (particularly high quality communication). With the increases in life expectancy observed in recent years, Uhlenberg and Kirby (1998) estimate that nearly 70% of individuals are born into families where all grandparents are alive, and this remains the case for approximately 40% at age 10. Estimates suggest that roughly 75% of all grandchildren at the age of 30 have at least one grandparent alive (Soliz, Lin, Anderson, & Harwood, 2006). Hence, for many, the grandparent–grandchild relationship is the first, most frequent, and most enduring source of intergenerational interaction (A. Williams & Giles, 1996). It is also a relationship with numerous positive consequences for the participants. Quality grandparent–grandchild relationships are associated with more effective transitions to adulthood for the grandchild (King, Russell, & Elder, 1998) and with higher social interaction and life satisfaction for the grandparent (Soliz et al., 2006). Therefore, it should be a place of considerable interest for those interested in communication and aging. Interestingly, though, a lot of the research on intergenerational communication has focused on other contexts (e.g., communication between young and old strangers: see Chapters 2–4). Recently, however, more work has emerged that focuses specifically on communication and grandparenting (Soliz et al., 2006), and this work draws on a longer tradition of work on grandparenting in psychology and sociology.

A lot of research has examined what predicts closeness in the grandparent relationship. Why are some of these relationships more intimate than others? Overall, grandchildren tend to be closer to their grandmothers than grandfathers, and also tend to be closer to **maternal grandparents** (i.e., their mother's parents; A. Williams & Nussbaum, 2001). Grandfathers can serve specific rewarding functions, however, for instance in exchanges concerning advice about finances or careers (Downs, 1989).

Grandchildren also tend to be fonder of younger grandparents and healthier grandparents, although *very* young (**"off-time"**) grandparents often resist their "unexpected" role (Burton & Bengtson, 1985). If you become a grandparent when you are 40, you might not feel "ready" for the role, and you might feel forced into an age identity that doesn't "fit" you (i.e., old!). In such cases, relationships may also be strained by the fact that the grandparent is still working full-time, and may even be raising young children of his or her own.

Not surprisingly, grandchildren are also closer to grandparents when their parents and grandparents get along with each other (McKay & Caverly, 2004; Uhlenberg & Hammill, 1998). Family feuds and parental divorce can result in loss of contact between grandparents and grandchildren (Drew & Smith, 2002), especially for paternal grandparents (Kruk & Hall, 1995). Recently, United States Supreme Court decisions have confirmed a grandparent's right to visit with his or her grandchildren after divorce. However, when the grandparent's child is not the custodial parent, retaining contact with the grandchild can often be a significant challenge (*Troxel v. Granville*, 2000), and the specifics of grandparents' rights vary state-by-state, as well as according to the individual situation

(Holladay & Coombs, 2001). Holladay and Coombs note the ways in which media coverage of grandparents' rights cases often give priority to parents' rights. When grandparents "win" such battles, the media will often frame such "victories" as a defeat for the parents' rights to raise their children how they want.

Findings concerning geographical distance generally indicate that increased frequency of visiting and closer **geographic proximity** between the grandparent and grandchildren are associated with emotionally closer relationships (Harwood & Lin, 2000; Hodgson, 1995; Uhlenberg & Hammill, 1998). Holladay, Lackovich, and Lee (1998) discovered that relationships were generally hurt by increases in distance and helped by geographical proximity. Furthermore, grandparents seem distinctly fond of grandchildren who live nearby (Falk & Falk, 2002).

To summarize, you are most likely to have a strong grandparent relationship when your grandparent lives nearby, is not too young or too old, is healthy, is your mother's mother, and has a good relationship with your parents.

So what about *communication* in the relationship? Some research has focused on *how* communication happens. Harwood (2000a) examined the types of communication media used in the relationship and found that frequency of telephone communication appeared to be associated with more satisfying grandparenting relationships among college students (more so than face-to-face or written communications). Recent work by Holladay and Seipke (2003) shows that communication using e-mail is also relatively frequent in the grandparent–grandchild relationship, and that it also predicts overall satisfaction and closeness in the relationship. We know very little about old-fashioned letter-writing and card-sending, but it is likely that these are important for current generations of grandparents.

More work has examined *what* communication occurs. Harwood (2000b) and Lin and Harwood (2003) have demonstrated that a variety of accommodative behaviors are associated with solidarity in the relationship. **Accommodating** the other (e.g., by complimenting), providing positive **self-disclosure**, and providing **social support** are all associated with positive relationships (Soliz & Harwood, 2006). Social support from the grandparent may be particularly important during times of family struggle or parental divorce (Cogswell & Henry, 1995). Very little work has examined whether particular topics of conversation are associated with positive communication in the grandparent–grandchild relationship, but at least one study indicates that they are not (Lin, Harwood, & Bonnesen, 2002). So perhaps it's not what you say, it's the way that you say it!

As noted in Chapters 2 and 3, **storytelling** is a type of communication that is associated with older adulthood (Ryan et al., 1994). Grandparent–grandchild interactions appear to uphold the importance of this behavior. Nussbaum and Bettini (1994) show that grandfathers and grandmothers have rather different storytelling styles. Grandfathers seem generally less willing to tell stories, and when they do talk, they tend to discuss historical issues (e.g., the war) and health issues. Grandmothers, on the other hand, talked more about relationships and family history in Nussbaum and Bettini's study. Grandchildren rarely tell stories to their grandparents. Grandparents' storytelling role is probably indicative of a function that they play in terms of mentoring (King & Elder, 1997) and transmitting and reinforcing family identity (Kornhaber & Woodward, 1981). Relatedly, a number of studies have reinforced the notion that grandparents play a **symbolic role** in the family, teaching family values and traditions (Brussoni & Boon, 1998), transmitting cultural/ethnic identity (Creasey & Koblewski, 1991; McKay, 1999; Wiscott & Kopera-Frye, 2000), and reinforcing religious traditions and values (King, Elder, & Conger, 2000). The role of grandparents in the intergenerational transmission of culture has received support from evolutionary studies (Hawkes, 2003).

Beyond these issues, Harwood and Lin (2000; Harwood, 2004) have pointed to four other key themes in the ways grandparents describe their relationships with their grandchildren. First, they talk about affiliation and the expression of love. Clearly, for grandparents the expression of affection in communication, and receiving such expressions from their grandchildren, are key to maintaining a quality relationship. Second, grandparents express considerable **pride** in their grandchildren's accomplishments and frequently recount the accomplishments as well as the grandchild's accounts of those accomplishments. Hence, expressions of pride appear to be key to the ways in which grandparenting is experienced and communicated. Third, descriptions of exchange are common in grandparents' accounts of the relationship. Grandparents describe things that they provide and do for the grandchildren (e.g., providing advice, or creating Web pages about the grandchildren), as well as things that the grandchildren do for the grandparents (e.g., making them feel in touch with today's world, providing computer advice). Finally, the theme of distance emerges. Sometimes this has to do with geographical distance as also described above: Grandparents who are geographically distant bemoan the negative influence on their relationship with the grandchild; those who are geographically close sometimes celebrate the fact. But other forms of distance are also raised (e.g., having a distant relationship because of the grandchild's parents, or the grandchild's behavior, or due to the generation gap). Uncovering these themes indicates that examining how people communicate about a relationship can reveal insights into their understanding of the functions and importance of the relationship, and what makes it work. Table 6.1 gives some example, of grandparents' communication of each of these themes.

Communication patterns that make age identities more salient tend to have a negative effect on the relationship. **Overaccommodation** and **underaccommodation** make the grandchild more aware of his or her grandparents'

Table 6.1 Affiliation, Pride, Exchange, and Distance: Themes in Grandparent Communication About Grandchildren

Affiliation:	"When I take the phone off the hook and hear 'Hi, grandma' my heart melts because I know she called because she wanted to." "I love you just the way you are."
Pride:	"We have 5 grandchildren and are very proud of all of them." "While in grammar school at age 13 he was elected Mayor for the Day of Harbor Falls, MI. He was very popular. In high school also in his Junior and Senior year he was voted Best Male Athlete by the coaches."
Exchange:	"The boys like to come over to Grandma's because there's lots of toys, a big yard to run in, dogs to romp with, a room of their own to sleep in." "Because he is bright, organized and ambitious, he's a great adversary: He makes me think about what I say."
Distance:	"I am on occasion, sorry that I do not feel that our relationship is such that I can feel free to tell her when she worries me with certain acts and behaviors." "Max has recently moved away, but I love spending time with him when possible and he loves spending time with his Nana."

age, and this awareness is associated with negative feelings about the relationship (Harwood, Raman, & Hewstone, 2006). As noted in the previous chapter, in making age salient, these sorts of behaviors may also make negative stereotypes salient. Once negative stereotypes are salient, the communication consequences tend to be bad. There is relatively little work on younger people's stereotypical communication toward their grandparents, but at least one study indicates that under some circumstances grandchildren will patronize their grandparents in the same ways that they patronize older adults who are strangers (Montepare et al., 1992). The next chapter will examine the question of whether having a good relationship with a grandparent changes how young people think about old people.

A final important note in this section: Grandparents are not all alike. Earlier in the book, I noted how diverse older people are. This **diversity** is reflected in the roles that grandparents play. Cherlin and Furstenberg (1986), for instance, note that grandparents may be very emotionally distant, very close, or may serve as authority figures similar to parents. Such findings illustrate that grandparents may be a lot more *interesting* to study than you might think: It's not all about stereotypes of grandma knitting by the fire in her fluffy slippers!

Why I Study Communication and Aging
Jaye Atkinson (Associate Professor, Georgia State University)

I had the most fantastic grandparents! Perhaps many of us think that, but Gram, Bo, and Nana were wonderful. Each had his/her own challenges—Gram was hit by a car on the day of her high school graduation so had mobility problems later, including being confined to a wheelchair toward the end of her life. Bo had a heart attack but remained an active gardener in his retirement, until his Alzheimer's disease progressed such that he couldn't make the 30-minute drive to the farm anymore. Gram took care of him as long as she could. Nana was a widow, retired teacher, and extremely active in her church and Sweet Adeline singing group, until her Alzheimer's disease progressed and required nursing care.

Because they loved me, I learned from them. I learned how to play gin rummy and dominoes from Gram and Bo. They were always ready for a game with me, and Gram made the BEST 50-cent pancakes on the planet! I learned how to play the piano and feed the birds from Nana. Their homes were always ready for an overnight guest, whether planned or not, invited or not. They loved me no matter what grades I received, what sports I played, or what state I called home (West Virginia, Ohio, Kansas, or Georgia). They welcomed any visits, cards, or phone calls. Gram, especially, would have loved e-mail, but none of my grandparents experienced home computers as commonplace.

Having such positive experiences with them, despite the various challenges they each faced, I was quite honestly shocked to discover the predominance of negative stereotypes associated with age. I was in graduate school before I recognized these perceptions existed! Mary Lee Hummert introduced me to her work on stereotypes of older adults, and I guess you could say, the rest is history! My grandparents did not have easy lives, but I truly believe they were happy. Now it's my turn to follow their example, persevere through life's challenges, love one another, and if I can debunk a few myths about aging along the way, that's all the better!

Reprinted with permission of Jaye Atkinson.

Grandparents Raising Grandchildren

A noteworthy trend in grandparents' supportive family roles is their increasing role as primary caregivers for their grandchildren: According to the U.S. Census Bureau, about 2.5 million grandparents were raising their grandchildren in the year 2000 (Hayslip & Kaminski, 2005). Such family arrangements often occur when there is a problem in the middle generation such as drug use, incarceration, mental illness, or the like (Dressel & Barnhill, 1994; Landry, 1999). Although a sense of pride and joy is typically associated with raising grandchildren, there are also less positive consequences. In addition to financial strains and legal issues (Waldrop & Weber, 2001), grandparent caregivers may experience shifts in their support networks, because their friends may no longer share the role of parent (Jendrek, 1993) resulting in a sense of social isolation for many (Landry, 1999). The physical, emotional, and psychological strain for grandparents taking on this role cannot be over-estimated (Hayslip & Kaminski), and they need considerable logistical and social support at a time when it is difficult for them to seek out that support (Kornhaber, 1996). A lack of effective support from friends and family has been linked to depression and poor physical health (Hayslip & Kaminski). Box 6.1 provides details of one particular study of grandparents in this situation.

Box 6.1   Effects of Support for Grandparents-Raising-Grandchildren

---

Gerard, Landry-Meyer, and Guzell Roe (2006) were interested in the types of stress that grandparents experience when raising grandchildren, and the ways in which social support might help grandparents during these times of stress. They studied 133 grandparents who were raising grandchildren ranging from infants to late teenagers. The grandparents completed a questionnaire that measured aspects of their relationship with the grandchild (e.g., daily hassles of being a "parent"), the level of social support from informal sources (e.g., friends) and formal sources (e.g., community agencies), and their level of stress. Not surprisingly, grandparents who experienced more hassles in dealing with the grandchildren also reported being more stressed. More interesting, use of formal support agencies (community groups, government support) significantly **buffered** the grandparents against the negative effects of raising grandchildren. That is, among grandparents who did not make good use of formal support, there was a very strong association between hassles with the grandchild and stress levels. However, for grandparents who made good use of formal support agencies, the connection between grandchild hassles and stress was a lot weaker. It seems that using government agencies and other formal help mechanisms helps protect grandparents against some of the negative consequences of raising grandchildren. Making use of family and friends didn't help in this particular study—the authors think that maybe these grandparents did not want to call on their friends and family for support. However, the perception that they *could* call on friends and family as a last resort did have a positive influence here. Grandparents who felt that their friends and family would help (even if they currently were not helping) were generally less stressed.

The Parent–Child Relationship in Older Adulthood

The relationship between parents and children is among the most commonly studied human relationship. However, the vast majority of research on this relationship has occurred with young children. Until recently, the assumption was that once children left home, not much of interest occurred between parent and child. Now, scholars realize that the parent–child relationship continues to develop during the child's adulthood, and that it may go through numerous interesting transitions during that time. In a sense, this relationship encapsulates a more general theme of a life-span approach to human development: Change, and therefore interest, does not stop at age 18! The parent–child relationship is dynamic across the life span, but it also offers continuity to both parties: Generally, it is a relationship with fairly consistent levels of affection and positive communication over a very long period of time. A lot of the research has focused on mother–daughter relationships, and it appears that these are the most stable parent–child relationships. Other combinations (father–daughter/son, mother–son) appear to have somewhat weaker ties that are more easily broken by events such as a parental divorce (Lye, 1996).

Let's get some misconceptions out of the way. First, at age 18 children don't run as fast as they can away from their parents and never look back. In fact, adult children generally remain emotionally close to their parents, and often remain geographically close as well (Lye, 1996). Second, aging parents do not inevitably become a caregiving burden for their children. Almost 85% of the 65+ population live either alone or with a spouse, and 75% of over-85s do the same (He, Sengupta, Velkoff, & DeBarros, 2005). Not all older adults need care (they may die suddenly, or may outlive their children), and not all look to their children for caregiving (they may have alternate paid or unpaid caregivers). The exchange of financial and practical assistance in this relationship is less common than most people think (Lye, 1996), and it is definitely a two-way street—often, older parents provide financial support to their adult children. In other words, as with other topics covered in this book, the key here is to recognize the variability in the older adult population, both in terms of their varying *need* for care, and the ways in which they receive and give it. In addition, caregiving is not necessarily a burden. While it is undoubtedly a difficult task under some circumstances, for some it is also a rewarding and enjoyable one (Williams & Nussbaum, 2001).

This relationship maintains its closeness throughout the life span via multiple mechanisms, and most of them are fairly common sense. From an

exchange theory perspective, parents invest considerable effort into the raising of their children, and hence children "owe" their parents continuing closeness and affiliation into their adult lives (Mancini & Bliezsner, 1989). **Evolutionary** approaches emphasize the investment that parents have in their children's success: Once parents are past the age of reproduction, their genetic legacy resides in their children, and so it is in their biological interest to maintain a relationship with those children (Eggebeen & Hogan, 1990). **Intergenerational solidarity** theorists focus on various dimensions of connections between parents and children over time, including geographic proximity, expressions of affection, and role relationships (Giarrusso, Silverstein, & Bengtson, 1996). For these scholars, the relationship is maintained by continuous patterns of behaviors like the expression of affection. **Attachment theorists** focus on the ways in which early parent–child connections are carried into adulthood as well-rehearsed and learned patterns of interpersonal behavior (Cicirelli, 1991). In other words, once you are close to your parent, why stop? Cultural explanations focus on how norms of **filial piety** (respect and responsibility for elders) play out in determining the need for continued parent–child contact into the child's adulthood (Gallois et al., 1999; see also Chapter 10). All are reasonable explanations. It is clear that maintaining strong parent–child connections into adulthood has been beneficial for the species dating back many thousands of years.

The volume of work examining actual communication in this relationship is relatively sparse. However, at least one article indicates that quality communication is central to determining a high quality parent–child relationship in adulthood, and that a quality parent–child relationship is very important for the older adult's overall well-being (W. H. Quinn, 1983). At the same time, achieving quality communication may present some challenges. For instance, Henwood (1993) suggests that communication between older women and their daughters might be a context in which the older women encounter "idealized grandmother" images, which can threaten a more sophisticated self-image they may wish to claim. Hence, for older women, communication with their daughters may be a battleground in which they occasionally have to defend themselves against being pigeon-holed (Noller et al., 2001).

A key tension or **dialectic** that encompasses many of the issues of parent–adult child relationships is that of **autonomy** and **connectedness** (Baxter, 1990). We all have a need for autonomy—to be independent of others and capable of looking after ourselves. Simultaneously, we all have the need for connectedness—to be in relationships with others, to exchange support and assistance, and to have sources for social contact. Autonomy and connectedness play out in interesting ways in the parent–child relationship. Young children seek autonomy (e.g., a 3-year-old will battle resolutely to put on his own shirt, even if it takes many minutes.) while also seeking connectedness (e.g., clinging to their parents in the presence of strangers). These tensions do not disappear as children enter adulthood: Young adult children may battle to buy a house without their parents' help to demonstrate independence, but may also call their parents for advice on dealing with their negligent realtor. At certain times, it is common for adult children to begin to question their parents' competence, and to begin to attempt to take control of financial and personal matters in their parents' lives. Ironically, this sometimes happens at the same time as they are asking their parents for help with things like taking care of grandchildren (Dickson et al., 2004).

Fingerman, Chen, Hay, Cichy, and Lefkowitz (2006) present information on an interesting concept relating to these issues: ambivalence. Ambivalence is defined as "having positive and negative sentiments toward the same object" (p. 152). These researchers argue that such ambivalence is common between parents and children, particularly those who are heavily invested in the relationship and who have fewer other meaningful roles. So, people are more likely to experience the combination of positive and negative feelings in the parent–child relationship when they are not deeply involved in things like a career. Ambivalence appears to increase if parents suffer from health problems. Presumably, if the parent is sick, positive feelings such as love will continue, but negative feelings caused by worrying about the parent or experiencing more demands from the parent might increase. The tensions between positive and negative feelings or autonomy and connectedness illustrate the complexity of this relationship into adulthood, and indeed demonstrate that it may gain complexity as we age.

Parents encounter the same tensions, delighting in their children's independence, while experiencing anxiety at the loss of control and some sadness at the loss of "their baby." Interestingly, even in adulthood, parents tend to provide more support to their children than the reverse (Lye, 1996). It is only in old-old adulthood that this pattern begins to reverse (Mancini & Blieszner, 1989). Interestingly, Antonucci (2001) notes that **perceived support** is more important than actual support (see also Box 6.1). That is, older adults who *think* that there are others willing to step up and take care of them are (ironically!) less likely to need that help. People who are unsure whether anyone would take care of them are *more* likely to need help (Krause, 1997). This illustrates a protective effect that having *perceived* social support may serve, even if that social support is never needed!

If older adults do reach a point where they need assistance, many are very resistant to placing a burden on their children. Many buy long-term-care insurance that will provide the ability to buy some level of care, thus hopefully minimizing a burden on their children. Others turn to social services or alternate sources (friends, siblings, spouses) for care, rather than their children. If children do end up providing care for a parent, the responsibility falls primarily on daughters, and given the demographics of the older population, they are generally caring for their mothers (Himes, 1994). In most cases, these responsibilities are taken on with a sense that it is appropriate and "fair" (L. Thompson & Walker, 1989), and some sense of reward is often experienced by the younger person (Walker, Pratt, & Eddy, 1995). Research shows that older people who are reliant on others for support tend to be less happy, because they perceive an inequity in their relationship. However, some older people who are cared for by their children perceive that they are drawing on a "support bank" account—the years they put in to supporting the children are now being paid back (Antonucci, 1985).

However, more negative outcomes are possible. Cicirelli (1993) notes the possibility that communication within the parent–child relationship can become strained by a parent's dependency, resulting in patronizing speech from the adult child to the parent. Given that stereotyping is a cause of patronizing speech (see Chapter 4), it is possible that this behavior is more common in relationships where the child comes to view the parent more as an "old person" than as a family member. In some instances, the negative treatment of the older parent may extend to emotional, verbal, financial, or even physical abuse. Some evidence links these abusive behaviors to earlier problems in the parent–child relationship (Parrott & Bengtson, 1999), including an inability for the child to psychologically separate from the parent (Noller et al., 2001). Again, we see evidence that amidst the change that occurs in this relationship there are also some stable features: Negative relationships do not magically improve. Abuse can also sometimes occur as a result of resentment (e.g., that caring for a parent is perceived to be damaging career plans). However, such resentment certainly doesn't always translate into abusive behaviors (Murphy et al., 1997). Chapter 11 contains more information about abuse of older adults.

The parent–adult child relationship encompasses numerous dynamics with the aging of the child from young adulthood into middle age and perhaps even old age, and the aging of the parent from middle age into young-old and old-old adulthood. Fluctuations in both parties' financial and marital status, and their changing health conditions, can dramatically influence the dynamic of dependency, autonomy, and connectedness. Golish (2000) provides a nice summary of various features that lead to "turning points" in the adult child–parent relationship.

Intergenerational Friendships

The discussion of friendship in the previous chapter was based on the idea that friendships are with people of a similar age, and that is often the case. However, some research has begun to look at friendships with people of different ages — intergenerational friendships. Such friendships are more common than perhaps you might think, and surprisingly they tend to be rather similar to intragenerational friendships. That is, they tend to be formed in similar contexts (workplace, church, school), and they serve similar functions (e.g., social support) (Holladay & Kerns, 1999). They differ in that they sometimes have a parenting/mentoring tone to them that is not common in intragenerational friendships. They also differ in that the "generation gap" sometimes impedes communication in such relationships: Partners may have trouble talking about issues that are unique to their generation. Nevertheless, such relationships do also offer unique opportunities for learning and growth, similar to those experienced in intercultural friendships, for instance. A. Williams and Nussbaum (2001) note that intergenerational friendships are sometimes treated judgmentally by those not in the relationship. People outside may question why someone would want to be hanging out with someone else of such a different age. Negative attitudes toward intergenerational friendships seem to mirror negative attitudes about aging. You may want to visit the "Generations Together" Web site to discover more about intergenerational relationships, including programs designed specifically to build such contact (www.gt.pitt.edu).

Summary

Intergenerational relationships are interesting in the ways that they can combine intimacy with a profound intergroup difference. People growing up in different historical times have some fundamentally unique experiences and understandings of the world, but in the context of certain relationships those differences can be overcome, or can become the fuel that sustains the relationship. The next chapter will discuss some of the ways in which intergenerational relationships might change how we feel about aging more generally. A final point needs to be made about both this chapter and the previous one. The organization of the chapters (and of most research examining relationships) has tended to focus on single, dyadic relationships, as if they existed in isolation (grandparent–grandchild, parent–child, sibling, etc.). Of course, they don't. Some research has broadened to examine more dynamic systems of relationships. A great example of this work is Michelle Miller-Day's (2004) examination of grandmothers, mothers, and adult daughters, which begins to capture the complexity of triadic family communication across three generations.

Keywords and Theories

Accommodating	Maternal and paternal grandparents
Accommodation theory	Off-time grandparenting
Attachment theorists	Overaccommodation
Dialectic (autonomy and connectedness)	Perceived support
Disengagement theory	Pride in grandchildren
Evolutionary	Self-disclosure
Exchange theory	Social support
Filial piety	Storytelling
Geographic proximity	Symbolic role of grandparents
Intergenerational solidarity	Underaccommodation

Discussion Questions

- How does the relative importance of different relationships change over the life span? Why?
- Discuss how age might be important, or irrelevant, to an intergenerational friendship. What effects might foregrounding or backgrounding the age difference have on the friendship?

- What do grandparents have to offer grandchildren that parents cannot provide? When could a grandparent serve a positive function in the parent–child relationship?
- What are some challenges for a grandparent raising a grandchild?
- What are some of the key transitions that occur to make a child begin to think of a parent as "old"?

Annotated Bibliography

Miller-Day, M. A. (2004). *Communication among grandmothers, mothers, and adult daughters: A qualitative study of maternal relationships*. Mahwah, NJ: Lawrence Erlbaum. As mentioned in the text, this book gets into some of the complexity of considering three generations rather than just two. The book makes for great reading due to, among other things, the extended descriptions of family communication (including family conflict). For a real sense of actual communication across generations within a family, this is a must read.

Szinovacz, M. E. (Ed.). (1998). *Handbook on grandparenthood*. Westport, CT: Greenwood Press. Probably still the ultimate book on grandparenting—the numerous chapters cover demographics, cultural variation, grandparents raising grandchildren, and pretty much any other topic related to grandparenting that you can think of.

Williams, A., & Nussbaum, J. F. (2001). *Intergenerational communication across the lifespan*. Mahwah, NJ: Lawrence Erlbaum. This book covers a broad range of issues relating to intergenerational communication. However, it has three chapters focused on family communication that provide excellent detail on issues like grandparent–grandchild relationships and adult child–parent communication.

⊰ SEVEN ⊱

Enhancing Communication
With Older Adults

This chapter describes a variety of ways in which we can challenge and change negative representations of older adulthood, as well as challenging and changing some of the negative communication styles that have been described in the previous chapters. By doing this, communication with older people should be improved. By the end of this chapter you should be able to:

- Outline the basics of intergroup contact theory and the implications of that theory for attitudes toward older people
- Differentiate between modifying *attitudes* toward older people and modifying *perceived variability* of older people

- Describe the communication enhancement model
- Describe various response options to patronizing speech and the consequences on those options for evaluations of an older person
- Describe some forms of communication training that might be useful in the intergenerational setting

I've been through two world wars, the Great Depression, taught 3,297 children, administered 4 elementary schools and outlived every one of the pastors I worked with. I'm 89 years old and you're telling me it's bedtime?

—Cartoon caption, Author Unknown

The previous chapters of this book have probably made clear that many people's attitudes about older adults are quite negative, and that these negative attitudes can have serious consequences for young and old alike. Indeed, beyond the individual, these negative attitudes are detrimental to society as a whole because they disenfranchise a large group of potentially productive people. Having demonstrated these negative issues, this chapter examines some ways in which negative attitudes and stereotypes can be counteracted, and hence ways in which positive intergenerational communication can be achieved.

Three main areas are described. First, I'll talk about the ways in which change can occur in younger people's attitudes about aging. If the predicament of aging model is correct (see Chapter 4), then positive changes in younger people's attitudes should result in more positive intergenerational communication experiences for young and old alike. I will focus particularly on work that looks at how communication between younger and older people can positively influence attitudes. Second, I'll focus on the types of communication that older people can use to neutralize some of the negative consequences of patronizing speech. It is important to remember that older adults are full and active participants in the process of intergenerational communication, and hence have the power to change interpersonal interactions with which they are dissatisfied. Third, I'll talk about some areas of communication skills development and communication training that contribute to a more positive intergenerational experience for everyone involved.

Change in Young People: The Influence of Intergenerational Contact on Attitudes

Intergroup contact theory was developed in the early 1950s by Gordon Allport (1954). Allport suggested that by having interpersonal contact with members of other groups, we could come to appreciate them more, and thus our negative attitudes toward those groups might improve. He suggested that structuring the contact such that it was cooperative and friendly would help. In addition, he claimed that if contact had "institutional support" (i.e., important people and institutions in society approved of the contact), then that would make the contact more effective. Support for Allport's theory has come from numerous places, including in the intergenerational area. A number of studies have shown that people who have more frequent intergenerational contact tend to have more positive attitudes toward older adults (e.g., Knox, Gekoski, & Johnson, 1986). However, exceptions to this rule exist— in certain contexts, intergenerational contact can reinforce negative stereotypes. If the majority of the contact, for instance, occurs in a medical setting, then it may reinforce the notion that older adults are mostly unhealthy (Fox & Giles, 1993, have a nice review of this work). The other disclaimer here is that **intergenerational contact** is relatively infrequent—especially for young people, and especially outside of the family. Young people don't talk to many older people, and when they do talk to older people it tends to be their grandparents (A. Williams & Giles, 1996). So even *if* we show that intergenerational contact has positive effects, those effects may be limited by the fact that the contact doesn't occur very much. My friend and research collaborator Angie Williams once said to me, "We're studying something that never happens!" Well, it does happen some of the time, but probably not as much as proponents of contact theory would like.

As a result of these issues, recent work has begun to examine intergenerational contact in the context in which it happens most often and is most positive—the **grandparent–grandchild relationship**. Recent developments in contact theory have suggested that contact is particularly effective in close relationships, because those relationships are places in which contact is low anxiety, rewarding, and allows people to confront group differences in a supportive environment. Data on the grandparent relationship indicate that it has the potential to change attitudes about aging. A number of studies have demonstrated this. In an interesting study, Silverstein and Parrott (1997) showed that having a good relationship with a grandparent influences not only how you feel about older people but also your support for public programs like Social Security that benefit older adults.

In recent work with a group of colleagues, I have shown that the effect of the grandparent relationship on ageist attitudes is particularly strong when the grandparent is seen as representative of older people, or similar to other older adults (Harwood, Hewstone, Paolini, & Voci, 2005). So, if you think of your grandma *just* as a grandparent, she may not influence your attitudes about older adults very much ("She's not old, she's just my grandma!!"). However, if you also consider her aging as part of who she is, then your feelings are likely to translate (generalize) from your grandparent to other older people ("She's old and she's cool. So I guess other old people can't be all bad!"). This is illustrated by Exercise 7.1.

Pettigrew (1998) has presented a version of intergroup contact theory that provides excellent directions for future work in this area—his theory derives from the issue of representativeness illustrated by Exercise 7.1, as well as the intuitive notion that contact will be most satisfying if we relate to one another as individuals. These two ideas are, of course, somewhat in

---

Exercise 7.1	**Intergenerational Contact**

This exercise reflects research done with research subjects who are not older adults. If you are an older adult, it might not work for you!

Think about the last conversation you had with an older person. Rate the conversation on the following scales.

How would you rate the <u>quality of communication</u> during this conversation?

1	2	3	4	5
Very poor	Poor	Neutral	Good	Very good

To what extent is this older person <u>typical</u> of older people in general?

1	2	3	4	5
Very little		Somewhat		A great deal

Your responses to these two questions tell you something about whether the conversation might have influenced your attitudes. The first scale tells you the **DIRECTION** of potential attitude change—if you had a BAD conversation (low number) then the interaction is likely to make your attitudes more negative; a good conversation (high number) will make your attitudes more positive. The second scale measures perceived typicality of the older person—is this person *like* other old people? This tells you the **extent** to which your conversation influences your attitudes. If you score LOW on typicality (e.g., a 1), then the conversation won't influence your attitudes much—whether it was positive or negative actually won't matter because you don't view this person as relevant to older people as a group. In contrast, if you scored a 5 on the second scale, your attitudes might be substantially influenced in whatever direction was indicated by the first scale.

conflict: It's difficult to orient to someone as a typical old person *and* as a unique individual both at the same time. An illustration and example of the model can be seen in Figure 7.1. Pettigrew suggests that the first stages of contact between groups such as age groups benefit from **decategorization**—people relate to one another as individuals *rather than* group members. So in an initial encounter between an older and a younger person, it is helpful if both people see each other in terms of factors other than age, and preferably as unique and interesting individuals. This will help to develop intimacy and liking. Once the relationship has developed to a point of mutual liking, trust, and comfort (i.e., a lack of anxiety), *then* it is important for group memberships to become salient (salient categorization; see Exercise 7.1 again). This categorization allows for feelings about the other person to extend beyond that individual to other people (e.g., from a single older person to older people as a group). Pettigrew argues that this has to come second: If group memberships are salient right from the start, then they will probably cause anxiety and make it unlikely that the contact will be pleasant and comfortable. Finally, once the individuals have a positive relationship and can see each other in terms of their group memberships, it is possible for them to **recategorize** in terms of some other dimension.

Figure 7.1　　Illustration of Pettigrew's (1998) Model of Optimal Intergroup Contact

Decategorization:	**Salient Categorization:**	**Recategorization:**
Informal contact involving non-age-related topics and resulting in liking and reduced anxiety.	Age becomes salient, resulting in generalization from target person to other group members.	The age distinction becomes replaced by another category in which both young and old person are members of the same group.
Example:	**Example:**	**Example:**
Repeated intergenerational contact in a work setting, with both people contributing to getting the job done.	A birthday party for the older person results in discussion of age, historical change, or disclosure of age-related status (e.g., being a grandparent).	As a result of frequent work-related interaction, young and old person begin to see themselves as a "team" and focus on their shared identity with the team more than their different ages.

Recategorization generally occurs in such a way that both people come to view themselves as members of the *same* group (e.g., "we're both Americans," "we're both Jayhawk fans"). This recategorization reduces the perceived importance of the age group membership, resulting in a reduced tendency to use age as a criterion for judging other people (i.e., less age stereotyping, prejudice, etc.).

Of course, the precise process outlined in Figure 7.1 is not going to occur every time a younger and older person come into contact with one another. In fact, it may be a rather unlikely sequence of events. What the model describes is an *ideal* process for such contact to result in positive attitude change. The process outlined in the model, however, may be facilitated by the way in which grandparent–grandchild relationships develop. Grandchildren generally get to know their grandparents at a very young age—probably before they even have the ability to distinguish between age groups, and certainly before they have been socialized into negative stereotypes of age. So, for many people, their relationship with a grandparent may be relatively close before they even have a concept of old age, and thus the initial stages of the grandparent–grandchild relationship match the initial stages of **Pettigrew's model**—decategorization. As grandchildren get older, they become more able to distinguish age groups. Simultaneously, their grandparents literally become older and hence more likely to be categorized as "older adults" (salient categorization). Hopefully, this categorization should not result in problems, because the solid foundation for a close relationship has already been laid. Thus, the positive relationship develops the ability to generalize to other older people as the grandparent becomes seen as in some way representative of older people as a group. If the relationship remains positive and is embedded in a positive family network, the possibility also exists for *recategorization* to occur along the lines of a fairly obvious shared group membership ("We're both members of the same family!"). My former students Jordan Soliz and Karen Anderson (Anderson, Harwood, & Hummert, 2005; Soliz, in press) have been studying the ways in which grandparents and grandchildren may come to possess a shared family identity, not only identifying with the family, but viewing one another as key elements of that shared identification. Thus, Pettigrew's model seems particularly useful in examining how grandparent–grandchild relationships develop over time and contribute to the grandchild's attitudes about aging.

Communication and Intergenerational Contact

Interestingly, most of the research on *contact* between social groups has been done by social psychologists. This is a little bizarre, given that "contact" is a communicative event. However, a couple of recent studies have begun to examine the types of communication in the grandparent relationship that make it particularly good as a predictor of positive attitudes. In one study, we found that a grandparent and a grandchild complimenting one another and talking about the other's interests were quite closely related to positive attitudes (Harwood et al., 2005). In a separate study, Jordan Soliz and I (2006) found that both **social support** behaviors and **self-disclosure** were closely related to positive attitudes. Social support relates to being able to turn to one another in times of trouble; self-disclosure involves grandparents and grandchildren sharing personal information with one another. It's worth noting that the type of self-disclosure we're talking about here is not the "painful self-disclosure" discussed in Chapter 4; rather we're talking about sharing the full range of one's life events, experiences, emotions, and so on, with one another in a reciprocal fashion.

So, a relationship that features positive communication behaviors (complimenting, social support, self-disclosure), and where age is salient (the grandparent is seen as representative of other older people), seems to be an excellent breeding ground for the grandchild to develop positive attitudes about aging and older people.

Perceptions of Variability

Finally, a few recent studies have begun to investigate the communication phenomena that lead to more variable perceptions of aging and older people. Underlying this research is the idea that it is not merely viewing older adults *positively* that is desirable. In addition, the perception that older adults are heterogeneous and diverse is important. Think for a moment about what has happened to society's perception of women over the past century. In the first half of the twentieth century, women weren't perceived particularly *negatively*. The problem with perceptions of women at that time was that they were incredibly narrow: Women were thought to be pretty to look at, good for having children and domestic duties, and not much else. In the intervening years (while things are still not perfect) we have moved to a point where women hold many prominent positions in government, run their own companies, and are involved in areas like the creative arts at a level on a par with men. What has changed is that the range of possibilities for women, the roles they can occupy, and their inherent capabilities are now perceived as more *complex and variable* than in the past. Imagining the same future for older adults is interesting. Right now, retirement, a brief period of gentle leisure, institutionalization, and death are the most common associations with advanced age. If perceptions of the possibilities and **variability** of older adults could shift in the same manner as has happened for women, that would be a good thing. Therefore, we need to start considering the **heterogeneity** of older people and the ways in which that diversity can function positively in society.

Two areas are worth comment here. First, research by Jordan Soliz has demonstrated that having diverse relationships with grandparents is important. His work has shown that students who have diverse communication with their different grandparents also have perceptions that older people are more heterogeneous. So, if younger people can have more diverse experiences with older people (perhaps particularly their grandparents), that will create perceptions of more exciting and diverse possibilities in older adulthood (Soliz & Harwood, 2003). Second, some of my research has shown that (non-painful) self-disclosure is important to perceptions of diversity—grandchildren who received more self-disclosure from their grandparents perceive older people as a group to be more diverse (Harwood et al., 2005). Why? Well, when they self-disclose, older people share different aspects of their experiences and feelings. The more of these that are shared, the more the older person appears to be a unique individual with specific characteristics that are different from other people's. The grandfather who tells you about his first crush, a conflict with his boss, and his trip to Lithuania becomes an individual who cannot be seen as "interchangeable" with other people. Once someone is perceived in this way, it becomes much more difficult to see their group as "all the same," and hence the tendency is to view the group as more diverse. As outlined a little earlier, self-disclosure is also related to positive evaluations of the grandparent–grandchild relationship and positive attitudes about aging. So, self-disclosure appears to be a very promising *communication* variable for future research. It would be fascinating to "train" grandparents and grandchildren to disclose more with one another, and examine whether the grandchildren's attitudes about aging became more positive over time, or whether they came to see older adults as more diverse.

As a whole, work on intergroup contact theory suggests that increasing levels of intergenerational contact would be beneficial. This does need to be done somewhat carefully, however. Forcing people to talk to older adults when they don't want to is probably not a good idea. Creating situations of intensive contact with severely impaired older adults would probably also be counterproductive, given that such contact will reinforce some of the more negative stereotypes of older people. Similarly, putting younger and older strangers together and expecting a beautiful friendship to emerge spontaneously is rather optimistic. Rather, encouraging and creating environments in which contact occurs naturally, and that are sufficiently structured so as to provide people with a focus for their interaction—a reason to communicate—is likely to be effective. As one example, consider the university setting. In recent years, "diversity" issues have become tremendously important in universities. Institutions of higher education have come to value the importance of a diverse student body, recognizing that students with different backgrounds bring different knowledge and perspective to the campus, thus resulting in a better learning environment for everyone. Very few, if any, of these initiatives have focused on enhancing *age* diversity on campus. This is unfortunate, as contact in the classroom, engaging in group projects, and the like have the potential to provide contact that would have very positive consequences. On the positive side, a number of state universities do offer reduced or free tuition to older people, and those incentives might have the effect of providing age diversity on campus. In addition, as emphasized in the earlier section, finding ways to capitalize on younger adults' existing close intergenerational relationships, particularly within the family, will be important.

Why I Study Communication and Aging
Susan Kemper (Professor, University of Kansas)

In 1980, I was teaching an undergraduate class on language acquisition. After a discussion of the development of narrative structure, Donna Kynette (an undergraduate student) asked whether older adults were "good" storytellers and able to create the sorts of elaborate story structures then popular in story grammars. I suggested she find out, so Donna spent the summer collecting stories from her older friends and neighbors. It took us a while to get around to actually examining the structure of these stories (Kemper, Rash, Kynette, & Norman, 1990) because we got distracted by other aspects of the language samples—more precisely, by the sorts of grammatical structures that didn't seem to occur. Donna's Honors Thesis (Kynette & Kemper, 1986) really laid the foundation for my research into the effects of aging on language. I'm still analyzing language samples in an effort to understand how older adults accommodate to task demands. But Donna has moved on—she now tells stories to her grandchildren.

Reprinted with permission of Susan Kemper.

Ending the Predicament: The Communication Enhancement Model

Inspired by some of the work already described, Ellen Ryan and her colleagues (Ryan, Meredith, MacLean, & Orange, 1995) have developed a model that is, in many ways, the perfect **complement to the communication predicament model** (Chapter 4). The **communication enhancement model** (see Figure 7.2) describes a similar cycle to the predicament model, but one that enhances communication and quality of life for older people (and their younger communication partners). The model was developed for the health care context (hence the use of the term "provider" in the model), but it applies equally well in other communication contexts. "Provider" in the model can be substituted for "young person" in any other type of intergenerational encounter.

Instead of emphasizing the role of negative stereotypes in intergenerational communication, this model delineates the ways in which younger people can recognize older adults' *individual* characteristics and modify their communication to reflect those factors. Thus, the model recognizes that *some* older adults may be suffering from hearing impairments and hence that additional clarity of speech may be appropriate. But it also recognizes that many older people do not require such accommodations and will perceive them as overaccommodative (patronizing). Accommodating to the older person as an *individual* is the key here. When individualized communication occurs, it optimizes the competence of the older person by empowering him or her. As opposed to the constrained opportunities for communication described in the predicament model, the

Figure 7.2   The Communication Enhancement Model

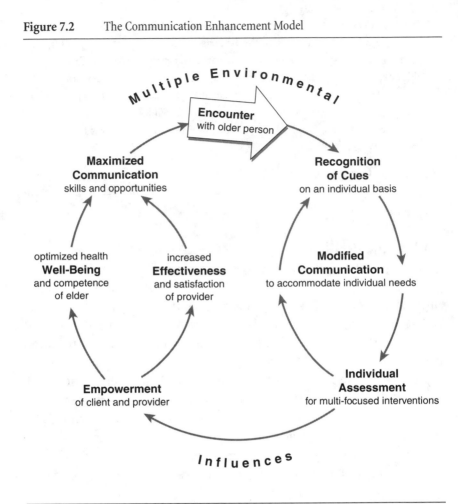

SOURCE: From Ryan, et al., Changing the way we talk with elders: promoting health using the communication enhancement model, in *International Journal of Aging and Human Development*, *41*(2), copyright © 1995. Reprinted with permission of Baywood Publishing.

enhancement model provides maximized communication opportunities, thus giving all older people (even those who *are* impaired) the greatest opportunity to express themselves and achieve fulfillment.

One of the most notable features of this model is that the positive consequences of this individualized approach for the *younger person* are emphasized. In the health care context, it is noted that the provider will achieve increased effectiveness and satisfaction. That is, when communication is tailored to the specific older individual, it increases the chances that the older person will understand what is being said (e.g., a diagnosis), take the appropriate actions (e.g., using medication), and achieve the desired outcomes (getting healthy again). For a health care provider, such outcomes are what is desired and should result in greater satisfaction. These ideas extend to other interpersonal contexts. In communication with a grandparent, for instance, a grandchild is more likely to enjoy the conversation and relate well with the grandparent if the grandparent has maximum opportunities for self-expression, if the largest possible range of topics is available, and if the grandparent is enjoying the interaction. All of those are most likely to happen when the grandparent is treated as an individual rather than stereotyped as an old person.

Of course, there is some conflict between the central idea embedded in the enhancement model and one of the key ideas of intergroup contact theory—salient categorization (described in the previous section). That is, the enhancement model focuses on treating the other person as an individual; intergroup contact theory, however, describes the importance of age salience and typicality. In part, this difference can be traced to the different goals of the two approaches. The enhancement model is solely focused on achieving positive *individual* experiences and outcomes. If a younger and an older person are seated next to each other on an airplane, and they manage to have a great conversation by dealing with each other as unique individuals, then the enhancement model has met its goals. Contact theory, on the other hand, is aimed at achieving more positive collective outcomes. This theory wants you not just to have a good feeling about the person you're talking to, but also a good feeling about their group. So if the young person walked away from the airplane ride without having really thought about the fact that they'd been talking to an older person, and without having changed their feelings about older adults, then contact theory would regard the interaction as a bit of a bust. However, the two approaches aren't as distinct as they may seem. Contact theory also emphasizes the importance of high quality contact between individuals, and (as in Figure 7.1) it also notes that forgetting about categories and dealing with people as individuals may be a crucial stage in developing quality contact.

Change in Older Adults: Confronting Patronizing Talk

In the previous chapters we examined the communication predicament of aging model and the ways in which younger people's negative attitudes about aging can lead them to use a patronizing speech style to older people. While the CPA model has been very important in the field, it has also been criticized because of its rather "passive" treatment of older people (Hummert & Ryan, 2001). In the model, the older people just sit there, get patronized, and end up suffering negative consequences. If you think about it, that's a rather patronizing view of older people, right there in the model! In reality, of course, older people have the power to express themselves in interaction and to respond in a variety of ways when they are patronized. These are discussed next and briefly outlined in Table 7.1.

Table 7.1   Examples of Different Response Types to a Patronizing Comment (e.g., "There you go, sweetie. You just sit there and I'll button your shirt for you!")

Type of response (example)	Likely evaluation of older person
Passive OK, that sounds fine.	Reinforces stereotype of dependence and incompetence.
Aggressive Don't call me sweetie and let me button my own shirt. I'm not incompetent you know, even though that's the way you always treat me.	Maintains perceptions of competence,but probably hurts perceptions of warmth.
Assertive Thank you, but I can button it so I'll just do it myself.	Increases perceptions of competence; tone of voice crucial in determining perceptions of warmth.
Humorous Oh, I'm sure you have more useful things to do. I'll button my shirt, and you go get us both a cocktail!	Increases perceptions of competence; should not hurt perceptions of warmth.

The table emphasizes two dimensions that are key in most interpersonal evaluations: **competence** and **warmth** (see also Chapter 3 for discussion of competence and warmth in stereotyping). Most of us would like to be seen as competent and also warm or likeable. A lot of the time, however, balancing these two is difficult—people who are seen as highly competent are not always seen as particularly likeable, and vice versa. The challenge of balancing these two is particularly troublesome for older adults when they are responding to patronizing speech. Trying to come out looking competent may make it difficult for them to appear likeable; being likeable may result in them looking incompetent. This is elaborated below; see also reviews by Hummert and Ryan (2001) and Hummert et al. (2004) for more detail. Also notable is Ellen Ryan and colleagues' (Ryan, Bajorek, Beaman, & Anas, 2005) application of some of these ideas to communication involving people with disabilities.

Passive Responses

A **passive response** to a patronizing comment is one that is nonconfrontational. It avoids addressing the patronizing behavior, either by "going along with" the talk or simply by avoiding addressing it. Passive responses confirm stereotypes of dependence and encourage more patronizing talk. If I address someone with a patronizing tone and they don't object, I assume that the tone is appropriate and perhaps even that the person appreciates it. When I address someone with a patronizing tone and they actually do what I ask, the patronizing style becomes "effective" communication for me and I keep doing it. A passive responder may be evaluated as warm, but certainly not as competent. This response style is probably characteristic of what would be expected from the *impaired* or *despondent* stereotypes described in Chapter 3.

Aggressive (Confrontational) Responses

Aggressive responses provide a direct attack on the patronizer and are generally not hedged with politeness or positive nonverbal behaviors. The recipient of a patronizing message simply attacks the patronizer and directly rejects the implication of his/her message. As you can probably guess, there are few benefits of this strategy in terms of warmth perceptions—the older person will generally be evaluated as ill-tempered. In some circumstances, these messages may have positive competence implications for the older person. The response certainly makes clear that this person is not going to stand for being treated like a child. However, they may also backfire on the competence dimension if the response is sufficiently aggressive to be seen as "crazy" or antisocial. Somebody who blows their fuse at what may appear to be minimal provocation will probably not emerge looking good on any dimension at all! The *shrew/curmudgeon* stereotype from Chapter 3 would probably be associated with an aggressive response style here.

Assertive Responses

An **assertive response** to a patronizing comment is one that directly challenges the implication that the older person is incompetent (i.e., challenges the stereotype underlying the message), while maintaining politeness. As noted in Table 7.1, such responses should enhance perceptions of the older person's competence. In the example provided, for instance, they are rejecting an offer of help and performing a task independently. Sometimes they may be rejecting use of a pet name, such as "sweetie," and asking to be called "Mr. _____" or "Mrs. _____," which should have positive implications for their status. The key balancing act that older adults have to perform when acting assertively is maintaining a polite and respectful tone that maintains perceptions of their likeability. Often this will depend on very subtle aspects of the message such as nonverbal communication (e.g., tone of voice, facial expression) and precise word choices (e.g., including politeness markers like "Thank you"—but not in a sarcastic way!). When these elements work together to provide a positive impression, then the assertive message will serve to enhance perceptions of competence while not damaging perceptions of warmth. When the appropriate nonverbal behaviors and word choices go wrong, the message may become aggressive. The quotation at the start of this chapter is perhaps an example of a good assertive response—depending on the nonverbals that accompanied the message, it might also be humorous (see below).

Humorous Responses

For older people who are patronized, humor offers an opportunity for them to reject the patronizing remark, while still keeping the tone "light." Ellen Ryan and her colleagues compared a **humorous response** to patronizing talk with a passive and an assertive response and found that the humorous response was rated as the most appropriate (Ryan, Kennaley, Pratt, & Shumovich, 2000). Using humor in this context is a great way to maintain the balance between competence and warmth. As can be seen from the example in Table 7.1, a humorous response can reject the implication of incompetence from the patronizing message. However, humor is almost always positive for perceptions of warmth: Funny people are almost inherently likable. And so the humorous response has positive possibilities for the older person on both key dimensions. Of course, the use of humor is not independent of assertiveness. Humor is most likely to be effective when used as part of a more generally assertive message, in order to buffer against any potential negative likeability evaluations. A brief side note here: In general, communication scholars have not done a good job of examining humor. For most people, some of their most enjoyable moments of communication involve sharing humorous stories or jokes, or enjoying another person's wit. However, in addition to providing enjoyment, humor can serve some important communicative functions as illustrated in terms of these responses to patronizing talk. Looking in more detail at humor as a communicative phenomenon in intergenerational contact would be a great project for an aspiring scholar!

Communication Skills and Communication Training

Finally for this chapter, I want to talk a little about **communication skills** and **communication training.** There are a number of aspects of what has been described up to this point that relate to more general notions of communication skills. You may already know about the communication notion of **person-centered communication** (e.g., Burleson, Delia, & Applegate, 1995). This is communication that focuses on the other person as a unique individual and that is tailored to his or her specific needs. Person-centered messages adapt to the context as well as to relevant people in the context and meet multiple goals (e.g., saying what you want to say, while maintaining a positive relationship with the other person). There are obvious links between this and the style of communication described earlier as part of the communication enhancement model. It is clear that people who are good at person-centered communication would be more likely to produce communication sensitive to an older person's needs and abilities. Similarly, older adults who are better at person-centered communication would probably be able to balance the competence and likeability demands of responding to a patronizing message.

Much of the literature on person-centered communication focuses on the concept as an individual difference variable (i.e., some people are good at it, and some are not). However, research also shows that it is possible to *train* communication skills, including person-centered communication. There are also now quite a few studies showing that communication training can be effective in the intergenerational setting. Kristine Williams and colleagues (K. Williams, Kemper, & Hummert, 2003) trained nursing assistants in nursing homes *not* to use patronizing talk. They used a short training course involving education and role playing, as well as watching videotaped interactions. The nursing assistants were shown patronizing and non-patronizing versions of the same talk (e.g., "Good morning *big guy.* Are *we* ready for *our* bath?" versus "Good morning, *Mr. Jones.* Are *you* ready for *your* bath?"). This training resulted in a significant reduction in patronizing talk. Significantly, the training program increased the respect apparent in the talk of the nursing aides, while *not* reducing the degree of caring in their talk. In other words, patronizing communication is not inevitable, and it is possible for people (even in a context such as a nursing home) to move away from such stereotyped forms of communication to more individualized strategies. Likewise, this study reveals that talk does not need to be baby-ish to be perceived as caring: In a nursing home, a degree of nurturing content in communication is important, but nurturing talk doesn't have to be condescending.

M. M. Baltes and Wahl (1996) also describe a training intervention to improve intergenerational communication. They trained staff in a long-term care setting to use more independence-supportive behaviors. Remember from Chapter 4, these are communication behaviors that "reward" older residents for performing independent behaviors. The training program not only increased the staff members' ability to engage in independence-supportive communication, but the researchers also showed that it increased the number of independent behaviors by residents in the setting. In other words, the training program not only had the desired effects on the staff members' communication but also had desirable follow-on effects on the behaviors of the residents.

Finally, it is worth noting that there are plenty of "practical" guides out there for effective communication. A particularly useful one is Barbara Dreher's short book *Communication Skills for Working With Elders* (2001). This book provides a wealth of information for dealing with communication issues that are more frequent with older people. The author is careful to acknowledge the importance of dealing with each person as an individual, while also providing hints for dealing with problems that are commonly encountered among those who work with older people on a daily basis. For instance, Table 7.2 provides Dreher's hints for talking with someone who has hearing impairments. Sometimes the most simple hints can be immensely effective. For instance, Dreher notes the importance of **rephrasing**, rather than simply repeating, when a first attempt at communication is unsuccessful. Repeating leads to frustration; rephrasing provides an opportunity to convey the message more effectively and achieve resolution. It's important to note that these skills would be useful to master no matter what the age of the hearing impaired partner.

Table 7.2   Ten Tips for Effective Communication With Hard-of-Hearing Persons

1. Stand at a distance of 3 to 6 feet.

2. Arrange to have the light on your face, not behind you.

3. Position yourself within the visual level of the listener.

4. Speak at a natural rate, unless you see signs of incomprehension.

5. Speak slightly louder than normal. Do not shout.

6. Always face the hearing-impaired person, and let your facial expression reflect your meaning.

7. Use short sentences.

8. Rephrase misunderstood sentences.

9. Do not talk while eating, chewing gum, clenching a pipe, or laughing.

10. Identify the topic of conversation so the listener has some contextual cues.

SOURCE: From *Communication Skills for Working With Elders*, by B. B. Dreher, 2001, New York: Springer.

Summary

This chapter has presented some of the ways in which we can start changing both attitudes about aging and negative communication patterns associated with old age. These changes will happen at the individual level through actions such as younger people considering factors other than age in making communication choices, and older people rejecting stereotypical communication in appropriate ways. Positive change may also be facilitated by better and more frequent contact between younger and older people—something that might be likely to occur in grandparent–grandchild relationships. Finally, communication in many settings (perhaps especially institutions like nursing homes) can be improved with tailored training programs that address problematic areas. A lot of the material in this chapter could be placed under the broad heading of "communication competence." Much of it is not rocket science: It is applying what we know about effective and appropriate communication in other contexts to intergenerational settings. In the context of this chapter, it's worth remembering some of the issues of collective action that were raised in Chapter 3. While the current chapter has focused on individual actions, positive changes will also occur through collective action and by challenging the messages our *culture* currently sends about aging. That's the focus of the next few chapters of the book.

Keywords and Theories

Aggressive responses
Assertive responses
Communication enhancement
  model
Communication predicament model
Communication skills training
Competence and warmth
Decategorization-salient categorization-
  recategorization
Grandparent–grandchild relationship
Heterogeneity
Humorous responses

Intergenerational contact
Intergroup contact theory
Passive responses
Perceived variability/heterogeneity
Person-centered communication
Pettigrew's model of optimal intergroup
  contact
Responses to patronizing speech
  (assertive, aggressive, etc.)
Self-disclosure (vs. painful
  self-disclosure)
Social support

Discussion Questions

- What are some aspects of your own relationship with your grandparents (or other older people) that you feel have changed your attitudes about older people as a group? Consider both positive and negative changes.
- Can you describe a "best case scenario" for the development of an intergenerational relationship that would positively influence a younger person's attitudes about old age?
- How could the enhancement model be used by a manager working in a restaurant frequented by a substantial older adult clientele?

- What are some elements of nonverbal communication that might make an older adult seem more aggressive (as opposed to assertive)?
- What are some ways in which someone working in a nursing home might engage in "independence supportive" communication?

Annotated Bibliography

Dreher, B. B. (2001). *Communication skills for working with elders.* New York: Springer. An easy-to-read, very practical guide for those who are working with elders. The book does not require any background in the discipline of communication and can easily be "dipped into" for dealing with specific situations. Dreher carefully avoids the tendency to suggest that all older adults are alike. She also provides some handy guides for communicating with older people who are suffering from rather specific health problems.

Harwood, J., Hewstone, M., Paolini, S., & Voci, A. (2005). Grandparent–grandchild contact and attitudes towards older adults: Moderator and mediator effects. *Personality and Social Psychology Bulletin, 31,* 393–406. A technical research report, but one that describes some of the recent research on contact theory and communication in the context of the grandparent–grandchild relationship. This article contains two studies that are mentioned in the text of the chapter.

Ryan, E. B., Meredith, S. D., MacLean, M. J., & Orange, J. B. (1995). Changing the way we talk with elders: Promoting health using the communication enhancement model. *International Journal of Aging and Human Development, 41,* 87–105. The original article introducing the communication enhancement model. This article provides some really nice case studies illustrating how the model might be applied in the health care setting. It is also clear, though, that it can be applied in non-health-related settings.

PART III

———•◦•———

Social Representations
and Mass Communication

This part of the book focuses on the "cultural" level of communication. It first outlines the ways in which mass media represent aging—whether old people are fairly represented on television, in magazines, in movies, and the like (Chapter 8). Chapter 9 then investigates the ways in which older people *use* the mass media, and the effects that the media might have on how all of us think about aging. Both of these chapters examine Western cultural representations of aging—the mass media are a very powerful cultural force in Western cultures, and this is where the majority of the research has been done. Chapter 10 describes cultural *variations* in the meaning of aging. While Western media provide one window into aging, other cultures have different ways of thinking about aging that deserve our attention. Hence, this final chapter of part III examines studies of media and other communication phenomena (e.g., interpersonal behavior, family relations) that tell us about different ways of growing old around the world.

⊰ EIGHT ⊱

Mass Communication
Portrayals of Older Adults

This chapter describes how older adults are portrayed in various media. By the end of this chapter you should be able to:

- Describe the meaning of the term "underrepresentation"
- Summarize the media contexts in which older people are underrepresented in the media
- Describe the situations in which older adults are positively and negatively represented in the media
- Talk about historical trends in portrayals of older people
- Understand the media *industry* dynamics that might influence portrayals of older adults

SOURCE: ©Gettyimages

*[Seniors] do not see themselves portrayed and when then do, it's in
a demeaning manner. They're referred to as "over the hill," "old
goats" and "old farts"—oh* please, *ugly ways of talking about us.*

—Doris Roberts [Marie Barone on *Everybody Loves Raymond*],
Interview with the Parents Television Council, 2003

I f we want to understand where a group stands in society, there are few
better ways of getting information than by watching television. If a group of
people is featured prominently on TV and is shown in a positive light, and the
main characters in most shows come from that group, you can probably safely
conclude that the group is valued by society and has power. Likewise, if you
don't see a group, or they tend to be shown in peripheral or negative roles, you
can conclude that this group lacks clout. In social science terms, the group
lacks **vitality**. Vitality refers to a group's strength, status, size, and influence in
a particular context. In the United States, white men as a group have the highest vitality (just look at the list of U.S. presidents: White men = 42, Others = 0).

So it is with age groups. Numerous scholars have examined different
media contexts, particularly television, with the goal of understanding how
and when age groups are shown, and thus drawing inferences about the relative power of different age groups in society. What they have found may not
surprise those of you who have read the earlier chapters in this book, or
indeed those of you who spend a lot of time watching television. In this
chapter, I describe some of these findings, focusing particularly on North
American and European media. Chapter 10 presents some cross-cultural data
on this issue.

Underrepresentation

One of the most common techniques for examining group portrayals on television is simply to count the number of members of certain groups in some
sample of programming. The proportions of different groups can then be compared to some baseline (generally the proportions of those groups in the real
population). Figure 8.1 presents such a comparison for age groups. In this case,
all prime-time major network television shows from 1999 were compared
with year 2000 census bureau data. As you can see, the TV shows contain many

more young adults (20–34 years old) than are actually present in the U.S. population. In contrast, the shows contain significantly fewer older adults. This phenomenon is called **underrepresentation**. Older people were about 3% of the television population, but almost 15% of the real population. Over the past 30 years, results consistent with this pattern have been fairly consistent in the research literature (Arnoff, 1974; Gerbner, Gross, Signorielli, & Morgan, 1980; Greenberg, Korzenny, & Atkin, 1980). In general, fewer than 5% of prime-time television characters are over 65. J. D. Robinson and Skill (1995a) statistically compared proportions of older adults in different studies over time and demonstrated that little change has occurred (at least up until that point in time). The same pattern emerges when television advertising is examined (Miller, Levell, & Mazachek, 2004; Roy & Harwood 1997), and similar patterns emerge in game shows and cartoons (Harris & Feinberg, 1977; Levinson, 1973). A recent analysis finds that about 8% of characters in children's cartoons are portrayed as over 55, as compared to well over 20% in the population as a whole (T. Robinson & Anderson, 2006).

Figure 8.1   Comparison of Prime-Time Television Population With Census Bureau Data

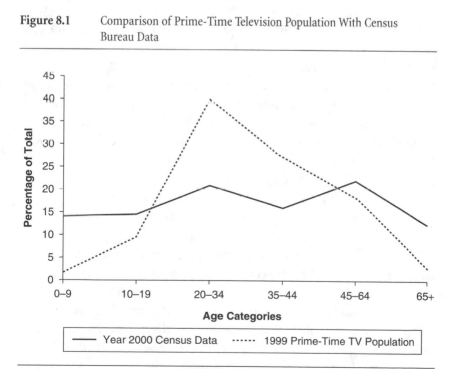

SOURCE: From Harwood, J., & Anderson, K., The presence and portrayal of social groups on prime-time television, *Communication Reports, 15*(2), copyright © 2002. Reprinted with permission of the Western States Communication Association.

Some exceptions have been claimed. For instance, Cassata, Anderson, and Skill's (1980) analysis of soap operas is sometimes cited as indicating better representation of older people in that type of programming. They found that about 16% of soap opera characters were over the age of 55. However, about half of those "older adult" characters were in their 50s, meaning that only about 8% of characters were over 60, and presumably even fewer over the age of 65. Elliott (1984) also found about 8% of soap characters were over 60 (as compared to about 14% of the population as a whole). These studies combined suggest that older adults may not be as severely underrepresented in soap operas as they are elsewhere, but they *are* still underrepresented (Cassata & Irwin, 1997). As you can see from this brief discussion, when interpreting this research it is very important to know what the "cut-off" is for someone to count as "old"—comparing people 55 and older on television with people 65 and older in the population will yield erroneous conclusions of "fair" representation on television. Petersen (1973) is often cited as the most dramatic illustration of older people having a substantial presence on television. Her study found almost 13% of television characters to be over 65, as compared to about 10% in the population at the time. She was working with a relatively small sample (only 247 characters) and did not report all the details of her method, but her results remain something of an aberration compared to the rest of the published literature. One final note: The vast majority of the literature has focused on entertainment television. Other areas of television may feature significantly more older people. For instance, in early 2005, Donald Rumsfeld (Former U.S. secretary of defense) appeared on CNN's *Larry King Show*. Both host and guest were in their early 70s, and both could be considered very significant cultural figures in the United States at that point in time. For half an hour, at least, cable news programming was dominated by older adults. We don't really know how frequently events like this occur.

Less work exists on media other than television, but that research also reflects the underrepresentation pattern. Magazine advertisements feature older adults at substantially lower levels than their presence in the population, even when a wide variety of magazines are examined (Harwood & Roy, 1999). For instance, Gantz, Gartenberg, and Rainbow (1980) found that older people are present in only about 6% of magazine advertisements that include humans. *Ladies' Home Journal*, *Ms.*, *People*, *Playboy*, and *Sports Illustrated* all recorded even fewer ads featuring older people, while only *Time* and *Reader's Digest* had somewhat larger numbers of such ads. Similar underrepresentation occurs in children's literature (Robin, 1977), children's magazines (Almerico & Fillmer, 1988), newspaper advertisements (Buchholz & Bynum, 1982), and popular movies (Lauzen & Dozier, 2005). Atkinson and Ragab (2004) examined the presence of older people in movies from 1980 to 1999, finding about 6% of the characters to be over the age of 60, a slightly higher number than that of television studies, but still a marked underrepresentation.

As you can see from the dates of the studies cited in the previous paragraphs, the patterns seem depressingly consistent over the years, with very little indication of trends toward increased representation of older adults, despite their growing presence in the population. Miller et al. (2004) examined television commercials across five decades and found no trend toward increasing portrayals of older adults (indeed, their data appear to indicate a peak in numbers of older people in ads in the 1970s). These data, unfortunately, are from a nonrepresentative sample, so the comparisons across decades may not be valid. Nevertheless, the media seem slow to recognize the growing presence and influence of this group.

Many researchers have further examined this phenomenon by examining proportions of men and women in these different media. Again, the findings have been relatively consistent across media and across time. Men are consistently represented in larger numbers on television and in magazines than are women, and this pattern tends to be exaggerated among older people. Gerbner and his colleagues (1980), for instance, showed a huge bulge of female television characters in their 20s, followed by a dramatic decline. Women over 40 were rare in their sample. Men, on the other hand, peaked in numbers in their late 30s, again followed by a relatively steep decline. Raman and colleagues (Raman, Harwood, Weis, Anderson, & Miller, 2006) show a similar pattern in magazine advertising, as do Stern and Mastro (2004) in television commercials (see also Box 8.1). Research has found that older men appear as much as ten times as frequently as older women (e.g., Petersen, 1973). The most recent research on this issue (T. Robinson & Anderson, 2006) shows a similar pattern among characters in children's television cartoons—approximately 77% of older characters on those shows are male. You can do your own informal survey of this issue using Exercise 8.1.

Interpretations of these findings focus on how men achieve a certain status with old age, whereas that status is not accorded to women. This relates, in part, back to some of the **evolutionary explanations** for differences in attitudes about older men versus older women (see Chapter 3). For instance,

Box 8.1   Women and Men in the Movies

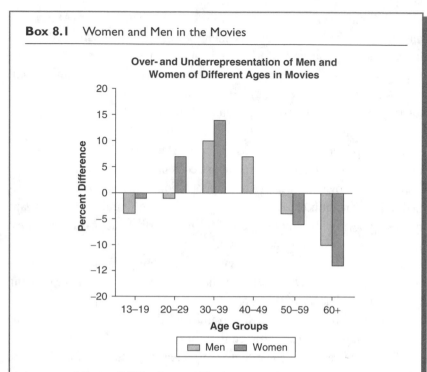

Over- and Underrepresentation of Men and Women of Different Ages in Movies

Lauzen and Dozier (2005) examined 88 of the top 100 grossing films in the United States of 2002 (think, *My Big Fat Greek Wedding, Spiderman, Lord of the Rings (Two Towers), Chicago*, etc.). They assessed the age and sex of all characters, as well as coding each in terms of leadership, role in the film (major/minor), and a number of other variables. The graph above shows the distribution of male and female characters across different age groups, as compared to those groups' actual presence in the population. So values above the zero-point indicate that groups are overrepresented in movies; below the midpoint indicates underrepresentation. As you can see, movies demonstrate a similar pattern to television and advertising. Women are overrepresented in their 20s and 30s, whereas men are overrepresented in their 30s and 40s. So men appear to retain a desirability and marketability for longer than women. Men and women are underrepresented in movies once they reach their 50s and 60s, but this underrepresentation is somewhat more severe for women. The authors of this study also found that men aged 40–69 were often powerful and in leadership positions, whereas women in these age groups were less powerful and had less in the way of personal goals. Similar patterns are shown in a study of 20 years of movie portrayals by Atkinson and Ragab (2004).

NOTE: Y-axis represents percent difference between presence in movies and in U.S. population. Negative numbers indicate underrepresenation in movies.

Exercise 8.1	Gender Bias in Media Portrayals of Age?

Recall the most recent movie you saw. Estimate the age and sex of the two or three major characters. If you are reading this book as part of a class, summarize this information for the whole class in the table below. What does it show?

	Male	*Female*
0–9		
10–19		
20–29		
30–39		
40–49		
50–59		
60–69		
70+		

Gerbner et al. (1980) note that "woman actually outnumber men among [television] characters in their early twenties, when their function as romantic partners is supposed to peak. . . . The character population is structured to provide a relative abundance of younger women for older men, but no such abundance of younger men for older women" (p. 40). In other words, Gerbner and his colleagues suggest that the television world is something of a fantasy situation for older men, who have a positive cornucopia of younger women from whom to pick a (fantasy) mate. Underlying this is, presumably, an ideology in which attractiveness as a mate (reproductive function) is valued above other factors in determining when and how women are shown on television. Accompanying this trend for younger women is the fact that women also seem to take on the more negative characteristics associated with age earlier than men—women in their 50s are more often categorized as fitting negative age stereotypes than are men (Signorielli, 2004). Thus, Paul Newman, Harrison Ford, Clint Eastwood, and many others retain a "sexy" image into their 50s, 60s, and even later, while thinking of their equivalents among Hollywood actresses is considerably more challenging.

Work on racial and ethnic disparities in portrayals of older adults is relatively rare and hard to interpret. As noted earlier, there are relatively few older adults on television, and among those the majority are portrayals of whites. For instance, Harwood and Anderson (2002) examined 835 television characters and found only *four* African American characters over the age of 60. Statistically it is virtually impossible to reach any conclusions about representations of older African Americans from such a sample; other ethnic groups were almost totally absent from the 60+ age group. Research aiming to examine ethnic variation among older television characters will either have to examine a gargantuan sample of programs and characters, or it will have to figure out a way of targeting specific portrayals of particular interest.

Negative Representation

In addition to the underrepresentation of older adults, it is important to look at *how* they are portrayed when indeed they are shown. Three predominant themes emerge suggesting that older people are **portrayed negatively** in most media. However, positive portrayals also exist (discussed later), and portrayals in most media are fairly complex and variable. Beyond the research described below, you may want to think about portrayals of aging in cartoons (Polivka, 1988), literature (Kehl, 1985; Woodward, 1991), jokes (Richman, 1977) or popular music (Leitner, 1983).

Health

As described earlier in the book, one pressing concern for social gerontologists is the almost obsessive societal link between aging and health. As was talked about in Chapter 1, our society finds it almost impossible to talk about aging without talking about health, and indeed "aging" is sometimes used to refer directly to declining health. The media also appear to fall for this link. Most research examining older people demonstrates that they are associated with ill health in a variety of ways in media portrayals. One of the best ways to demonstrate this connection is with advertising portrayals. Raman and colleagues (2006), for instance, examined the types of products that feature older adults in their magazine advertisements. In North American **advertising,** older people were overwhelmingly associated with health-related products. Interestingly, many of these products were for ailments that are not particularly age-related (e.g., allergy medications), although some were for products with clear age connections (e.g., incontinence treatments, Alzheimer's drugs). As will be described below, the individual portrayals of older people in these ads are not necessarily negative. The concern is with the perpetual linking of age and health, which reinforces the connection between those two things. Sometimes, we see dramatic illustrations of ways in which individual decisions such as those of headline writers can change whether a media portrayal emphasizes decline in old age—often a subtly different spin can have dramatic consequences (see Box 8.2). Chapter 11 has more detailed coverage of specific communication and health issues in older adulthood.

Box 8.2   Mass Communication About Aging: A Case Study—Are Older Surgeons' Patients More Likely to Die?

In early September 2006, I noticed a headline in my local newspaper. "Study: Aging Surgeons Less Effective in Some Surgeries." Being interested in aging, I read the article. It appeared to report that patients of older surgeons die more often, but the exact findings of the original study on which the article was based weren't entirely clear. Google news quickly directed me to other articles based on the same original study. All of the articles included basically the same information, but the headlines varied quite dramatically in terms of their implications about older surgeons' skills. Consider the following:

Study Raises Questions About
    Aging Surgeons' Last Years
Older Surgeons Not
    Necessarily Better
Old Surgeons Still Good—If Busy
Are Older Surgeons Better?
Study: Surgeon's Experience
    as Important as Age
Study: High-Volume Surgeons Best
Age of Surgeon Is Not
    Important Predictor of Risk
    for Patient

With Surgeons, Older May Not
    Be Better
Aging Surgeons Under
    Scrutiny
Surgical Work Can Outlast
    Skills
When Should Surgeons Hang
    Up Their Scrubs?
Study Questions Surgeons' Last
    Years Behind Scalpel

I was immediately struck by how the same original information could be presented in so many different ways, and I was particularly concerned about the impact that these different headlines might have on a reader who was quickly

(Continued)

(Continued)

scanning the newspaper. Some appear to suggest that there are significant problems with older surgeons, while others explicitly say that age is not important, and some don't mention age at all. In this case, the headline writers have interpreted the results of the original study and either emphasized or deemphasized the role of age. What was the actual finding of the study? Older surgeons' patients *did* die more often for three of eight types of surgery examined (they were equal on five of the eight). *But* that death rate was because more of the older surgeons were performing relatively few operations—they were getting less "practice" than younger surgeons. Older surgeons who maintained a regular surgical load had performance that was as good or better than younger surgeons. There are three morals to this story: (a) If you're getting a surgery done, you should ignore the surgeon's age but make sure you ask how often the surgeon performs the specific procedure that you're about to undergo, (b) when you read a newspaper headline suggesting a link between age and some other variable, try to dig a little deeper and see what the original research actually found, and (c) if you are *writing* newspaper headlines, don't jump to a conclusion based on one piece of information—consider the effects on your readers when stating a conclusion like "aging surgeons less effective."

Lead Versus Peripheral Roles

A frequent observation of scholars examining older adults on television is that they are rarely shown in major roles. J. D. Robinson and Skill (1995b) have developed a theoretical perspective surrounding this phenomenon: **peripheral imagery theory.** This theory suggests that minor or peripheral characters in a media presentation may be more revealing than central characters as concerns societal portrayals. Specifically, major characters in television shows, for instance, tend to develop over time, have idiosyncrasies, and have a detailed back story that allows us to view them as a complete person. Minor characters, on the other hand, are present for a short period, serve some rather specific plot function, and then disappear. As such, they need to be processed and understood rather quickly by the audience. In doing this quick processing, it is likely that the audience relies on schemas or stereotypes about the groups that the characters come from. Thus, the writers will create characters that fit with the audience's schema. For instance, if you need a character who is hard of hearing in order to make a joke work, having an older person serve that function will work best. Their poor hearing fits the viewer's schema of old age, and hence the writer doesn't have to spend valuable time explaining that they are deaf. Thus, the fact that older adults are often present in peripheral roles enhances the likelihood that they will be portrayed in a stereotypical fashion. One disclaimer: Some studies do not support the contention that older adults are shown more frequently in peripheral roles (e.g., Harwood & Anderson, 2002). The diverging findings on this issue may be a function of the relatively small number of older adults on television; when we are only looking at a relatively small number of older characters, it becomes statistically challenging to examine subtle issues like whether they are portrayed peripherally in larger numbers than other age groups. Either way, peripheral characters are important to examine because of the ways that they reveal stereotypical images (J. D. Robinson, Skill, & Turner, 2004).

Humor

Funny messages are a media staple: From blockbuster comedy movies and network situation comedies to basic cable's *Comedy Central* channel, comedy is ubiquitous. Older people and aging are used a lot for comic effect, often in less than flattering ways. Comedy can be achieved by having a stereotypical older character who is the butt of other characters' jokes (e.g., the dirty old man, the forgetful aging parent). Such messages obviously rely on shared knowledge of the stereotype for their **humor** and almost certainly serve to reinforce that stereotype. An advertising campaign for baseball on the Fox network featured an 89-year-old ex-baseball player supposedly making a comeback. One spot showed the man attempting to pitch: "After lobbing a massive gob of spit onto a baseball, he weakly throws the ball a mere couple of feet" (Petrecca, 1999, p. 8).

Messages About the Aging Process

In addition to actual portrayals of older people, the media send a variety of messages about the aging process that can be construed as negative. Perhaps most salient here are the advertisements for cosmetics that promote "younger" skin, moisturizers that have "anti-wrinkle" formulas, and dyes developed specifically to hide grey hair. While we have grown accustomed to these products and probably don't think twice about them, the marketing of them is explicitly ageist. The premise is that we all want to hide any signs that we are aging, and that this is natural and normal. Justine Coupland (2003) makes a powerful argument that cosmetics advertisers not only want to make aging skin seem pathological but also want to induce guilt in women by making women themselves feel "responsible" for wrinkles. Note that this is a very gendered discourse, with women being targeted massively more than men for such products. The message is one that is clearly opposed to the visible manifestations of aging, and hence is ageist. All this occurs, despite the fact that (to quote J. Coupland), "to live in the world is to age, day by day, from birth. How can advertisers persuade women that stopping the ageing process or, rather, disguising its effects on the body is achievable?" (p. 128).

Other troublesome messages about aging occur in the media's use of phrases like "senior moment" (Bonnesen & Burgess, 2004), descriptions of the physical status of "veteran" athletes (often in their late 20s!), and perhaps even in advertisements for financial services for retirees that tend to focus on leisure activities and do not portray the many constructive ways in which older people contribute to society. Even more destructive messages are present in media like birthday cards, but of course such messages are intended to be funny, and hence their creators would perhaps argue that they are harmless. I would disagree! There is very little research on these kinds of portrayals or their effects on people who see them. If you are reading this book as part of a class, you might want to discuss some ways in which some of these forms of communication talk about the aging process: Take a look at Dillon and Jones's (1981) study of birthday cards and then visit your local Hallmark store to sample the wares.

Positive Portrayals

There are a few areas in which it is possible to identify positive elements in portrayals of older people, although in some cases these need to be subject to some critical thinking. Some researchers describe **positive media portrayals** of aging without a clear comparison point. For instance, Vernon, Williams, Phillips, and Wilson (1990) describe positive portrayals of older people in prime-time television on a variety of dimensions. However, they have no comparison with the portrayal of younger people, so we can't know whether these "positive" portrayals are different from (i.e., less positive than) portrayals of younger characters. Likewise, Cassata et al. (1980) describe generally positive portrayals of older people in daytime soaps, but again without a comparison to younger people. Kessler, Rekoczy, and Staudinger (2004) engage in a rather complicated analysis attempting to compare older adults' portrayals to some objective standards of life success. They suggest that portrayals of older adults in German television are positive. Again, however, we do not know whether portrayals of younger people are even more positive because portrayals of younger people were not examined. This is a crucial point: It may be that older adults are *not* portrayed in an overwhelmingly negative fashion, but they are nevertheless portrayed less positively than young people.

Certain apparently positive portrayals also require a somewhat more detailed examination to understand the complex ways in which older people are shown. Next we consider some common areas of apparently positive portrayals. The filmography in Box 8.3 provides a list of movies that should lead to interesting discussion about portrayals of aging.

Box 8.3   Filmography of Interesting Portrayals of Aging

The following are movies with positive, interesting, or controversial portrayals of aging. I am not recommending these as the best images of aging that are out there. Rather, they are movies that give interesting starting points for discussing how the media portray aging. In many cases, they also provide interesting perspectives on intergenerational relationships, something that has not been studied extensively. I have also included films on different portions of the life span: Portrayals of middle age (e.g., *The Big Chill*) are interesting in that they often present people first coming to terms with their own aging. It is crucial to watch the movies critically, considering the ways in which they present aging as a diverse and positive experience, the ways in which they stereotype the older characters, and the ways in which aging is at times sentimentalized. If you are reading this book as part of a class, you might want to watch one of the movies and discuss its portrayal, or divide them up among the class, and share the different narratives of age that you see with one another. I have also included a few television shows that have interesting portrayals of older people.

(Continued)

(Continued)

A Woman's Tale	Space Cowboys
Babette's Feast	The Big Chill
Cinema Paradiso	The Dresser
Crimes and Misdemeanors	The Gin Game
Curtain Call	The Notebook
Dad	The Straight Story
Driving Miss Daisy	Tuesdays With Morrie
Fried Green Tomatoes	The Golden Girls (TV)
Grumpy Old Men	King of Queens (TV)
Innocence	Frasier (TV)
Iris	The Simpsons (TV)
Lost in Yonkers	Murder, She Wrote (TV)
Rocket Gibraltar	Everybody Loves Raymond (TV)
Something's Gotta Give	

Exceptional Characters

Older adults who have engaged in activities that are dramatically **counter-stereotypical** (going against the stereotype) are a staple of "human interest" sections of newspapers and local TV news—the classic case here is the 83-year-old grandma who jumps out of an airplane. Older adults who run marathons, cycle across the Rocky Mountains, climb Everest, or get shot out of canons are subject to similar treatment. Little research has been done on these portrayals, but they do seem to share similar features. Most notably, the *exceptionality* of these achievements is a common theme (the older adults concerned are described as remarkable, amazing, fantastic, and the like). Most of the stereotype violations are positive, but sometimes these individuals have violated stereotypes in a negative fashion (e.g., in December 2005, a 70-year-old grandmother achieved some notoriety when she stole the baby Jesus from a nativity scene: "Granny Lifts Baby Jesus," 2005).

Clearly such portrayals might have the capacity to change our perceptions of aging, given that they feature individuals who have ignored the constraints that society places on old age, instead choosing to pursue exciting and generally personally rewarding activities. However, the very *newsworthiness* of these achievements, and the way in which these older people are portrayed as *exceptional,* tends to discount any positive impact that the stories might have on our more general views of older people. The focus on the individuals as exceptional makes it clear that a typical older adult *does not* do these things, and perhaps that they *should* not. One skydiving grandma is on the news precisely because she is doing something that is not representative of most old people. You may wish to refer back to Chapter 7, which discussed the role of representativeness or typicality of older adults in having the potential to change attitudes.

Central Characters

The exceptional or atypical portrayals described above are also apparent in some fictional characters—generally they tend to be the lead characters in shows. While older adults are rarely lead characters in shows, when they are the leads, they often portray older adulthood in apparently positive and almost always **counter-stereotypical** ways. The most commonly discussed of these in recent years is *The Golden Girls,* which aired on NBC from 1985 to 1992 but is still showing in syndication. Other similar shows are *Murder, She Wrote, Diagnosis Murder, Matlock,* and *Jake and the Fatman.* These shows often capitalize on particular star power. A show like *The Golden Girls* that features four older women would be a very tough sell to most network executives (see below). However, when it includes recognizable stars like Estelle Getty, Bea Arthur, and Betty White, it comes with a built-in audience of people who like those actresses, and thus is sustainable. Similar star power is apparent on *Murder, She Wrote* (Angela Lansbury), *Matlock* (Andy Griffith), and other such shows. These shows thrive among the older audience because, as will be elaborated in the next chapter, older people generally like shows that feature older characters. Hence, while *The Golden Girls* was popular across the whole television audience ("Best and Worst by Numbers," 1989), it was consistently a huge ratings winner among older viewers (Mundorf & Brownell, 1990). This audience can be attractive to certain subsets of advertisers (e.g., financial organizations offering retirement planning).

Bell (1992) examined a number of shows featuring older characters as the leads in the late 1980s and concluded that the older characters were shown as affluent, healthy, active, admired, and sexy. Such portrayals are in stark contrast to the "average" portrayals of older adults that are negative (as described above; remember that J. D. Robinson and Skill (1995b) suggested that peripheral characters tend to be more stereotypically portrayed than leads). Lead characters necessarily involve more complexity than peripheral characters, and they also need to be more likeable. Thus, in the rare instances where older characters get to be the lead in the show, they are likely to be positively portrayed.

Unfortunately, a few factors make these lead characters' positive portrayals less exciting than we might hope. First, as described in more detail in the next chapter, younger people are unlikely to watch these shows. Hence, no matter how positive the portrayal, younger people are unlikely to see it or be affected by it! Second, such portrayals may be less positive than you might imagine for some older people. In particular, Mares and Cantor (1992) show that some older people (those who were coping less well with their own aging) found the highly engaged, active, and competent characters on television to be somewhat threatening. Third, there appears to be a decline in this kind of programming. During the late 1980s and early 1990s a number of shows with older adult leads maintained lengthy prime-time runs (see those listed above). In contrast, it is difficult to think of a current prime-time network show with a lead character over the age of 60. A fourth concern is that these portrayals (as well as the news portrayals of exceptional older adults described in the previous section) may at times have a humorous intent, an issue that we turn to next.

Humorous Characters

In some of my earliest research, Howard Giles and I looked at images of aging in *The Golden Girls* (Harwood & Giles, 1992). We concluded that the show did do a good job of contradicting a number of stereotypes of old age (for instance, the characters are shown as active, healthy, and sexual). However, we also expressed concern that the humor in the show often centered around ageist stereotypes in unfortunate ways. For instance, the character Blanche is the most sexually active of the characters, and her sexual exploits are often the subject of jokes in the show, which might serve to reinforce the idea that all sexual activity in older people is absurd. Indeed, when characters engaged in activity or said something that was counter to age stereotypes, the vast majority of the time it was associated with laughter on the show's laugh track.

Advertising messages also sometimes capitalize on portraying older adults in ways that violate our stereotypes, and again, these messages often rely on humor. A 2005 beer commercial features an older woman (fairly short and plump, with grey hair) in a martial arts class. Her instructor is clearly very skilled, but the older woman appears passive. However, when her instructor takes her beer away, the older woman immediately launches into a series of violent and very effective martial arts moves, bringing her black belt instructor to his knees. The message relies on violating the stereotype of "grandmotherly" behavior to achieve its humor. While it might superficially be seen as a positive portrayal of aging (the woman is physically strong and powerful), the humorous intent removes any likelihood that it might be interpreted in a liberating way for older people. This is, of course, only one advertisement. The next section concerns more general patterns in advertising.

Advertising

In contrast to the negative portrayals commonly found elsewhere, advertising images of seniors tend in large part to be positive. For instance, Roy and Harwood (1997) found that older characters in television ads tended to be happy and active (see also Atkins, Jenkins, & Perkins, 1991; Swayne & Greco, 1987). The same has been found with magazine advertising (Harwood & Roy, 1999). In part, of course, this can be explained by the nature of advertising. Ads are trying to sell products, and it is pretty rare for advertisers to want to depress their audience or make them unhappy. Indeed, in a recent examination of magazine advertising that I was involved in, we found happy, smiling older adults in advertisements related to Alzheimer's disease, long-term institutionalization, and loss of bladder control (Raman et al., 2006).

Currently, there are some interesting trends in the ways that ads are using the grandparenting relationship to sell products. A number of recent ads include the implicit message: "Use our product and you can have a better relationship with your grandchild." Figure 8.2 provides one example. The product being advertised is designed to help improve lung functioning for people with a specific ailment. The improved lung function is illustrated by the ability to blow bubbles and hence entertain the granddaughter. Obviously, being able to blow bubbles is not the primary advantage of having good lungs. But the image in the ad provides a positive spin on the product—rather than emphasizing current limitations and problems, it emphasizes future possibilities. And in presenting this somewhat idealized image of the relationship, it manages to associate the product with an uncontroversially positive thing: Very few people are opposed to grandparents and grandchildren having fun together, and so people should be in favor of this product.

Figure 8.2   Advertising Featuring the Grandparenting Relationship

Researchers in Britain have recently begun looking at advertisements featuring older adults in a more detailed, qualitative fashion, focusing especially on visual communication cues in the advertisements. This work has begun to provide some categories in which we can place different kinds of portrayals. For instance, sometimes older people are shown as comic or ridiculous (e.g., a very old man dressed in teenage clothing styles), other times they are shown as glamorous and wealthy (e.g., a well-dressed couple dressed up for a night on the town), and sometimes they are celebrities endorsing a product (Ylänne-McEwen & Williams, 2003). These researchers have suggested that some advertisements are now featuring older adults in an "age incidental" fashion—the age of the characters in the ads is irrelevant to their portrayal. This is an interesting trend in that old people are (too) often portrayed precisely for their age status—that is, the fact that the person is old brings some humor or information to the ad, and the older person would not be there otherwise. To have older people in an ad in a non-age-relevant fashion perhaps demonstrates some more general acceptance of aging and old age in society such that these people are welcome to simply play the role of a *person,* rather than always being an *old* person.

Miller et al. (2004) present data suggesting that older adults are being shown more positively in commercials today than they were in the past. Using Hummert's "multiple stereotypes" perspective (see Chapter 3), they coded older characters in television commercials over five decades. The results indicate that, for instance, an active "golden ager" stereotype is represented by about 50% of older characters in the 1980s and 1990s, but less than 30% during the 1950–1979 period. Conversely, negative stereotypes of older adults seemed to be used a lot in the 1970s but not at other times. These results are intriguing, and this study also represents one of only a few pieces of research that incorporate some of the stereotyping work from Chapter 3 into media content analysis. The samples of ads from each decade are not necessarily comparable, however, because they were not randomly sampled.

Overall, though, advertising does appear to be one area in which positive portrayals are fairly common. Indeed, there are some indications that advertising may be at the leading edge of genuinely positive, and even liberating, portrayals of older adults. A recent billboard for a soap product shows a woman's face with visible wrinkles and long grey hair: She is probably in her mid to late 50s, so she is not "old" in the sense that is typically used, but she is definitely showing signs of aging. She is smiling, and beside her are two simple check boxes saying:

☐ Grey?
☐ Gorgeous?

The message is a new one: That it's OK to celebrate the physical manifestations of aging, and that it might even be possible to see some of those markers as attractive. Unthinkable? Think again! See Exercise 8.2 for some recent advertisements: Are these sending positive or negative messages about age?

Exercise 8.2   Portrayals of Aging in Advertising

Compare and contrast the advertisements on the next two pages. What message(s) does each send about getting old? Consider alternatives, and think about why the creators might have made the messages ambiguous and what they were trying to achieve. When examining the advertisements, consider the following issues:

a. What is the visual image of the older people? What are their facial expressions? How are they dressed?

b. Does the text make reference to age or aging? How? Does the language that is used in the ad send any messages about aging?

c. Are there similarities between these ads and the one shown in Figure 8.2?

d. How are relationships portrayed in the advertisements? Which relationships are described/discussed, and with what effect?

e. Overall, what effects might come from exposure to multiple similar messages? How might these messages make younger and older people think about aging, personal relationships, or the products/services being advertised?

THANKS TO DR. JERMAN, THIS GRANDPA CAN STILL COME OUT TO PLAY.

He had his first heart attack at 79. But thanks to Dr. Jerman, he's still playing with his granddaughter at 92.

Although it's easy to attribute patient longevity to advances in medical science, those advances would be nothing without Dr. Jerman's skill, diligent observation and dedication to his patients. In the care of Dr. Jerman, this spry fellow has more time to play expert bridge, more time to go bird watching, and more time to goof around with his granddaughter.

Dr. Jerman wouldn't consider himself a hero. But to a certain three-year-old girl, he definitely is.

Michael Jerman, MD
Cardiologist
AMA member

AMA
AMERICAN
MEDICAL
ASSOCIATION

Helping doctors help patients.

Tell the AMA about the doctors who've been heroes in your life.
Share your story at
www.ama-assn.org/go/stories

Political Power

Holladay and Coombs (2004) discuss some common media images of older adults' political power. These authors note that the media present groups like the AARP as "nearly omnipotent" in Washington, DC, driving policy making and striking fear into legislators with threats of how their older constituents will vote based on senior-related policy issues. The AARP certainly does exercise political power in Washington: It is a respected authority on aging issues, and it has the ability to mobilize large numbers of seniors on particular issues. However, as Holladay and Coombs note, older people virtually never vote as a block—older adults' political attitudes and voting behavior are at least as diverse as any other group. Hence, the AARP has not demonstrated the power to shift election results. Perhaps as a consequence of this, its direct effects on new policy have been limited. The frequent overstatements of the AARP's influence in Washington do, however, have some rather negative consequences. In particular, Holladay and Coombs note that these portrayals reinforce notions that older adults are "greedy geezers," and that their political activities are entirely grounded in self-interest. More broadly, the portrayals of the AARP's political power reinforce ideas that older adults are being looked after in the political realm, which is at best only partially true.

The Media Industry

We turn now to a brief discussion of media industry issues to help understand what has been described in this chapter. The low levels of older adults' media portrayals and lack of positive change over time might be seen as somewhat surprising given that the U.S. media examined in most of these studies are private, commercial enterprises. U.S. commercial media rely on attracting audiences, and older adults are a large and growing audience. The U.S. population 50 and older owns $7 trillion in assets and has around $800 billion in personal income (70% of the total net worth of American households: L. Davis, 2002). Such a group would seem like a good target for television programmers and advertisers alike. So why are older people being ignored?

Obviously, decisions about the content of television shows (what the show is about, who the main characters will be) are made by groups of people. The decision to **"green light"** (approve for production) a television show is an expensive one for a media organization, and one that is only made when the organization is confident that the show will gain a viewership, and thus be attractive to advertisers. Don't forget: The main goal of network television is not to make shows that entertain you. Their main goal is to deliver an audience of people to advertisers.

One commonly cited issue with portraying older people on television is that such characters do not appeal to younger viewers, and many advertisers are very concerned with getting their products in front of younger consumers. Adults aged 18–49 are often referred to as **"key demographics"** (or just "key demos") within the media industry. The show that wins among the key demos can be a bigger deal than the show that gets the most viewers overall. Why?

Young people are also often believed to have more *disposable* income (i.e., they have cash in their pocket that they are willing to spend). It is true that a greater proportion of older people's assets is tied up in things like stocks and real estate. If you have paid off your mortgage and own your home outright, you have control of a very significant asset, but you can't buy a can of soda with that asset! However, in terms of pure dollars, older adults control more discretionary income than any other group (Polyak, 2000). While we don't have a lot of research to go on, it seems likely that older adults are somewhat smarter with their discretionary spending than young people, however. So, while younger people might be attracted by a well-made commercial, older adults have a lifetime of experience with consumerism and may be somewhat more skeptical of advertisers' claims. Perhaps they are less likely to be influenced by a 30-second advertisement and hence are less attractive to advertisers trying to sell things to us. There is also the impression (largely false) among advertisers that older consumers have decided on their brand and are unlikely to switch (e.g., if she's driven a Buick all her life, she's not going to change now!). David Poltrack (a researcher for the CBS television network) has argued against this by citing the example of the Lexus car brand, driven mostly by people over 50. In 2000, he said: "Lexus is a car that didn't exist four years ago, so how did these older people come to buy it; did they think they were buying a Cadillac?" (quoted in Briller, 2000). Perhaps the philosophy of targeting key demographics has reached its pinnacle with Fox's *American Idol,* a show in which anybody over the age of 28 is *too old* to participate (http://www.idolonfox.com/).

A final problem is that the desire for younger viewers may drive a desire for younger people to write and produce media content. Thus, not only are older adults excluded from media content, they may also be excluded from the process of media production: People who have worked hard to "make it" in Hollywood may suddenly find themselves kicked out once they pass a particular age hurdle (see Box 8.4).

Box 8.4   Age Discrimination and Media Writers

In October 2000, in the case *Wynn et al. v. NBC et al.*, a group of TV writers began a discrimination claim against the television industry. Over the subsequent years, this case has grown into one involving 23 separate class action lawsuits filed against numerous television production companies and involving hundreds of television writers. The claim is one of age discrimination: that television companies and talent agencies denied opportunities to writers and paid writers less for their work based purely on their age (see www.writerscase.com for current status information). The case is still in the legal system, but academic research on the topic suggests that the plaintiffs might have a case. Bielby and Bielby (2001) studied employment and monetary compensation for writers across different age groups. The graphs below show somewhat dramatically what was found in terms of compensation. There is a steady decline in the amount that writers are paid as they get older. Also, note that the declines are steepest for the most recent date (1997) implying that discrimination got worse between the mid 1980s and the early 1990s. Whether or not illegal discrimination has occurred is up to the courts. But it is clear that the people who determine the content of the media do not represent the diversity in their audience, and this may play a role in explaining the relative homogeneity in the messages we see. While organizations like the NAACP have been successful in increasing the presence of African Americans both in front of the camera and in the creative process, there is little in the way of such advocacy for older adults.

Net Age-Earnings Profiles of Film and Television Writers
for Selected Years, 1985–1997 Predicted Dollar Earnings by Age Category

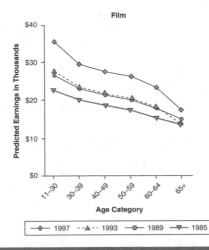

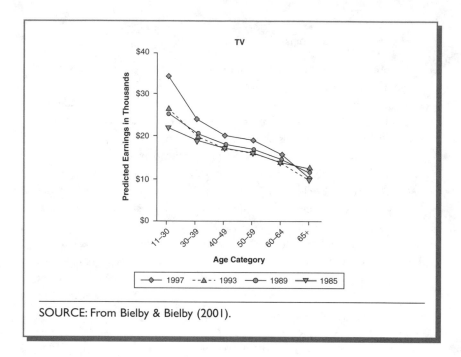

SOURCE: From Bielby & Bielby (2001).

Summary

The work described in this chapter demonstrates conclusively that media portrayals of older adults are neither fair nor realistic. Older adults are not portrayed in accord with their real presence in the population, and they are rarely shown in ways that represent the true experience of being old in all its depth and breadth. In large part, this unfortunate pattern of portrayals is reinforced by the commercial demands of the industry, as well as ingrained patterns of industry behavior, including perhaps age discrimination against writers. Future research on portrayals of older adults could usefully focus on three issues. First, it would be useful to develop ways of measuring variability in portrayals of older people. As was talked about in Chapter 7, our under-standings of social groups don't just consist of positive versus negative. We also have perceptions of how much variation there is within groups ("Oh, they're all the same"). Television portrayals may contribute to homogeneous perceptions of older people if the portrayals lack variation. Right now, we don't know much about how *varied* television portrayals of older people are, relative to variation among portrayals of younger people. My hypothesis is that older people are portrayed as being rather similar to one another.

Second, it would be useful to examine whether the older people who *do* exist on television are clustered in a limited number of shows. This is clearly the case with other groups; for example, although African Americans are now present on television in larger numbers than in the U.S. population, they are not evenly distributed. Certain shows on certain networks are "black" shows and feature almost entirely black casts, while the majority of shows are "white" shows. It's not clear whether this pattern also occurs with older characters.

Finally, we need more systematic research on messages about aging. When do words like "old" or "elderly" or "aging" get used on television and in other media, and in what context? The media clearly inform our understanding of lots of topics, and it's time to understand in more detail exactly what the media are telling us about getting older.

Keywords and Theories

Advertising

Counter-stereotypical

Evolutionary explanations (for sex differences in portrayals of age)

Green lighting

Humor

Key demographics (key demos)

Negative and positive portrayals

Peripheral imagery theory

Underrepresentation

Discussion Questions

- Which current shows feature older characters? Which of those characters would you regard as positive portrayals, and which as negative? Are the portrayals lead characters or peripheral characters?
- Do members of your family watch shows featuring different aged characters? Which shows? Why?
- Examine the advertisement in Exercise 8.2. What are the possible messages that they are sending about old age?
- Think about a recent portrayal of an older person that you saw in a television or magazine advertisement. What message(s) is it sending about aging?
- Do you agree that women should buy products to reduce the visible signs of aging?

Annotated Bibliography

Bielby, D. D., & Bielby, W. T. (2001). Audience segmentation and age stratification among television writers. *Journal of Broadcasting and Electronic Media, 45,* 391–412. A fascinating article on the age of television writers and their employment status and pay. While at times it gets a little technical, it is one of the few articles to address issues of age behind the camera, compared to a relatively large number of studies that examine portrayals of age.

Kessler, E.-M., Rekoczy, K., & Staudinger, U. M. (2004). The portrayal of older people in prime time television series: The match with gerontological evidence. *Ageing and Society, 24,* 531–552. An article presenting a very detailed analysis of older adult portrayals on German television. The approach of the authors is novel, in that they attempt to compare older people on television with the "real" status of older people in society. They conclude on this basis that certain portrayals are overly positive: that television in some cases may actually be too positive about aging issues. Such conclusions are unusual in a literature that is obsessed with how negative most portrayals are, so the article deserves reading.

Neussel, F. (1992). *The image of older adults in the media: An annotated bibliography.* Westport, CT: Greenwood Press. This book is now a little outdated, but still an amazing resource. It contains citations and brief descriptions of a massive range of studies of how older adults are portrayed across multiple media contexts. It provides particularly thorough coverage of the wide range of studies on portrayals in literature. The current chapter did not examine that work because much of it is in the form of a more "literary" perspective rather than a communication perspective. Nevertheless, such work is very interesting.

NINE

Uses and Effects of Media

This chapter covers the ways in which older people use the media, including how age-related uses of the media are associated with factors such as age identity. It also examines how the media might influence people's attitudes about aging. By the end of this chapter you should be able to:

SOURCE: © Gettyimages

- Understand some reasons why data show older people watching more television (on average) than younger people
- Describe the media that older people use more and less frequently than younger people
- Distinguish between informational and entertainment motivations for media use
- Explain what uses and gratifications theory and cultivation theory bring to discussions of aging and the media
- Be able to look at messages that feature older people and hypothesize some likely effects for different kinds of younger and older adults

I didn't know anything about anything before. The whole world has opened up to me.

—"Barbara," a self-described C-SPAN junkie in her mid-70s, describing the impact of watching more public affairs television programming in her later years (from Riggs, 1996)

T oday's older adults have seen the world change from one in which radio was the dominant medium, through the heyday of television, into our current world where media choices saturate almost all elements of our daily lives, and no one medium can really claim dominance. The World Wide Web has gained tremendous power over recent years, but it's clearly still developing, with almost daily changes in the availability of video and interactive media on the Web, and continuing debates over the extent to which the Web will supplant traditional media. Accompanying this have come questions about whether watching television shows on the Web is really any different from watching them on TV. In the context of such remarkable change, it is important to understand older adults' contemporary media use and the likely effects that media consumption may have on them and on the age-related attitudes of those around them.

In this chapter, I will explore older adults' media use, focusing particularly on television (because that's where the majority of research has been done). There are a lot of connections between this chapter and Chapter 12 (Technology); however, it is useful to keep them separate because the types of research being done are quite distinct. Nevertheless, when you get to Chapter 12, I will be reminding you of some key issues from the current chapter. First, we'll look at age differences in media use, and then the chapter will move to a discussion of the effects of the media. Remember— the comments above about changes in the media environment have implications for the data in this chapter. Most investigations that I will be reporting concern media use between 1970 and 2000. By the time you read this book, some of these patterns may have changed dramatically: At the time of writing, it's impossible to know what impact Internet radio, satellite radio, podcasts, TiVo, and video iPods might have on the data to be presented below.

Age Differences in Media Use

Different age groups show dramatically different patterns of media use. This is apparent even in young children, who move from extreme interest in television in early and mid-childhood, to a greater interest in music and video games in the teenage years. Likewise, when we compare older adults with other adults, we find interesting differences, some of which are revealing in terms of the nature of aging in today's society.

Quantity of Television Viewing: Older People as "Embracers" of Television

One of the most discussed issues with older people is the amount of television they view. Research has consistently found that older people watch more television (on average) than younger people. This has led to descriptions of older people as "embracers" of television. Figure 9.1 illustrates this pattern. You can see that adults in their 20s watch just over 3 hours of television per day, and that number goes down through the 30s and 40s. Once people reach their 50s, however, it starts to creep up again, and it jumps quite noticeably into the 60s and 70s, with a slight drop-off among people 80 and older. Notice, though, that the differences in absolute time are not huge—adults in their 40s (the lowest viewing age group) are watching about 2½ hours a day on average, while those in their 70s (the highest viewing group) are watching just over 3½ hours a day—the difference is about 1 hour a day.

Numerous explanations have been forwarded for the age differences in television consumption. Perhaps older adults are lonely and go to television for company; perhaps they are sick or disabled and so television is one of the few activities that they can do; perhaps they simply have more leisure time than younger people, and so have more hours in the day that they can devote to television. While all of these are plausible explanations, there is not a great deal of evidence to support any one of them, and some research actually negates some of these explanations. For instance, even when health is statistically controlled, older people's viewing is still higher than younger people's (Mares & Woodard, 2006). A typical 75-year-old with a particular level of health will watch more television than a 55-year-old with the same level of health. Health-related issues do influence television viewing for people of all ages—research by Alan Rubin (1986) showed that older *and* younger people who are unhealthy and have mobility problems watch more television and view television as more important in their lives as compared to those who are healthier and more mobile.

Figure 9.1   Television Use Among Different Age Groups

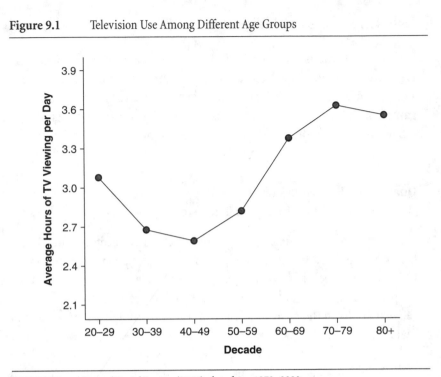

SOURCE: From General Social Survey (2006); data from 1972–2000.

So what is going on here? One explanation that has received some support derives from television's unique combination of sound and video. These
visual and auditory cues are somewhat **redundant**—when you see an explo-
sion, you also hear it, so even if you weren't looking at the screen, you know
what happened. As described in Chapter 2, many older people have some high
frequency hearing loss (presbycusis) that can impair their ability to understand speech. Some older adults (particularly in the older age ranges—80+)
also have significant visual impairments. For individuals in either group, and
particularly those who have vision *and* hearing impairments, television is a
particularly appealing medium because if you mis-hear something you can
probably follow from the visuals, and if you miss seeing something, you can
probably follow from the sound. This redundancy is absent in most other
media that are solely visual (e.g., books, magazines) or auditory (radio).

Other suggestions include the stereotype that older adults tend to be
lonelier than younger people, so television provides companionship. Recent
research does not support this explanation for age differences (Mares &
Woodard, 2006), but there is some evidence that *among* older people, those

who are experiencing more loneliness also tend to watch more television—particularly entertainment television (Perloff & Krevans, 1987).

There are also some statistical issues that need to be considered. Relying on **average** levels of television viewing can be deceptive—sometimes a difference in the "average" viewing for two groups doesn't tell us very much about most members of those groups. Consider Table 9.1. This table shows that more than 70% of all age groups watch 0–4 hours of television a day. The most dramatic differences between age groups come in the proportion that watch 5–8 hours of television a day—that's a lot of television, but perhaps not an extreme amount. Less than 10% of people in their 40s watch that much TV, but over 20% of people over 70 do so. Only very small numbers of any age group watch more than 8 hours a day, but you can see that more older people (particularly those in their 80s) are at this very heavy level of television viewing.

More detailed examination of these same data (beyond what's shown in Table 9.1) reveals that there is more **variability** in television viewing among older people than among younger people. The proportion of people 80 years and older watching NO television is higher than any other age group, *and* the proportion watching more than 9 hours a day is also higher than any other age group. At both extremes of television viewing, people 80 and older are the largest group. Again, we return to one of the themes from the first chapter of the book: Older people are incredibly diverse, and it is problematic to make any "average" statements about them. One cause of this may be the diverse living environments occupied by older people. Some older adults may live in

Table 9.1   Hours of Television Viewing per Day by Age Groups

		Hours of TV viewing per day			
		0–4	5–8	9–12	13+
Decade	20–29	81.2%	16.0%	2.3%	.5%
	30–39	87.4%	10.8%	1.4%	.4%
	40–49	88.7%	9.5%	1.4%	.4%
	50–59	86.4%	11.4%	1.6%	.7%
	60–69	78.6%	18.3%	2.2%	.8%
	70–79	73.8%	22.8%	2.5%	.9%
	80+	73.3%	22.4%	3.5%	.7%
Total		83.5%	14.1%	1.9%	.6%

SOURCE: From General Social Survey (2006); data from 1972–2000.

residential institutions. In some of these places, many common areas will have televisions that are on almost all of the time. So if you go to the lounge area, the television will almost certainly be on, whether you are really interested in it or not. Other older adults live independently and have much more *choice* about whether they turn the television on.

Nevertheless, there is still considerable interest and some controversy about what explains the differences in average television viewing across age groups. Two very recently published pieces provide good "state of the art" reviews of this issue (Mares & Woodard, 2006; Van der Goot, Beentjes, & van Selm, 2006).

What Older Adults Watch

Beyond questions of how *much* television older people watch, there is interest in *what* they watch. Older people tend to pay more attention to news shows, game shows, educational programs, and community access programming, whereas younger people watch more sitcoms and television dramas (J. D. Robinson et al., 2004). Overall, older people tend to prefer programs that provide **information**, whereas younger people prefer **entertainment** programming. Of course, there are substantial gender differences in viewing: Older men watch *Monday Night Football* substantially more than older women—just as with younger men and women (Burnett, 1991; J. D. Robinson et al., 2004)!

It is not always clear *why* these age differences in viewing exist. Some research indicates that the news/public affairs programming offers older people social opportunities. For instance, Riggs (1996) demonstrates that knowledge of current events is essential in order to participate in conversations in retirement communities. Individuals in these settings will watch the news and C-SPAN so that they don't feel left out of discussions over lunch. It is also important to remember that younger people may learn a lot of news and community information through their workplaces or contacts at school. For older people who are no longer working, such daily contacts may be missing; informative television programming (and particularly local news) may hence fill a specific gap in their social networks.

Again, though, it is worth reinforcing that these statements do not apply to all older people, many of whom have very active social networks. And as with everything else, remember that these are averages, and there is considerable variation among older people. For instance, upper and lower income older adults watch quite different types of programming—PBS for the wealthy, late night syndication for the less well-off (Burnett, 1991). Riggs (1996) discusses the ways in which watching public affairs programming provides "serious and purposeful" leisure activity for older adults: a way of relaxing while also being intellectually challenged and stimulated. For the upper-middle-class, educated older adults studied by Riggs, informational and "elite" programming probably also carries with it a cultural prestige/cachet: If it is no longer easy to physically attend the opera, you can still watch opera on PBS. Hanley and Webster (2000) make a similar point, although with a slightly different "spin": They say that older adults' viewing of quiz shows provides a defense against charges of watching television as wasting time: The informative content of the viewing means that it is defensible as an educational activity.

Research has also examined the characters in shows that are watched by older people, focusing particularly on those characters' ages. As might be expected, older people view shows with characters who are of similar ages to themselves (and indeed, younger people do the same). Table 9.2 shows the ages of lead characters in shows popular among viewers of different ages. The data are broken down by the age of the characters. So, for instance, among shows popular among child viewers, 20 of the lead characters were 0–20 years old. Younger adult viewers watch shows with mostly younger adult lead characters, and only older adults view *any* shows that feature older adult lead characters. Now take a look at Table 9.3, which reports the top ten shows for people of different age groups in 1994. While a number of these shows are now off the air, many of them are still probably familiar to you. Notice that shows with large numbers of children in the cast (*Full House, Home Improvement*) and shows set in schools (*Boy Meets World, Hangin' with Mr. Cooper*) are popular among children. Similarly, shows with lots of teens and young adults (*Melrose Place, Beverly Hills 90210, Friends*) are popular among those 18–29 years old. Most important for this discussion, notice that shows with older adults in the cast (*Murder, She Wrote, Matlock, Diagnosis Murder*) are *only* popular among people over the age of 65. J. D. Robinson et al. (2004) provide similar information about the 1997 television season, at which time older adults' favorite programs starred Bill Cosby (60 years old at the time), Chuck Norris (57 years old), and Dick Van Dyke (72). Meanwhile, younger adults were enjoying *Friends*, *Seinfeld*, *Home Improvement*, and *The Simpsons*, none of which feature older adults in any significant roles. We will get into *why* this might occur just a little later.

Other Media

Older adults listen to less radio than younger people, and when they do listen they prefer AM radio to FM radio, whereas younger people prefer the latter. Older and late middle-aged individuals (55+) tend to prefer talk radio and

Table 9.2   Age Distribution of Lead Characters in Shows Popular Among
Different Viewer Age Groups

	Age of characters		
	0–20 years old	*21–60 years old*	*60+ years old*
Child viewers	20	13	0
Younger adult viewers	4	21	0
Older adult viewers	2	11	3
U.S. Census Data	*28.63%*	*54.62%*	*16.75%*

SOURCE: From "Viewing Age: Lifespan Identity and Television Viewing Choices," by J. Harwood, 1997, *Journal of Broadcasting and Electronic Media, 41,* 203–213.

news programming relative to younger adults—a finding that is consistent with television content preferences (i.e., informative rather than entertainment programs). **Readership** of books and newspapers generally increases across the life span; however, it decreases in older adulthood if significant vision problems occur—older adults without vision problems read substantially more than those who experience such problems. Age differences in reading are particularly strong when it comes to newspapers: Newspaper reading is strongly related to age, with older adults reading newspapers substantially more than the young. There are also substantial age differences in magazine preferences—J. D. Robinson et al. (2004) report that older people read *Reader's Digest, National Geographic,* and *Good Housekeeping,* whereas younger people read more *Sports Illustrated* and *Cosmopolitan.*

Some of these differences can be explained by the change in proportion of women to men across the life span. Older men, for instance, read *Sports Illustrated* quite a bit, but there are relatively fewer of them in the older population, and so for older people as a whole it doesn't appear that they read that magazine as much as younger people. J. D. Robinson et al. (2004) report popular magazine readership among older people, broken down by sex. While both older men and older women enjoy *Reader's Digest* and *People,* there are a number of magazines that only older women read in large numbers (*Women's Day, McCalls, Family Circle*). Similarly, there are a unique set of magazines that older men read much more than older women—particularly news magazines (*Newsweek, Time, U.S. News and World Report*). Chapter 12 examines technology issues concerning older adults in detail, and so discussion of the Internet will be held until then.

Table 9.3   Top Ten Rated Shows Across Four Viewer Age Groups (September 19, 1994 – November 27, 1994)

Rank	2–11 year olds	18–29 year olds	35–54 year olds	65+ year olds
1	Boy Meets World	Seinfeld	Home Improvement	Murder, She Wrote
2	Home Improvement	Beverly Hills 90210	Grace Under Fire	60 Minutes
3	Step by Step	Grace Under Fire	NYPD Blue	CBS Sunday Movie
4	Full House	Melrose Place	Seinfeld	Diagnosis Murder
5	Hangin' with Mr. Cooper	Home Improvement	E.R.	Dr. Quinn, Medicine Woman
6	Family Matters	Roseanne	Roseanne	Matlock
7	Me and the Boys	E.R.	Monday Night Football	Under Suspicion
8	Simpsons Two	Simpsons	Frasier	Due South
9	ABC Saturday Movie	Ellen	Murphy Brown	CBS Tuesday Movie
10	Simpsons	Friends	Earth 2	Dave's World

SOURCE: From "Viewing Age: Lifespan Identity and Television Viewing Choices," by J. Harwood, 1997, *Journal of Broadcasting and Electronic Media, 11,* 203–213. Data originally provided by Nielsen Media Research.

The move to online newspapers and other online news sources may influence the relative readership of such information across the generations.

Uses and Gratifications Theory

Of course, one reason why we are interested in the media is because the media provide rewards to those who use them. **Uses and gratifications theory** was developed in the 1970s to help us understand the different rewards that come from using media (e.g., providing information, relaxing, excitement, etc.). This theory is based on the assumption that viewing of television is **selective**—people pick and choose shows and channels that provide them with particular rewards.

In some of my work, I have attempted to explain older adults' preference for same-age television characters by considering what they get out of viewing such characters. At least in part, the preference seems to be explained by a sense of identity with these characters—the more people like their age group and are proud of belonging to a particular age group, the more they like to watch television characters belonging to that age group. This applies to younger people too, who seek out shows featuring their own age characters and report receiving rewards from such viewing (e.g., many younger people strongly agree with statements like "I watch television because I enjoy watching people at my time of life"). For young people, those types of gratifications explain some unique aspects of their television viewing— particularly viewing of MTV and shows like *The O.C.* It seems likely (although we don't have the data) that **age identity** gratifications also explain some of older people's viewing of shows like *Murder, She Wrote* or *Matlock.* So, television viewing of same-age characters may reinforce and support age group identities.

There are also other reasons that explain the age differences in certain shows' popularity, of course. Shows are **marketed** to certain age groups—so CBS might put an ad for its Sunday night movie in a magazine targeted at seniors, whereas it's unlikely that NBC would do the same for *Friends.* Almost all of MTV's marketing is aimed at young people. People of different age groups are also interested in thematically different content—as noted earlier, older adults seek information content, and this probably explains their viewing of *60 Minutes* more than an identity explanation.

Our discussion of selective viewing (picking which shows to watch) has important consequences for the previous chapter's discussion of the **underrepresentation** of older people on television. Notice that while older people are underrepresented on TV *as a whole,* they are not as underrepresented in the television that older people actually watch. Hence, while we are concerned with the negative effects of underrepresentation, those effects might be moderated by the fact that older people are creative and strategic in their television viewing, and they manage to find the "ingroup" portrayals even if they are fairly rare. The flip side of this is that younger people choose not to watch shows that feature older adults (see Tables 9.2 and 9.3 again). So, even if older adults were present on television in larger numbers, young adults would probably avoid shows featuring older characters, and hence still not be exposed older people on television.

Exercise 9.1	Selective Television Viewing by Age of Character

For the next week, keep a diary of your television viewing. For each show that you watch, list the "star" character(s)—the people who appear in that show every week and are the primary focus of the show. At the end of the week, go back and guess the age of each of those star characters. Ask yourself the following questions:

- How many of them were under the age of 10?

- How many are over 40?

- Why is it that the population of television characters that you watch looks like this?

- If a similar show was on that featured older adult characters, would you watch it?

- Can you imagine "American Idol" with contestants in their 40s?

Media Effects

Implicit in the previous chapter and this chapter is the idea that media have consequences for consumers. If our consumption of television, newspapers, magazines, and the like never had any effects on us, then we probably wouldn't pay that much attention to it. However, there is quite a bit of research demonstrating that the media do have consequences for people, including in terms of their thinking about old age. We'll consider this separately for younger and older people.

Effects on Younger Viewers

Cultivation theory states that the media (and particularly television) shape our beliefs about the world, particularly in areas where we either have no outside experience, or we have experience that "fits" with television's version of reality. So, for instance, we might believe from the television (*America's Wildest Police Chases!*) that police officers spend a lot of time involved in car chases, and television's influence would be enhanced if we have little other contact with police officers, or if we have a police officer friend who also enjoys exaggerating the exciting nature of his or her work.

Older adults are not shown in large numbers on television (see Chapter 8), so cultivation theory predicts that people who view a lot of television will emerge with the impression that there are not many older adults in our society. In a 1980 study, George Gerbner and his colleagues demonstrated exactly that effect: Teens who watched lots of television estimated that older people were a smaller proportion of the population than teens who watched less television. Given that younger people generally have relatively little contact with older people in other contexts, we might expect television to be particularly powerful in shaping images of older adults. Also, a lot of what we hear about older people and aging even away from the media tends to reinforce the idea that they are not particularly important. So, the media send messages about getting old, and younger people absorb these messages. If you like debates, you might want to look at Passuth and Cook (1985) for discussion of the *size* of Gerbner's effect: While Gerbner found that television influenced younger viewers' perceptions, the **effect size** was pretty tiny—young people who watched a lot of television were *statistically* more negative about older adults, but only by a small amount. Passuth and Cook suggest that Gerbner's effects may be small because (a) older people aren't present on television very much (see Chapter 8), (b) portrayals of older people are often quite positive (see Chapter 8 for debate on this point), and (c) because interpersonal contact, particularly in the family, is more important (see Chapter 7).

Effects on Older Viewers

Relatively little work has examined the effects of the media on older people. In general, researchers work on the assumption that the negative portrayals and underrepresentation on television will have negative effects on older adults. Donlon, Ashman, and Levy (2005) provide some support for this claim. Controlling for age, depression, education, and health, they found that older people (aged 60–92) who watched more television also had significantly more negative attitudes about aging. Television also had *larger* effects on older people's attitudes than age, depression, education, or health.

However, these effects certainly depend a lot on what is viewed rather than merely total viewing time. As described above, older people are pretty good at finding portrayals of older characters that are not demeaning, and watching those shows in large numbers. Indeed, such selectivity may play a role in explaining older adults' preference for information (e.g., news) shows. One study shows that older people who watch television for information tend to perceive television portrayals of older people more positively and tend to have a more positive self-concept. In contrast, those who watch television for fantasy or entertainment tend to perceive portrayals of older people on television as more negative and tend to have more negative self-concepts (Korzenny & Neuendorf, 1980). In other words, information programming may be appealing in part because it tends to avoid the most negative and stereotypical portrayals that are common in fiction programs, and hence older people can avoid the negative effects of being exposed to such content. As was noted in the previous chapter, for older men at least, information programming can yield some high-status portrayals of older people: newsreaders, presidents, and the like.

However, older viewers' responses to older characters can be quite complex. One of the most revealing instances of this is some work by Mares and Cantor (1992). These scholars examined two groups of older viewers: those who were experiencing loneliness in their lives and those who were not. They then offered them the opportunity to choose between watching a positive (socially involved and happy) or a negative (lonely, not happy) portrayal of an older person. They then actually showed them a negative or a positive portrayal of an older person. The older viewers who were not lonely showed the expected pattern—they chose to watch the more positive portrayal and showed positive responses to that portrayal (e.g., they were in a better mood after seeing that than after seeing the negative portrayal). In contrast, the lonely older viewers selected the negative portrayal to view and felt better after seeing the negative portrayal. Any idea why?

The authors say that it's because the viewers compared themselves to what they saw in the television show, and they felt better about their own position in life relative to that of the television character. That didn't happen with the older viewers who were not lonely because they were relatively satisfied with their lives anyway. They didn't need to see someone in a worse position to improve their mood, and so the negative portrayal just depressed them. One message of this study, of course, is that we should not simply be concerned with whether portrayals of older people on television are positive or negative. We should also attend to **variability** in portrayals. Simply having all portrayals of older adults be wonderfully positive would not be accurate and would not provide viewers with the kind of viewing they sometimes desire. Some older people on television should be lonely, and some should be mean, and some should be unhealthy. And some should be healthy, active, funny, and strong. Providing diverse portrayals gives all viewers an opportunity to understand the complexity of aging, provides viewers with the types of portrayals that will meet their psychological needs, and gives television *programmers* the opportunity to capture a diverse audience of older people to their shows.

Older People as "Embracers" of Television?

Interestingly, older people are pretty aware of the potential negative effects of television. Most older people, when asked, reject TV's image of aging and are quick to comment that they think it affects older adults' attitude toward their own aging (Bleise, 1979), as well as affecting younger people's attitudes toward older people. T. Robinson, Popvich, Gustafson, and Fraser (2003) found that respondents were concerned that politicians' decision making concerning older adults might be influenced by negative media portrayals. A majority of these research subjects indicated that they would not buy products that were advertised in ways that were offensive to older people, including ads that ridiculed older adults, or negatively stereotyped them as grouchy or nosy. Healey and Ross (2002) found similar responses to television programming and advertising among older viewers in England. Returning to themes from the previous chapter, older people in these studies were well aware that two significant reasons for underrepresentation and negative representation of older people on television are (a) a lack of older people working in the media industry and (b) a lack of desire among advertisers to court older consumers.

Such criticism of portrayals is somewhat at odds with the data presented earlier indicating that older people watch *more* television than other age groups, and the related claims in the literature that older adults are **embracers of television**—meaning that they enjoy and approve of television content more than other groups. There are quite a lot of data to support the "embracer" conception, with most studies indicating that older people are quite satisfied with television content (e.g., R. H. Davis & Westbrook, 1985). In part, these differences are a function of how the question is asked. A general question about enjoyment of television results in positive responses. A more specific, pointed question about portrayals of older people encourages a more critical perspective in the audience, and results in more negative evaluation.

It is unclear the extent to which older adults criticize portrayals of older people "spontaneously" while viewing, rather than when asked explicitly about them by researchers. This ties into issues of **media literacy**—the extent to which we understand media at different levels, including how they were created, how they try to influence us, and the hidden implications in media messages. James Potter, in his 2004 theory of media literacy, distinguishes between **conscious** and **unconscious** modes of viewing: In the unconscious mode, viewing is partly "mindless," and content is not processed critically. Older adults, for instance, may be unlikely to consider the implications of a negative portrayal for their own self-concept or for the image of their group. In the conscious mode, viewers become more overtly aware of content, processing it at a deeper and more critical level. It is likely that researchers who ask older adults about media portrayals are shifting their research respondents from the unconscious to the conscious mode, causing them (at least retrospectively) to delve deeper into the nature of portrayals and consider television's older characters in the context of their implications for aging. Long term, it would be interesting to see whether more extensive application of more "conscious" media processing would lead older adults to "embrace" television just a little less!

Summary

This chapter has covered the uses and effects of mass media, with particular emphasis on older adults. It has shown that older adults show some predictable patterns of media use, including "embracing" television and avoiding radio. Research demonstrates that older people use media for information reasons and enjoy informational programming more than entertainment. Older adult portrayals on television influence younger people to have more negative attitudes toward older people and to believe that older adults are a smaller part of the population than they really are. Effects on older people are more complex, but television clearly has the potential to harm older people's self-concept if they are exposed to too many of the negative images. Fortunately, older people are selective in their viewing and tend to orient to shows featuring positive portrayals of older people. Research shows that older adults are aware of negative portrayals of their group on television and are particularly critical of advertising images.

Keywords and Theories

Age identity
Age-related marketing
Conscious and unconscious modes
   of viewing
Cultivation theory
Embracers of television
Entertainment
Information

Media literacy
Readership
Redundant cues
Selective viewing
Underrepresentation
Uses and gratifications theory
Variability in viewing

Discussion Questions

- What are some reasons for older people watching more television than younger people?
- Why do older people prefer shows that provide information?
- Consider one of the movies listed at the end of the previous chapter. What effects might viewing the movie have on younger viewers? Older viewers? How might the effects differ based on the type of person watching (e.g., lonely versus socially engaged)?
- Which current television shows might be most harmful to an older audience?
- What does cultivation theory say about the size of the effects that television has on its viewers? Discuss why the effects are not bigger.

Annotated Bibliography

Mares, M. L., & Cantor, J. (1992). Elderly viewers' responses to televised portrayals of old age. *Communication Research, 19,* 459–479. A classic research study (described in the chapter) that looks at how lonely and non-lonely older adults respond to positive and negative portrayals of old age on television. Very interesting methodology, and some profound conclusions for television programmers.

Riggs, K. (1998). *Mature audiences.* Piscataway, NJ: Rutgers University Press. A fascinating description of different ways in which older adults use television creatively, both in terms of viewing (e.g., fans of *Murder, She Wrote*) and creating (e.g., producing a public access television show). The book is more empowering for older people than most research on older adults and the media.

Robinson, J. D., Skill, T., & Turner, J. W. (2004). Media usage patterns and portrayals of seniors. In J. F. Nussbaum & J. Coupland (Eds.), *Handbook of communication and aging research* (2nd ed., pp. 423–450). Mahwah, NJ: Lawrence Erlbaum. Relevant to this chapter and the previous one, this is an excellent and relatively up-to-date summary chapter. The authors include particularly detailed and relevant information on older adults' media usage, including numerous tables on things like magazine preferences and radio station listening.

TEN

Culture, Communication, and Aging

This chapter addresses in detail the ways in which different cultures orient differently to age and aging processes, and the influence of that on intergenerational communication. It also considers the role of cultural change in affecting the place of older people in society over time. By the end of this chapter you should be able to:

SOURCE: © Istockphoto.com

- Describe important dimensions that differentiate cultures in terms of attitudes about aging
- Talk about some culture-specific patterns of family life that influence intergenerational communication in the family
- Provide examples of differences and similarities in ways of *thinking* about aging across cultures
- Describe at least one pattern of intergenerational *communication* that is unique to a particular cultural context
- Describe how cultural change (e.g., urbanization) might influence intergenerational relations

I have had more salt in my life than you have eaten grains of rice.

—Chinese Saying

C ulture is one of those words that can mean a lot of different things to a lot of different people. It might mean the opera or art galleries to some people ("High Culture"), while to others it might mean buying a candlestick from Bangladesh at *Pier 1 Imports*. For this chapter, I'm using **culture** to mean a shared set of ideas, values, or behaviors that originate in the shared geographic associations of a group of people. So, when a group of people live and associate in the same geographic region, they will come to adopt similar values and behaviors. Those values and behaviors will be taken with them and maintained, while also no doubt changing in certain ways, even when they leave the shared origin. The word "associate" is important here. It's certainly possible for two groups of people to originate from the same geographic region, but to have very different sets of cultural values: People from groups that do not freely associate or are in conflict might have quite divergent value systems even if they live in very close proximity (e.g., Jews and Palestinians in Israel). Finally, this definition means that "culture" can be used to describe general patterns in a very broad area (e.g., East Asian culture), or fairly local patterns that are embedded within a broader culture (e.g., Navajo culture, which is distinct, but which also shares elements with other Native American cultures and with the broader U.S. culture). The latter type of cultural group is sometimes called a "co-culture."

Why does a book on aging need a chapter about culture? It should be clear from what you have read in previous chapters that North American beliefs and values concerning aging (a) are shared and (b) influence the experience of aging. On the whole, the belief that old age is associated with ill health, for instance, is widely held and shapes many people's expectations for aging. It also influences intergenerational communication in some of the ways described in Chapter 5, as well as being associated with mass media messages about aging as described in Chapter 8. Hence, attitudes about aging and intergenerational communication norms are elements of culture. Given this, examining cultural differences tells us various ways in which people get old, and shows how cultural values placed on aging result in different outcomes for old people as well as different patterns of intergenerational communication.

Three dimensions of culture will be particularly important in this journey. First, cultures differ along a dimension called **power-distance** (Hofstede, 1980). This refers to the degree of "hierarchy" in a culture—the extent to which some people have a lot of power and control, while others have very little. In very egalitarian cultures (low on power-distance), nobody is seen as having inherently much greater status than anyone else, and people value ideals of equality. In contrast, in very hierarchical cultures some people are seen as inherently more important and valued than others, and everyone agrees to defer to those people (high power-distance). Because age is often used to indicate status, the role of age in these cultures will be different. If age indicates power, and everyone agrees to respect power, then old people will have inherent status simply due to their age. Japan is an example of such a culture—age *is* power in many Japanese contexts.

Second, cultures differ in their levels of individualism versus **collectivism**. Collectivist cultures (East Asian and Central American cultures in particular) believe in maintaining harmony between individuals, supporting and nurturing social relationships, and valuing success of the group over the individual. In contrast, individualist cultures (which would characterize North Americans of European origin) believe in striving for individual success, valuing individuals' unique characteristics, expressing oneself, and placing one's own needs above those of surrounding groups. So, for instance, individualist parents tend to urge their children toward independence, celebrating and encouraging attempts to operate without the parents' help and become a successful *individual*. In contrast, parents in collectivist cultures are more focused on establishing the child as a well-integrated and contributing member of the family—someone who will bring respect and even resources to the family unit. Collectivist cultures tend to endorse **filial piety** norms. Filial piety (*xiao* in Chinese) is a culturally defined set of respect norms with regard to age. According to filial piety, it is the responsibility and obligation of younger people to take care of their elders, particularly within the family context. Hence, cultures with high levels of filial piety will often strongly endorse family caregiving for older people. Moreover, these cultures prescribe respect of older adults. This can change the dynamics of intergenerational communication within the family, as well as changing socio-structural arrangements concerning older people. For instance, when cultures are high in filial piety, nursing homes tend to be relatively rare and are associated with stigma. You only end up in a nursing home if your family didn't care enough to look after you personally. Indeed, in some East Asian

Figure 10.1   Xiao Shuen. The Chinese symbols for Xiao Shuen, literally "filial piety." These symbols represent the honor and respect due elders from younger people in traditional Chinese society.

cultures, responsibility to care for one's parents is legally required (Liu & Tinker, 2001).

Third (and related to filial piety), cultures differ in **co-residence norms**. In some cultures, it is typical for multiple generations of families (the "extended family") to live together in a single residence. In others it is typically just the nuclear family (parents and children) that share a residence. Patterns of intergenerational communication within the family obviously change quite dramatically based on these norms. For instance, grandparents and grandchildren in a typical North American family might see each other once a week or once a year, but seeing each other all the time at home is unusual. Co-residence is associated with more daily contact and hence a more established relationship, but also may be associated with more everyday conflict. Co-residence patterns can change based on other cultural changes. For instance, societies that move from rural to urban patterns of life may undergo shifts in co-residence as a result of younger generations moving to the city while the older generations remain in the rural areas.

The rest of this chapter examines attitudes about aging and intergenerational communication patterns in four regions, or broad cultural groups. I have selected cultures that display some contrasts and some similarities with the patterns described in previous chapters—the earlier chapters focused largely on research from North America and Europe, generally research that was done on people of European origin. In each section it is important to bear in mind the substantial **variation *within*** each of the cultures being examined. While I am describing some commonalities among East Asian or Native American cultures, for instance, it is crucial to remember that Japan is not the same as Taiwan and Navajo culture is not the same as Lakota culture. Finally, it is important to remember that other cultural groups may provide other insights on aging and intergenerational relations. You may wish to explore the nature of aging in African American (Slevin, 2005), Moslem (Salari, 2002), Scandinavian (Lund, Avlund, Modvig, Due, & Holstein, 2004), African (Cliggett, 2001), or Pacific Islander (Gattuso & Shadbolt, 2002) groups. In this chapter I can just give you a flavor of some groups that have been studied, but there are plenty of ways to extend what you learn here into other cultural contexts.

Why I Study Communication and Aging
Hiroshi Ota (Associate Professor, Aichi Shukutoku University, Japan)

I guess I had always been interested in the effects of age as well as culture on how people talk to each other, even before I started doing research on communication and aging. This is perhaps where I came from culturally, i.e., Japan. In Japan, people beautifully change the way they talk depending on who they talk to. When you find your interlocutor is older than you, even by one year, you are expected to increase the level of linguistic politeness in communication. On the other hand, you may use less polite language to somebody who is younger than you, without offending the person. Age conscious speech is seen in every aspect of our communicative life in Japan. I was following the norm when I met Howie Giles. He asked me if I was interested in aging research in communication. At that time, I had no option other than say "yes" so to be polite to "Dr. Giles" (not Howie) who was older than I. Things worked out all well and beautiful in the end. I am still doing research on communication and aging, and also have learned a lot about my aging process from what I found in my research with a number of my colleagues in different parts of the world. This is the story.

Reprinted with permission of Hiroshi Ota.

East Asia

In this section, I focus on areas such as China, Japan, and the Korean peninsula. Cultures in these regions share some norms derived from the religious/philosophical basis of **Confucianism**, as well as other traditions such as Buddhism. Of course, some dramatic differences exist both between and within Japanese, Chinese, and North and South Korean cultures, and you should not interpret this section as suggesting that people from this region are all alike.

Confucian teaching specifies obeying superiors, particularly those who are older. The idea of filial piety is central to Confucian teachings. For instance, in the *Analects,* a central book in the Confucian tradition, the "master" says, "A youth, when at home, should be filial, and, abroad, respectful to his elders" (*Analects,* 1893, Text 9). It is interesting that respect for all elders is noted, but in addition there is special provision for family elders ("at home")—family elders require filial behavior, not merely respect. Indeed, the book is careful to note that just *supporting* one's parents is not sufficient, that there should also be veneration (worship or adoration): "The filial piety nowadays means the support of one's parents. But dogs and horses likewise are able to do something in the way of support; without reverence, what is there to distinguish the one support given from the other?" (*Analects,* 1893, Text 41). Hence, a high level of respect for all elders and a responsibility for caring and veneration within the family are established in these cultures through historical tradition. Combined with this, East Asian cultures tend to be relatively high on power-distance. They value hierarchy and explicit respect for those who are above you in the hierarchy. Thus, younger people will honor their elders by using specific forms of language and addressing them with honorific terms (the equivalent of "sir" or "madam" in English). In South Korea, the government and big corporations sponsor filial piety awards for individuals who have displayed an exceptional degree of devotion in support of older family members. These prizes receive major national news attention, and the winners become the subject of educational materials designed to encourage similar behaviors in the young.

Notably, even very small age differences will suffice to justify expression of filial piety—in Japan, an age difference of just one year is sufficient for one adult to use an honorific term and defer to another (although it is important to note that other issues such as organizational seniority also influence the appropriate use of honorifics). In Chinese, using the correct *chenghu* ("form of address") is extremely important, and failing to do so results in extreme dissatisfaction for older people (Zhang & Hummert, 2001). Age may also be taken into account explicitly in considering who should receive a promotion within an organization, for instance.

As might be expected from some of these norms, Chinese families have typically lived together in extended family units, with the older parents preferably living with the son and daughter-in-law. Similar patterns exist in Japan, and the patrilineal nature of this society means that the eldest son is very likely to host the parent—the husband's mother is about 13 times more likely to live with the family than the wife's mother (Kojima, 2000).

The power of filial piety in determining attitudes toward aging has been revealed by research. For instance, Levy and Langer (1994) show that Chinese older and younger people hold more positive attitudes toward aging than old and young Americans. Moreover, these differences in attitudes appear to influence aspects of older adults' functioning. For instance, age differences in memory performance that are seen in the United States do not appear in Chinese people (i.e., on the memory tests in the Levy and Langer study, Chinese older adults did as well as Chinese young people).

However, the situation becomes a little more complex when examined more closely. Even within the Confucian tradition, there are exceptions to the filial piety rule. For instance, Confucian teachings state that the greatest priority is placed on "greater truths" (*Tian Ming*—the mandate of heaven). So if an older person asks a younger person to do something that goes against higher principles of good and evil, the younger person may refuse. Hence, Tian Ming provides a way out of unquestioning filial piety.

In addition, recent developments in East Asia have fueled changes in the traditional structure. This region of the world is now home to some of the largest and fastest growing cities in the world (Beijing, Hong Kong, Taipei, Seoul, Tokyo, etc.), and in many cases these are places with very high housing costs. As younger people move to the cities seeking work, they are often not able to support their older relatives in terms of providing housing. Hence, the older people may remain in rural areas. Thus, traditional patterns of extended family living are declining somewhat as a function of **urbanization**. Such trends are contributing to growth in care institutions such as nursing homes in East Asia (Ikels, 2004). Combined with this urbanization, there are trends of **Westernization**. The influence of Western media, through satellite television, advertising, and the exports of television and movies, has led to increased awareness of non-traditional cultural patterns, and hence to cultural and value change in some of these cultures (see Box 10.1).

Box 10.1   Age-Related Cultural Values in Television Advertising

Carolyn Lin (2001) examined television advertisements in the United States and China to see whether values differences in the two cultures were apparent in advertising. Among her hypotheses, two relate fairly directly to the themes discussed in this chapter. Specifically, Lin hypothesized that commercials in the United States would include more appeals to "modernity/youth." Given Chinese culture's traditional emphasis on filial piety, it could be expected that a youth appeal would be more likely in the United States. In a complementary fashion, Lin also hypothesized that more "veneration of elderly models" (filial piety) would be displayed in Chinese advertisements. She examined a random sample of prime-time (8–11 p.m.) television from both countries. In the United States, she examined network programming (e.g., NBC) and cable (e.g., ESPN). In China, she examined the two main government channels (CCTV1 and CCTV2) as well as a local station (Beijing TV). In all, she examined 206 commercials from the United States and 195 Chinese commercials. The cultural values were coded from 0 (none) to 3 (strong) by independent coders (one native Chinese speaker and one native English speaker). The coding was done based on carefully developed conceptual definitions of these values. For instance, veneration of elderly is defined as occurring when "wisdom and the elderly, as well as the veneration of that which is traditional, is stressed. Older group members are depicted being asked for advice, opinions, and recommendations. Models in such advertisements tend to be older" (p. 94). An advertisement in which a younger person used a product to care for an elder, or gave the product to an older person as a gift, would therefore reveal high levels of this value. As predicted, the veneration of the elderly value was significantly stronger in Chinese commercials than commercials from the United States (means on the 0–3 scale were .50 in the United States and 1.5 in China). In contrast, however, there was no difference in the two cultures in terms of the youth theme (means of about 1.1 in both cultures). So, this study provides evidence that some traditional values are reflected in Chinese advertising, but also suggests that some Western values may be infiltrating Chinese advertising. Lin says that the "youth" trend may be in part due to the one-child policy—when families only have one child, that child becomes much more important, and perhaps even a "little emperor/empress." Such a family role makes these children important determinants of consumption, and hence targets for advertisers. Lin is careful to note that the Western "youth" values appeals are often "localized" in China; so, while the youth value is prominent, it has a uniquely Chinese flavor to it.

Finally, there are more specific societal influences on patterns of inter-generational relations and age-related values. In China in the mid 1970s, for instance, the government actively promoted socialist ideologies and engaged in ideological attacks on traditional Confucian values. The attacks on Confucianism have almost certainly had some consequences for endorsement of these values among the population, although the populace largely resisted the government attacks and most aspects of Confucianism remained strongly endorsed. More recently, the government has been actively promoting Confucian values. As noted earlier, the South Korean government also engages in very active promotion of filial piety practices. In addition, the Chinese **one-child policy** has been in place since 1979—families are required (or at least encouraged) to have only one child so as to limit explosive population growth. This policy means that in coming years the network of children to whom older people can look for support will be shrinking. In turn, this will increase the financial and emotional strain on younger family members attempting to pro-vide support for elders. The one-child policy has also meant that many families do not have sons—thus the default place of residence for aging parents will not be available to some families in the future. These factors illustrate how the political environment can change family relations and norms for intergenera-tional relationships. Current debates about Social Security in the United States might have similar implications. Government policies that result in reduced financial support for older adults will have unknown consequences for the population. The policies might cause older people to remain in the workforce longer, or policy change could place more of an onus on younger people to sup-port their parents financially in old age. Hence, you can see that there are inter-personal and relational consequences of broader public policy changes.

When we gathered data on attitudes toward older people at a wide vari-ety of cultural sites, we found that Hong Kong had some of the most negative attitudes—more so than North America, Australia, and other East Asian sites such as South Korea (Harwood et al., 1996, 2001). Hong Kong is one of the most urbanized and Westernized regions in East Asia. It is also a place that reveals the ways in which cultural change can yield a generation "gap" of dra-matic proportions. Visitors to Hong Kong will see young people talking on cell phones, wearing Western clothes, shopping at The Gap, and eating McDonald's. In contrast, the older people in Hong Kong appear (at least on the surface) to be living lifestyles more reminiscent of quite traditional Chinese life: buying food from open markets, wearing traditional clothing, and the like. It is likely that this pattern has played out in similar (if perhaps milder) forms across many areas of East Asia. More generally, our examination of cultural differences revealed that many cultures share fairly similar patterns of attitudes, albeit with subtle differences. Most cultures view aging as associated with a general decline in physical strength and fitness, and an increase in certain social characteristics such as wisdom and generosity.

Mei-Chen Lin has examined **schemas** of intergenerational communication in Taiwan in a way that parallels my earlier study in the United States (see Chapter 3, especially Table 3.4). Her research uncovered the schemas shown here in Table 10.1 (Lin, Zhang, & Harwood, 2004). One of the most notable differences between this work and the work in the United States is that

Table 10.1   Intergenerational Communication Schemas in Taiwan

1. ***Mutually satisfying conversation.*** Young person is interested in conversing with the older person and respects the older person's life experience. Young person doesn't need to adapt conversation manners to show proper respect—there is not a large "generation gap." Young person learns from older person.

2. ***Helping conversation.*** Young person feels sympathetic toward the older person and feels that talking will make the older person happy. Young person picks topics carefully and is careful with his/her manners; believes that older person lives in the past. The generation gap is very large. Older person is mildly *laodao*.

3. ***Mixed feelings conversation.*** Older person loves young person's company. Young person doesn't enjoy conversation very much, is intimidated, and feels a need to be very polite. This older person has a tendency to complain or disclose unpleasant life experiences in the conversation.

4. ***Small talk/disinterested conversation.*** Young person is indifferent toward the conversation, is clearly not satisfied. The conversation is just small talk. The older person seems to enjoy the conversation and is not bitter. Young person is not very satisfied and has little to say about the experience.

5. ***Mutually unpleasant conversation.*** The older person is stubborn, meddling, and *laodao*. She or he tends to correct younger person's behavior and extends negative comments to young people in general. The conversation is unpleasant and dissatisfying for both people. Young person tends to avoid such conversations; she or he feels restrained and intimidated in the conversation, and feels the need to be polite.

SOURCE: Adapted from *Young Adults' Intergenerational Communication Schemas in the Taiwan and the US*, by M.-C. Lin, J. Harwood, and M. L. Hummert, 2006, unpublished manuscript, Kent State University, and from "Taiwanese Younger Adults' Intergenerational Communication Schemas," by M.-C. Lin, Y. B. Zhang, & J. Harwood, 2004, *Journal of Cross-Cultural Gerontology, 19,* 321–342.

the *range* of intergenerational schemas appeared to be somewhat narrower in Taiwan. In particular, the extremes of positive and negative were less apparent in Taiwan. Lin suggests that this is because Chinese culture has more explicit prescriptions for what is appropriate (and what isn't) in intergenerational settings. These prescriptions "structure" the contact to some extent, hence making it more difficult to have the "overwhelmingly positive" conversations found in some North American responses, while also preventing the most negative of interactions from occurring. When culture defines particular patterns for communication and dictates who is in charge, conflict is kept under control. If you contrast the most positive and most negative schemas from Table 3.4 with those in Table 10.1, you'll notice considerably more "extremes" in the U.S. data.

Nevertheless, it's important not to become focused solely on the cultural differences. There are also remarkable similarities in the schemas across these cultures. Similarly, it's possible to identify communication behaviors that are quite similar across cultures. For instance, recent work by Matsumoto (in press) has examined painful self-disclosure among older women in Japan. You'll remember from Chapter 4 that older adults in some Western cultures will sometimes talk about rather personal and apparently painful aspects of their lives. Matsumoto demonstrates that very similar patterns occur in the conversations of Japanese older women, including some specific features that are common to the Western observations of this phenomenon. For instance, the Japanese data reveal many instances where the older speakers would present very painful information (e.g., about a husband's dying moments) in a very humorous fashion, along with considerable laughter. At times, the humor is used to enhance sharing and coping with these difficult events. However, Matsumoto also suggests that the laughter is simply a device to make such speech more "vivid and interesting" to the listener. So, far from the notion that this talk reveals a self-centeredness in the speaker, it is actually produced in ways that are entertaining and engaging for the listener.

Zhang and Hummert (2001) describe one pattern of intergenerational communication in China that is not immediately apparent in Western intergenerational interaction. They note that young Chinese people are very bored and frustrated when older people engage in **laodao**. *Laodao* is a distinct style used by Chinese older adults that involves repetitive complaining, often concerning the younger person's behavior—literally the word means "endless repeating." Sometimes, Chinese older adults' criticisms can appear surprisingly blunt from a Western perspective. For instance, Zhang (2004) writes about an older person describing a younger person's hair as "like hair from a cow," while a grandmother describes her granddaughter as less respectful than the family dog. If you can't imagine your grandma comparing you to the family dog, you're probably not Chinese! It is likely that this very explicit criticism is another result of the way that age status is "built in" to the culture. The explicit age hierarchy gives older people a lot of license in expressing their feelings. The *laodao* style is distinct from similar patterns in the United States in that it is often perceived by younger people to originate in the older person's caring for or loving them. Thus, despite their frustration, younger people attribute some positive motivations to the communication. In addition, given the norms for avoiding intergenerational conflict and respecting elders, younger people will tend to respond in a nonconfrontational way to this behavior, often trying to change the topic, or just "tuning out" by watching television.

Even some of these norms may be changing, in parallel with the attitudinal changes described above. Some recent research suggests that younger people in China may be becoming more willing to engage in **conflict** with their elders, perhaps as a result of Westernization of value systems in China (Zhang, Harwood, & Hummert, 2005). Older Asians also report a decline in filial piety (Ingersoll-Dayton & Saengtienchai, 1999). Zhang and Hummert's (2001) study revealed Chinese younger people complaining about older adults' acting "superior" to them (e.g., "Older adults are not democratic. They do not treat young people as their friends, they act like superiors"). From a traditional standpoint, of course, the idea that older adults *should* be democratic is ridiculous! Hence, these comments perhaps indicate a decline in these young people's belief in those traditional values. Whether the young people express this directly to older people is, of course, another matter.

A final note here: There are crucial differences between feelings about older adults *within* versus *outside* the family that need further investigation. As noted earlier in the chapter, differences exist in prescriptions for treatment of older adults outside (respect) versus inside (filial piety) the family. East Asian cultures are collectivist. The family is a very important group to many people in these cultures, and hence older family members are likely to be treated as members of the "ingroup" by their young relatives—"we are both members of the same family." This relates to the issue of decategorization discussed in Chapter 7. The young person in this situation is not thinking of the grandparent in terms of the age categorization. In contrast, older *non-family members* are members of the outgroup on *two* dimensions (family and age), which can result in substantial problems in intergenerational communication (Giles et al., 2003)—the situation lacks the immediately accessible dimension for a shared identification that is provided by the family in a grandparent–grandchild dyad.

South Asia (India)

While East Asia draws extensively on Confucian traditions, India is influenced most heavily by **Hinduism** (although, of course, there is a large Muslim population in India, as well as other groups). Hinduism shares with Confucianism the idea that the son should care for the parents (Sharma, 1980). However, Hinduism presents a more explicit life-span approach to human development, outlining four stages (Bhat & Dhruvarajan, 2001). From birth until leaving school, people are students (*brahmacârin*) who are supposed to live with teachers (*Guru*). Following this, people are supposed to marry, have children, and be householders (the *Gârhastya* stage). Then comes the *Vânaprastya* during which a couple retires to the forest and engages in religious practice—this stage coincides with the arrival of grandchildren. Finally, during the *Sannyâsa* stage people are required to renounce material things—men are supposed to become monks at this point, while women are cared for by their sons' families. In modern Hindu society, the latter two phases have merged into a "retirement" period that would seem fairly familiar to North Americans, but still one that is infused with the idea that old age is a time for spiritual seeking and growth. For men this transition comes at the point of retirement from work, whereas for women it comes when their eldest son gets married. Old age in Indian culture is associated with wisdom, and older people (particularly parents) are supposed to be respected by younger people. Traditionally parents in Indian Hindu society are revered—filial piety is a strong value here too (Giles, Dailey, Makoni, & Sarkar, 2006).

As with China, however, trends of modernization and urban living have led to changes in Indian culture. Elders' spiritual roles have been marginalized in the new retirement, and so it is more difficult to identify unique contributions that older people make to the family. They are more dependent on younger family members, who increasingly view them as a burden rather than with the traditional values of filial piety. In modern Indian society, older people have fewer meaningful roles. They are marginalized in everyday family decisions and are dependent upon their children, emotionally and financially. From some perspectives, the traditional notion of filial piety is steadily eroding in modern Indian society (Bhat & Dhruvarajan, 2001).

Some of the origins of this erosion might come from media exposure (Parameswaran, 2004). Indian media have been substantially more open to foreign content than, for instance, Chinese. Hence, satellite television is more widespread than in other Asian cultures and is largely unregulated. In addition, significant portions of the Indian population (particularly the middle and upper classes) speak English, and hence media content from the United States and England is directly comprehensible. The Indian education system has also grown massively in recent years, and an increasingly educated society is always one that will import ideas from other cultures and become aware of different perspectives. Thus, philosophies like individualism and questioning authority have become more widespread.

A number of examinations of Indian media have shed some light on how aging is represented in South Asia. Interestingly, similar patterns as in the West emerge in terms of quantity of portrayals. Older adults are underrepresented in Indian media relative to their presence in the population at large (Raman et al., 2006). In addition, older women are more heavily underrepresented than older men, while young women (in their 20s) are hugely overrepresented. This pattern is substantially stronger in the Indian media than in the West, perhaps reflecting the greater paternalism in India (i e , men have substantially more status and power than women). Similarities between the United States and India also emerged in various connections between aging and health (for instance older characters being shown as unhealthy in both cultures). However, preliminary results from India don't indicate that older characters are shown disproportionately in ads for health products, which is certainly the case in the United States (Raman et al.). Finally, some interesting patterns have been shown in portrayals of relationships. Most interestingly, products in both cultures are sold to grandparents on the premise that if they use the product, they will be able to spend more time (or enjoy their time more) with their grandchildren. For instance, the Raman et al. paper describes the advertisement shown in Figure 10.2. The thematic portrayal of grandparenting here appears quite similar to such portrayals in the United States (e.g., see Figure 8.2, in Chapter 8).

Traditional Indian culture, therefore, values aging in a manner that contrasts with East Asia—while East Asian cultures emphasize veneration

Figure 10.2   Advertisement From Indian Magazine

Why should joint pain
stop you from playing
with your grandchild ?
Try the
*pure concentrate
of Shallaki.*

Introducing Himalaya Pure Herbs *Shallaki, for joint pain relief.* Shallaki is proven over the ages, for its anti-inflammatory and analgesic properties. Now Shallaki's natural goodness has been fortified by Himalaya using advanced scientific processes to give you

Pure and concentrated. Scientifically tested.
Your guarantee for the highest quality and potency.

its concentrated strength and assured purity in the right measure. This includes maintaining absolute freshness, extracting the optimum strength from the herb using a proprietary technique and continuously testing to maintain consistency in every batch.

This is what makes Himalaya Shallaki special. What you get is the pure and measured concentrate of Shallaki, in its most effective form. In a convenient capsule. Himalaya Pure Herbs Shallaki. It's nature's

gift to your body. Make it a habit. In two weeks, you'll feel the difference in every step.

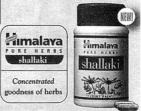

Himalaya PURE HERBS
shallaki

Concentrated
goodness of herbs

11 other products from the Himalaya Pure Herbs range. | Available at all leading chemists. Ask for your free leaflet.

Dosage: One capsule twice a day. Price: Rs.50 per pack of 60 capsules.

| AMALAKI | ARJUNA | ASHVAGANDHA | BRAHMI | KARELA | LASUNA | NEEM | SHUDDHA GUGGULU | TAGARA | TRIPHALA | TULASI |
| Anti-Oxidant | Blood Circulation | Anti-Stress | Alertness | Regulates Metabolism | Cholesterol Protection | Skin Care | Lipid Regulator | Relaxant | Bowel Cleanser | Cough & Cold |

For more info: The Communication Cell, The Himalaya Drug Company, Makali, Bangalore-562 123. Tel: 080-371 4444 E-mail: write.to.us@himalaya.ac Visit us at: www.himalayahealthcare.com

CONTRACT-1417-2002

and caregiving, Indian culture emphasizes spirituality and wisdom in old age. However, modern India presents stark patterns of change in older adults' place in the family and society. In contemporary urban, upper class, Indian families, the position of the grandparent might look quite familiar to an average North American. Indian media portrayals, such as the one in Figure 10.2, might also seem quite familiar if you have read Chapter 8 of this book!

United States Latino Cultures

Prior work has made mixed claims about the values placed on aging in Latino cultures (Markides, Martin, & Gomez, 1983), but there is at least anecdotal evidence that filial piety is more strongly emphasized as an important value in these cultures (Bastida & Gonzalez, 1995). Burr and Mutchler (1999) indicate that Hispanics are more likely than some other groups to advocate co-residence between older and younger generations, although they also note a lack of differences on other dimensions of filial piety (e.g., financial assistance). N. Williams and Torrez (1998) note that Hispanic grandparents and grandchildren are more likely to live together than non-Hispanic Whites, but less likely than Asian or African Americans. They also suggest that some of the differences in filial piety that have been observed may be a result of other variables. For instance, when statistically controlling for variables like a person's income, some cultural differences in people's filial piety disappear. These authors suggest that high levels of filial piety may in part be a response to financial and social inequities—when you don't have much money, reliance upon family members for support is likely, as is an acceptance that everybody has to help take care of each other.

Grandparents do appear to play different (and perhaps more significant) roles in Latino grandchildren's lives than in non-Hispanic grandchildren's lives (e.g., providing day care, living with the family: Raphael, 1989). However, there may also be additional barriers to the development of grandparent–grandchild closeness (e.g., language barriers from monolingual Spanish grandparents to monolingual English grandchildren: Schecter & Bayley, 1997). Families are better able to communicate and establish cultural continuity (pass along traditions, feel connected to one another) when the grandparents and grandchildren share a language. Having bilingual children or grandchildren is also useful to Spanish monolingual older Latinos, in that their (grand)children can serve as **linguistic brokers**. That is, if they need access to services or information that is only available in English, the younger bilinguals can act as translators.

It is notable that Central American nations such as Guatemala are among the most strongly **collectivist** in the world, and even Mexico is very much more collectivist than the United States (Hofstede, 1984). These cultures value social groups and family more highly than others (even more so than cultures in Asia that we often think of as highly collectivist). One manifestation of this collectivism is in the emphasis placed on family in Latino cultures. Extended families are valued, and often include godparents and other close friends who are treated as part of *la familia* (Vidal, 1988). So, we might predict that Central American and Mexican cultures would have the highest levels of respect for elders at least within the family. Research by Kwak and Haley (2005) suggests that this family-centeredness extends to the very end of life. Hispanic Americans want family involvement in end-of-life decision making more than almost all other groups.

However, some debate is still ongoing in the literature about the nature and extent of differences in grandparent–grandchild relations in Latino versus Anglo families, with suggestions that researchers are "overstating familial bonds among the Mexican American elderly" (N. Williams & Torrez, 1998, p. 91). In part, this debate may be because work has paid insufficient attention to diversity *among* Latinos in the United States. Work on Cuban Americans is lumped together with work on Mexican Americans, and the research often does not distinguish between families of recent immigrants and families that have been in the United States for many generations. Equally important, the work does not consider regional differences within the United States. Even among Mexican Americans, there is considerable diversity between those residing in South Texas and those residing in Southern California. All of this diversity means that drawing firm conclusions about one group being more or less family-centered is very difficult.

Portrayals of Latinos in the media are sufficiently infrequent that it is difficult to examine how such portrayals differ across the life span. Mastro and Stern (2003), however, do demonstrate that television advertising features proportionately more *younger* Latinos than African Americans or Whites. In other words, the well-established pattern of overrepresenting younger people appears to be even stronger for Latino portrayals. This may reflect a broader stereotype of Latinos as being associated with sex and sexuality, which in turn is stereotypically associated with youth (Berg, 2002). Glascock and Ruggiero (2004) have provided one of the only examinations of portrayals on Spanish language television in the United States. This examination suggests that quite familiar patterns appear—women on Spanish language television are younger than their male counterparts (see also Mastro & Ortiz, in press). Remember from Chapter 8 that this is also the pattern on English language television.

Native American Cultures

Aging in Native American cultures has traditionally been viewed positively (Hedlund, 1999). The term "**elder**" takes on a very specific meaning in these cultures, indicating an individual with great knowledge both about the world in general and also about the tribe, including family relationships within the tribe and tribal history. In cultures that have been primarily oral (and at times have been suspicious of written communication), the role of the elder has been to pass this information on to younger generations. Interestingly, despite the connotations of the term, "elders" do not have to be chronologically old. The term "elder" is used to indicate someone with wisdom, not simply someone with age. Graves and Shavings (2005) note that an elder must be someone who "maintains a healthy lifestyle and has a wealth of cultural information and knowledge . . . their lifestyle is held up as an example for others to follow" (p. 37). Thus, not all older adults are "elders." Ganje (2004) notes that the idea of a birthday—of tracking chronological age at all—was only introduced to most Native American cultures fairly recently.

In understanding American Indian cultures, it is important to recognize that there is substantial variation in the degree to which people from these groups have acculturated to "mainstream" America. The level of **acculturation** is related to where people live—about 60% of Native Americans live in urban areas, are geographically separated from other Native Americans, and tend to be largely assimilated into the "mainstream." In contrast, about 40% live in rural areas, primarily on reservations. For these individuals, the geographic proximity to other members of their culture has led to greater cultural maintenance. Traditional patterns of Native cultures are easier to see in rural Native Americans, and the vast majority of research has been done on reservations. Thus, for instance, extended families tend to live together on reservations, with grandparents and grandchildren sharing a residence a lot of the time. However, among the majority of American Indians who do not live on reservations, grandparent–grandchild co-residence is significantly less common (Scharlach, Fuller-Thomson, & Kramer, 1994).

A lot of social representations of Native Americans focus on connections to nature, harmony with the universe, and perhaps somewhat sentimentalized notions of the spiritual side of Native American life. Media images contribute to this (e.g., *Pocahontas:* Fryberg, 2003). However, there are some, more down to earth (and realistic) contrasts between Native American life and typical Euro-American patterns. For instance, many Native societies are **matrilineal**—women are the focus of family relationships and the "line" through which family is traced. In contrast, White Americans traditionally trace descent through both lines, and regard the mother's and father's ancestors as equally part of their family history. One consequence of matrilineal descent is that considerable research has been done on older women in Native American families, while relatively little work has focused on older men. Older women play a substantially more significant role in childrearing than in many other cultural contexts. Older American Indian women often become a surrogate mother to one or more of the daughter's children (Hedlund, 1999).

One of the roles played during childrearing is the transmission of cultural values and practices (Graves & Shavings, 2005). One unique way in which this occurs is in the artistic realm. Hedlund (1999) describes how older women will often incorporate their artistic practices (e.g., weaving among the Navajo) into everyday childcare. By being surrounded by this artistic production, the children learn more about the culture and develop expertise in the practice. At the same time, the older person produces items that are of cultural and economic value to the family and tribe. Thus, older women in such contexts are serving childcare, cultural production, economic production, and cultural transmission functions simultaneously!

More generally, attitudes about aging are traditionally positive and respectful in Native American cultures. A. Williams and Nussbaum (2001) quote work indicating that the Navajo elder is seen as wise and a source of important and useful information concerning links between past and future (Barusch & Steen, 1996; McGoldrick, Pearce, & Giordana, 1982; see also Graves & Shavings, 2005, for similar discussions relating to Alaska Natives). Interestingly, this value, along with other traditional Native American perspectives, may be stronger among younger than older American Indians.

For instance, Jackson and Chapleski (2000) examined older and younger members of the Anishinaabeg (members of the Chippewa, Ottawa, and Potawatomi tribes) living in Michigan. They found considerably more cultural activity (particularly organized group activities) among younger and middle-aged tribe members than older people. For instance, the younger people were more involved at the summer powwow than older adults, and were more likely to organize activities like a Native American drum group. The authors suggest a historical reason for this. The older members of the tribe lived most of their adult life during a period where the U.S. government was actively trying to assimilate Native Americans, depriving them of access to their own culture, discouraging native language use, and the like (see also Shaver, 1997). The younger tribe members, in contrast, have grown up during the period of **"self-determination,"** with the U.S. government taking a somewhat more "hands off" approach. As such, the younger people have had more freedom to engage their culture, and also have had some motivation to reclaim it. Other authors have also noted a resurgence in the use and study of native languages in younger generations (Graves & Shavings, 2005). Closer examination of the older people indicated that they had also retained aspects of their culture (e.g., language use), but that it manifested in much more private ways. The historical times they had lived through made them reluctant to engage in more public cultural activities.

A final area of some current research activity relating to older Native Americans is in health care. Both Shaver (1997) and Barker and Giles (2003) have provided some fascinating insights into how older Native Americans deal with the health care environment. Both note that dealing with doctors can be extremely problematic for these individuals. Particularly on reservations, doctors tend to be quite young and are almost all White—it is common for newly qualified doctors to take positions on reservations that provide them financial benefits to help pay off student loans and the like. This can lead to some interesting and problematic miscommunication. In general, Native Americans are more reluctant to share personal information than European Americans (Polacca, 2001), and so what might be perfectly normal questions for a physician to ask a White patient are seen as intrusive or overly personal in Native American settings. Of course, the degree of perceived intrusiveness is enhanced by the fact that it's a younger person asking the question. Shaver describes one physician in the following fashion:

When the physician interacts with elder women, he displays the following behavior: his voice becomes more highly pitched, he uses a sing-song voice that is used with small children, he calls the women by their first name ("Hellooooo, Gladys!"), he refers to them with terms of endearment that a close relative might use ("dear," "babe," and "Sweetheart"), he makes personal comments about their hair or clothing, and he teases them about their behavior or their activities. (p. 172)

This communication is highly reminiscent of the **patronizing communication** described in Chapter 4. In this context, its negative effects are exacerbated by the cultural difference and the traditional respect for age in Native culture, such that the behavior is seen as clearly inappropriate.

In the previous sections on culture we have discussed media portrayals of older adults among those cultural groups. That's not possible for Native Americans. There are so few portrayals of Native Americans in the media, that trying to further break them down by age group and attempt any systematic examinations is impossible. For instance, Mastro and Stern (2003) found that only 9 out of 2,290 television characters that they studied were Native American. Future work might be able to do detailed analysis of portrayals of older Native Americans in the media by targeting specific movies or television shows that feature such characters, but it's clear that very few such portrayals exist.

Globalization and Transcultural Themes

It is easy to read the descriptions of cultures above and think that cultures are fairly static and unchanging. In fact, though, cultures are always changing. Indeed, you'll notice that in the descriptions of China and India, the Westernization and urbanization of those cultures are noted as having a profound impact on the role of older people in those societies. Likewise, culture changes on the individual and family level. Within Latino families in the United States, for instance, the intergenerational dynamics can be dramatically different depending upon when the family arrived in the United States and which family members speak Spanish and/or are bilingual. Similar dynamic patterns have been examined in other immigrant cultures (for instance, Chinese immigrants to New Zealand: see Ng & He, 2004). In many cases, it is possible to identify something similar to a culture gap that mirrors the generational difference—grandchildren may be quite different from their grandparents in terms of a broad array of cultural values. Native American culture has obviously been massively influenced by the arrival of Europeans in North America. Along with the destruction of so many other aspects of these cultures, we have probably lost certain ways of thinking about the role of older adults in society. Some of the most dramatic cultural changes can be observed in **multicultural families**, where different traditions come into contact on a daily basis. How does a Korean American mother-in-law deal with her African American daughter-in-law when it comes to taking care of grandchildren? What happens when an older Navajo woman expects to live with a Caucasian son-in-law, but he is not interested? These are the types of issues that will become more widespread as multicultural families become more common.

There is no doubt that the world is becoming (metaphorically) smaller, and so cultures are coming into contact more and more, both on a macro level (e.g., via satellite broadcasting of programming from one culture into another) and on a micro level (e.g., via the processes experienced by a single tourist visiting another country and absorbing something of that nation's culture). This process of **globalization** carries with it the promise that we will learn tolerance of one another and gain understanding of some of the positive elements of other cultures. However, it also carries the threat that ways of life are being lost. One common theme across many cultures is that filial piety or respect for older people is declining (Graves & Shavings, 2005). Even among Europeans, for whom filial piety is not a hugely culturally important value, it is not unusual to hear that respect for older people is not what it used to be. If a decline exists, it may perhaps be traced to some of the phenomena that accompany "modern" living. Nuclear families, urban lifestyles, and geographic mobility all probably take their toll on intergenerational relations, no matter what culture you are from. This perspective is described more fully by **modernization theory** approaches (Cockerham, 1997). My children live 500 miles from one set of grandparents and 5000 miles from the other set—that's pretty different from living down the street! Of course, the other possibility is that throughout history, people have *always* thought that respect for elders is declining—perhaps overestimating the amount of respect they themselves showed to their grandparents when they were younger. The following quotation may be informative: "Children today are tyrants. They contradict their parents, gobble their food, and tyrannize their teachers." These words are attributed to Socrates, who lived about 2,500 years ago!

Summary

Each of the cultures examined features some unique cultural elements (e.g., *laodao* in China), but they all also exhibit some commonalities (e.g., a concern that traditional respect for elders is declining). As cultural contact continues, it's easy to think that cultural groups will begin to merge more and more. However, contact between groups sometimes energizes groups to retain their cultural traditions, and may strengthen cultures. As we examine the different philosophical and practical approaches to aging in these different cultures, it can make us aware of how the ways our own cultures approach aging are not the "right" or only way to think about getting old.

Keywords and Theories

Acculturation	*Laodao*
Collectivism	Linguistic brokers
Conflict	Matrilineal
Confucianism	Modernization
Co-residence	Multicultural families
Culture	One-child policy
Elder (Native American)	Patronizing communication
Filial piety (*Xiao*)	Power-distance
Globalization	Self-determination (Native
Hinduism	American)
Intergenerational communication	Urbanization
schemas	Variation within cultures

Discussion Questions

- Is there an equivalent of *laodao* in your culture?
- How does communication occur in families where the grandparent and grandchild don't share a language? What are some consequences of that for the grandparent–grandchild relationship?
- What might be the consequences of the one-child policy (instituted in 1979) for elder co-residence in China? When might the effects of this be felt most strongly?
- Why is there less intergenerational conflict in high power-distance cultures? What sorts of government policies relating to aging would you expect to see in high versus low power-distance cultures?
- Do you believe that people today have less respect for their elders than in the past? Why/why not?

Annotated Bibliography

Jackson, D. D., & Chapleski, E. E. (2000). Not traditional, not assimilated: Elderly American Indians and the notion of "cohort." *Journal of Cross-Cultural Gerontology, 15,* 229–259. This research is described briefly in the chapter; however, the article is worth reading in its entirety. It covers a number of interesting methodological issues concerning work with different age groups (most notably, cohort versus developmental explanations for age differences), as well as summarizing the historical experiences of current older Native Americans very nicely.

Pecchioni, L. L., Ota, H., & Sparks, L. (2004). Cultural issues in communication and aging. In J. F. Nussbaum & J. Coupland (Eds.), *Handbook of communication and aging research* (2nd ed., pp. 167–214). Mahwah, NJ: Lawrence Erlbaum. Perhaps the most recent review of cultural issues in intergenerational research. This chapter focuses particularly on the body of research examining intergroup and accommodation processes. It also takes some time to examine the meaning of culture and different cultural ways of understanding age, aging, and successful aging. Finally, the chapter considers the role of culture and aging in areas such as organizational, political, and health communication.

Szinovacz, M. E. (Ed.). (1998). *Handbook on grandparenthood.* Westport, CT: Greenwood Press. This book is now almost 10 years old. However, it is a great review of a huge body of work done examining grandparents. Most notable in the context of this chapter are individual sections of the book devoted to examining grandparenting among African Americans, Asian Americans, and Hispanic Americans. These chapters provide excellent coverage of cultural issues. A chapter by Ikels also provides some coverage of the broader issues underlying the examination of cross-cultural differences in grandparent relations.

PART IV

Contexts of Communication in Older Adulthood

This part considers two contexts in which substantial recent research has emerged—health communication and technology. Both are crucial to cultural conceptions of aging (i.e., as a period of ill health and technological incompetence). The specific findings in each area have nice connections to the earlier sections (e.g., how technology is used to support the grandparent–grandchild relationship, how patronizing speech is directed at institutionalized older adults). Thus, this part provides some "in context" applications of previously discussed phenomena.

ELEVEN

Health and Health Care

This chapter focuses on the communication and aging issues relating to health and health care, focusing particularly on doctor– patient communication, communication in support groups, and elder abuse. By the end of this chapter you should be able to:

SOURCE: ©Tomaz Levstek/Istockphoto.com

- Describe some ways in which communication between doctors and young patients differs from communication between doctors and older patients
- Discuss some ways in which a "third party" or companion might influence interaction between a doctor and an older patient
- Describe how the communication enhancement model might be applied to physician–patient communication in older adulthood
- Describe how older people and their physicians might improve communiction during a visit to the doctor
- Understand why support groups may be effective for caregivers, including some of the contrasting features of online and offline support groups
- Discuss some of the causes of elder abuse, and how communication factors into abuse situations

If I'd known I was going to live this long, I'd have taken better care of myself!

—Eubie Blake, noted pianist and composer, age 96

P revious portions of this book have made clear that there is a well-established psychological link between old age and health: We find it very difficult to think, talk, or write about older people without mentioning health. I have argued (and I hope you've been convinced!) that this can often be a bad thing. Obsessively linking aging with ill health can mean that we forget about the positive aspects of old age and ignore the potential of older people. If ill health is what immediately leaps to mind when we think about older people, then consideration of the aging population translates into thinking about available hospital beds and prescription drug coverage; we forget how older people contribute to society in ways that benefit those around them, grow the economy, and make the world a better place.

Nonetheless, as things currently stand there are good reasons to focus on health issues pertaining to older adulthood for this chapter. Older adults' medical issues are different from other age groups in a number of ways. Figure 11.1 describes how the prevalence of various ailments changes with age. Note that certain classes of disease (e.g., respiratory diseases like asthma) remain relatively stable in prevalence across the life span, while others (e.g., arthritis, hypertension) are clearly age-related. Some diseases are *almost* exclusively diseases of old age (e.g., Alzheimer's). The figure also illustrates that a lot of those 75 and older suffer from multiple health problems. If you add the numbers for the columns representing people 75 and older, you'll get a number much larger than 1000, indicating that some people must have more than one of these ailments. In fact, certain of the problems are interrelated—blindness can occur as a consequence of diabetes while strokes and heart problems can both be consequences of high blood pressure. Hence, physicians dealing with older patients will often be dealing with people who have multiple chronic conditions, whereas younger people more often show up at their doctor's office with single acute problems. (In medical terms, a chronic condition is one that is long term and generally has no simple treatment to make it go away. These are the kinds of maladies that are "managed" rather than "cured." High blood pressure is a classic chronic condition. In contrast, acute problems are more short term, albeit perhaps serious for that period of time. A broken bone or the flu are acute conditions.)

This chapter examines how communication issues are related to some of the health-related experiences of older adults. While illnesses are essentially biological, social processes are crucial to our health, both in terms of those social processes influencing health (e.g., a friend persuading you to exercise more, or an ad campaign persuading you to quit smoking), and in terms of how social processes influence how people cope with being sick (e.g., interactions with physicians, communication within support groups, etc.). This

Figure 11.1   Prevalence of Chronic Conditions by Age

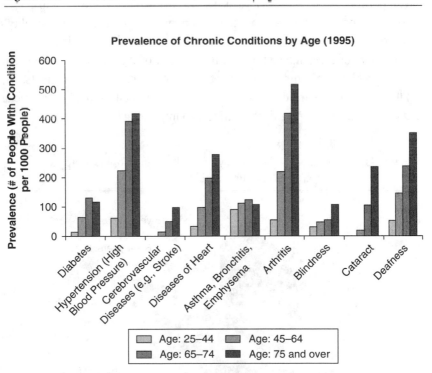

SOURCE: National Center for Health Statistics, Data Warehouse on Trends in Health and Aging. Retrieved June 2005 from http://www.cdc.gov/nchs/agingact.htm

chapter focuses primarily on **physician–older patient communication**. This is the area in which the most research has been done on older adults and health-related communication. Following this, however, I will discuss two other areas in which some research has been done, and where more communication research is needed: **caregiver support groups** and **elder abuse.**

Physician–Older Patient Interaction

Few interactions carry the direct life-or-death implications of conversations between a physician and a patient. Making the correct diagnosis and ensuring that the treatment occurs are obviously incredibly important. Older adults visit doctors more frequently than other age groups (T. L. Thompson, Robinson, & Beisecker, 2004). Figure 11.2 shows that people over 75 have over 800 visits per year per 100 people, or about 8 visits per year per person, whereas 18- to 44-year-olds have only 2 or 3 visits per person on average. As a result, the quality of doctor–patient interaction may be *more* important for older people because they have more of these interactions. In this section of the chapter, I will describe some problems in communication between physicians and older patients. Then I'll discuss some of the causes of those problems, and talk about how physicians *and* their older patients might contribute to improving the situation.

Figure 11.2   Number of Visits to Physician Offices and Hospital Outpatient Departments per 100 People

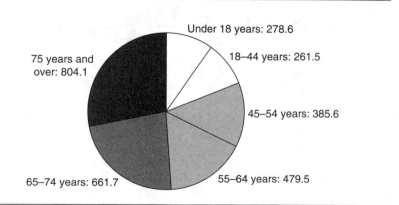

SOURCE: "Health," by Centers for Disease Control and Prevention (National Center for Health Statistics), 2005, Figure 24 data.

The Nature of Physician–Older Patient Interaction

Researchers have examined patterns of communication between physicians and older patients using both direct observation (e.g., video or audio recording of actual conversations) and questionnaires (asking physicians and/or patients about their experiences). Among the conclusions from this research are (Haug & Ory, 1987; T. L. Thompson et al., 2004):

Physicians' talk to older patients is more condescending than to younger patients.

Physicians spend less time with older patients.

Physicians ask older patients fewer questions.

Physicians take a more **authoritarian role** with older patients (e.g., they do not engage in joint decision making as much of the time).

Physicians are less patient with older people.

Physicians and older patients tend to disagree about the goals of the medical encounter more often than physicians and younger patients.

Physicians often provide less information to older patients, particularly about medication.

The importance of physical exercise to health is discussed in a small minority of encounters between physicians and older patients (3.7% according to Greene & Adelman, 2001).

Physicians only talk about **psychosocial issues** (e.g., relationships, living situation, depression) when they are raised by the physician. When patients raise such issues, they are largely ignored.

Older patients fail to raise issues of concern to them in encounters with doctors 50% of the time, even when they said those issues were important immediately prior to the encounter.

Physician Factors

Doctors undoubtedly have some responsibility for these problems. First, medical schools do not always do a great job of training physicians in communication skills, and particularly in communication skills relevant to older adults (Fallowfield et al., 2002). There is also relatively little in the way of training in **geriatrics** (health issues specific to older adults), unless physicians select that as their specialty. In general, geriatrics is a less glamorous and less profitable specialty than, say, brain surgery, and so it is less appealing to many medical students. One side effect of this is that there are relatively few people equipped to *teach* geriatrics. A 2003 report from the Association of American Medical Colleges reported that only 1% of faculty in U.S. medical schools reports geriatrics as their specialty. Thus, there is a vicious cycle whereby medical students don't tend to be interested in geriatrics to start with, and their medical schools lack many faculty who are likely to spur their interest.

In addition to a lack of training, ageist biases underlie some of the communication issues described above. As noted in Chapter 4, ageist stereotypes can be a basis for condescending or patronizing speech. Some of the myths of aging from Chapter 3 might underlie the lack of information some physicians provide about exercise or smoking. If physicians believe that behavior change won't help older people ("the horse is out of the barn"), then they will be less likely to talk about it. Similarly, if physicians don't believe that older people *can* change ("you can't teach an old dog new tricks"), then they may also not recommend positive changes. Notice how the doctors' actions serve to reinforce the stereotype in this case—if doctors don't push older patients to change their behaviors, chances are they will indeed remain "stuck in their ways."

Finally, physicians' use of overly technical language and jargon impedes communication with all patients, but may be particularly damaging to interactions with older adults—specifically older adults with short-term memory or mental processing problems. Physicians are trained in biomedical language, but the ability to translate that into speech that is comprehensible to the layperson is key to successful patient care (Aronsson, Sätterlund Larsson, & Säljö, 1995).

Patient Factors

We should not assume that all negative elements of these interactions are because of the physician. Older patients also contribute to these negative outcomes both directly and indirectly. Older patients tend to prefer a different style of interaction with their doctors. They adopt a more **authoritarian** approach to the medical encounter: "The doctor is the expert, I'll just sit here and she or he will tell me what to do." In part, this may be a cohort effect, stemming from historical orientations to doctors—today's more egalitarian and consumeristic approach to health care is relatively new and substantially different from the medical system into which today's seniors were socialized (Beisecker & Beisecker, 1993). Hence, older adults often ask fewer questions in medical encounters, and some older people do not desire to be "involved" in ways that today's physicians might expect. The change to a **managed care** system has also affected medical consultations in ways that older adults might have trouble adjusting to (e.g., dealing more with nurses, having relatively short periods of time for the physician encounter, etc.: Nussbaum, Pecchioni, & Crowell, 2001).

Some older adults also have ageist attitudes that can negatively influence the quality of care that they receive. Many are resigned to experiencing ill health, viewing it as an inevitable part of the aging process. As a result, they may fail to inform their physicians about certain symptoms, or they may wait longer than they should to see a doctor as a result of thinking that a particular symptom is "normal" for their age (Ory, Abeles, & Lipman, 1992). Sometimes doctors may attempt to overcome these attitudes in their patients, telling them that a symptom is *not* normal for someone of their age. N. Coupland and Coupland (1999) demonstrated that some patients are very resistant to this information! Indeed, N. Coupland and Coupland noted the complex ways in which allowing certain symptoms to be attributed to age might be functional for older people (at least relative to attributing them to something more serious). In one poignant exchange, a physician points out that getting older is "not the reason that you should get tired," in response to which the patient comments, "Well I'm hoping it is." So, on the one hand attributing pain or illness to age might be dysfunctional because it results in not seeking treatment. On the other hand, it might be psychologically functional at times to believe that what you are experiencing is "normal" rather than pathological. It's probably a case-by-case decision as to which strategy is functional, and hence when to discourage the age attribution.

In addition, as described earlier, older patients may often have multiple chronic ailments, and are more likely to be using **multiple medications** than younger people. These issues complicate the medical encounter in predictable ways. For instance, older people who come to an encounter with more issues to discuss are likely to find that a subset of those issues are not addressed, perhaps because time runs out. Older patients are also more likely to have sensory impairments (e.g., hearing problems) and cognitive impairments (e.g., mild memory loss as part of normal aging, or even dementia for a minority of older patients) that can further complicate the medical encounter (Adelman, Greene, & Charon, 1991). Gender issues can also complicate communication between physicians and older patients. Haug and Ory (1987) showed that when patient and physician were the same gender, patients tended to disclose more information and the interactions went more smoothly. While I don't know of research on the issue, gender mismatch might be a particular problem for older men who might be faced with a considerably younger female physician. For many older men today, the women they have run into in health care contexts have largely been nurses. As a result, they may have particular difficulty in relating to a female physician.

Companions

One final element can seriously complicate the physician–older patient encounter—other people. As many as 40% of older adults' visits to physicians involve a companion (J. Coupland & Coupland, 2001). These companions are most often an adult daughter of the patient, but may also be other family members (particularly a spouse), friends, or assistants from a residential care center (e.g., a nursing home aide: Adelman, Greene, & Charon, 1987). Recent research has focused on the nature of these "**triadic**" encounters, examining different roles that the third person can take and influences that they can have. J. Coupland and Coupland conclude that the third person can serve positive and negative functions. On the positive side, third parties can provide information (speaking for the patient) in situations where the patient is impaired or anxious. Beisecker (1989) described one situation in which a patient is being somewhat evasive in answering a doctor's question and the companion jumps in with, "Tell him the true story. He tried [working] for three days and is utterly fatigued. He's not able . . . it's taking too much out of him." In this case, the companion may be providing very useful diagnostic information for the physician that the patient was reluctant to share. In ideal circumstances, the patient and the third party can collaborate in telling the doctor the symptoms, providing the doctor with more complete information than she or he might have received from just one person. For instance, consider the following example (edited here for length):

1. *Doctor:* And, [to daughter] how's she been?

2. *Daughter:* Yeah, [to mother] you had a bit of er . . .

3. *Patient:* Oh, er er

4. *Daughter:* Yeah, giddy

5. *Patient:* Just a little, not er a pain, but, just a pressure, you know

6. *Daughter:* A pressure, you know in her head, she, for a couple of days, it's passed now

7. *Doctor:* Did you actually have the dizziness?

8. *Patient:* No giddiness

9. *Daughter:* No

10. *Doctor:* The sickness that you had before?

11. *Daughter:* No

12. *Patient:* No

SOURCE: From J. Coupland & Coupland, 2001.

As can be seen, in line 1 the doctor asks the daughter a question about the mother. Rather than simply answering *for* her mother, the daughter turns to the mother and talks to her directly, thus encouraging her involvement in the encounter. In lines 2–6, mother and daughter *jointly* tell the doctor about the problem, and in 8–9 and 11–12, they jointly respond to the doctor's questions. While at times such collaborative responding might take more time, it almost certainly results in better information being conveyed.

In contrast, though, third parties can sometimes serve negative functions, particularly when they form an alliance or coalition with the doctor that works against the patient. J. Coupland and Coupland described an instance where the patient is taken by a nurse to undress for a physical exam, and the daughter and the physician are left together. Almost immediately, the daughter begins describing her mother in patently stereotypical ways, including lumping her mother together with other older people (e.g., "She is a worrier . . . I think when you get to her age you get a bit confused actually . . . when they get to their age they think, well, why are they doing it"). Note the way that the talk moves from talking about the patient ("She") to comparing the patient to other people of a similar age ("her age") to simply talking about all old people as a homogenous mass ("they . . . their age . . . they"). Such communication can have negative consequences for the patient's chance at a good medical and social outcome from the visit given that the companion is effectively encouraging the doctor to stereotype the patient. More generally, negative outcomes are possible when the physician and the third party end up excluding the patient. For instance, the patient and companion may refer to the patient as "he" or "she" and thus talk as if the patient isn't even there (even though the patient is still in the room)— "**communicatively disenfranchising**" the patient, to use J. Coupland and Coupland's phrase.

The companion can also take away *time* that the patient could spend talking to the physician. A recent study from Japan found that older adult patients seeing a doctor alone talked for about 46% of the medical visit. In contrast, patients who had a companion with them talked for only 29% of the time (Ishikawa, Roter, Yamazaki, & Takayama, 2005). This same study also found that patients and companions often disagreed on the companion's role, with the companion generally expecting to play a more extensive role in the encounter with the doctor than the patient was expecting of the companion. Hence, the presence of a third party is not inherently bad, but it has the potential to have negative effects, and it is yet another complicating factor in interactions between older patients and physicians.

Improving Physician–Older Patient Encounters

All of the factors described above are a recipe for complicated communication between physicians and older patients, with the possibility for negative outcomes. As a result, it's important to consider ways in which both parties can contribute to more positive outcomes.

For the physician, it's clear that experience with older patients and specific training can help. Trained geriatricians display considerably more positive behaviors in interactions with their older patients, as do physicians who see more older patients as part of their general practice (Radecki, Kane, Solomon, Mendenhall, & Beck, 1988). Some relatively simple things can also improve the effectiveness of these encounters (e.g., providing treatment and medication information in written *and* verbal form). Greene and Adelman (2001) make a number of recommendations for helping physicians negotiate these encounters more effectively. They advocate for taking non-ageist approaches to the encounters. This involves doctors making conscious attempts to recognize the heterogeneity of the older population, and to avoid ageist assumptions in what they discuss with their patients. Perhaps the most vivid example of this is that doctors sometimes do not discuss obvious health promotion factors like exercising and quitting smoking with their older patients. These factors make a dramatic difference in health status for people of *all* ages, so doctors' failure to recommend them to older patients is probably driven by ageism.

Physicians should also acknowledge the patient's **personhood**. As recommended by the **communication enhancement model** (see Chapter 7, Figure 7.2), effective physician–patient communication is helped by treating the patient as a person rather than as a disease, and helping the patient plan for his or her specific future. Encouraging the patient to ask questions, being responsive to issues raised by the patient, and attending to the **patient's agenda** are also extremely important. Patients are particularly responsive when doctors check that all important issues have been covered, and do so in a way that reflects a genuine interest (e.g., "What other questions do you have for me?" as opposed to "OK, so is that it?"). Patients also appreciate physicians who address them in a manner they deem appropriate. For some older people, being addressed by their first name is disrespectful—they expect to be called "Mr./Mrs." and have a negative view of physicians who do otherwise (Allman, Ragan, Newsome, Soufos, & Nussbaum, 1999). Physicians should probably assume that older patients prefer the more formal form of address until such a time that the patient indicates that they prefer to be on first name terms.

It is also important for physicians to encourage talk of sensitive issues, and to create an environment in which such talk is relatively easy for the patient. Issues of sexuality, neglect/abuse, incontinence, or death are often of importance to older people, but they are not easy topics for any of us to discuss. Doctors need to be clear with their patients that the discussions are confidential, they need to create environments that are private, and they need to discuss such topics in ways that encourage patient disclosure. For instance, maintaining eye contact, nodding the head, and other nonverbal behaviors can indicate that what the patient is saying is important, and not weird or strange, and that the doctor is attending to it. Over the long term, such discussions become more likely, of course, when a relationship of trust is developed between physician and patient.

Finally, physicians need to attend to broader contextual issues. Older adults may come to a physician with a health problem that results from abuse, neglect, or insufficient self-care (perhaps precipitated by depression, for instance). Treating the *symptom* in such circumstances only goes part way toward dealing with the underlying problem. Physicians should be able to sensitively raise discussion of the older person's living environment and whether broader lifestyle changes are needed. Doctors should also be aware of other resources (social work, psychiatric services, law enforcement) whose involvement might be needed to deal with the broader issues. Here, of course, the importance of physicians *listening* carefully to older adults is crucial. What may seem like a meaningless tangent to a doctor rushing to get to the next patient may actually be the crucial information that communicates the cause of some health problems. For instance, a story about crime in the neighborhood might be indicative of somebody who is finding it hard to get out of the house, is frightened, or is suffering from a lack of social contact due to others' unwillingness to visit.

Older patients, too, must contribute to a more positive communication climate in the health care encounter. First, they should prepare for visits to the doctor. Greene and Adelman (2001) recommend that older people identify an **agenda** for the visit and write it down. This agenda should include a *prioritized* list of questions so that the most important issues are dealt with first. Patients may need to be aware that all issues can't be dealt with in one visit, and they should be prepared to make multiple visits if there are a large number of issues to deal with. Sometimes, it can be useful to provide the physician with a written list of the questions/issues, so that the physician is "on the same page." If older patients need someone to give them a ride to the office, or to help them in talking to the physician, they need to find that person and make arrangements with him or her. Importantly, the older patient should carefully negotiate the companion's role with that person. It is undesirable to think that someone is just giving you a ride to the office, only to find them coming in to see the doctor with you! This is particularly the case if a sensitive or confidential health issue is the reason for the visit.

During the visit, it is important to let the physician know about any sensory impairments. For instance, if the older patient has a hearing problem, it's crucial that the doctor be told so that it can be accommodated in whatever ways are necessary. Patients also need to pay attention to the listed agenda/questions that they have brought along, and possibly may need to keep written notes. A certain degree of assertiveness is also essential for all patients in medical encounters. Physicians only know that they are not being understood if patients tell them, so it is crucial for older patients to ask for clarification or repetition when something is not understood or is "missed." Patients should also follow up on any lingering issues with a phone call or an additional visit after their physician visit.

Finally, patients should always be aware of their ability to switch physicians. Patterns of physician–patient interaction, once established, rarely change very much (Greene & Adelman, 2001), so a patient who is not happy with a physician should not keep visiting that physician in the hopes that things will improve. That said, patients should also be aware of the important of a good long-term relationship with a physician. As noted above, older patients are often trying to manage multiple ongoing, chronic conditions, conditions for which a long-term physician relationship is very helpful. Any doctor can see you once to prescribe an antibiotic for a sinus infection, but managing high blood pressure requires a longer term history of your health status such as knowledge of prior medications that have been tried and didn't work. The idea of having a relationship between patient and health care provider so that the provider is familiar with the patient's history is often called **continuity of care** in the health care industry. Patients who repeatedly switch physicians because of minor inconveniences or dissatisfactions may be hurting themselves, given the disruptions to continuity of care that result from such switches.

Satisfaction

While there are numerous outcomes that are important from physician–patient interactions, **patient satisfaction** has consistently emerged as important. Satisfaction has been linked to patient adherence to treatment regimens (e.g., taking medication appropriately), positive health outcomes, reduced anxiety, and keeping future appointments. For physicians, patient satisfaction has been linked to their own satisfaction, as well as reduced malpractice lawsuits (something most doctors are concerned about). In general, older patients are more satisfied by encounters that are longer, that involve more humor and shared laughter, and that involve more questions from the physician, particularly negatively worded questions such as, "No chest pain?" Older patients are also more satisfied with encounters that include high levels of information from the doctor. Physicians in satisfying encounters do not dominate the encounter, and also tend to provide "orienting" statements such as, "Next I'm going to listen to your lungs, and then the nurse is going to come in and check your blood pressure." Of course, none of these issues are unique to older patients—probably all of us would like to be treated in this fashion by our doctors!

Beyond Communication:
Other Medical Manifestations of Ageism

Ageism in medical settings can be observed in ways that go beyond communication. Given the focus of this book, these issues will not be examined in detail; however, they are worthy of brief mention. Research has demonstrated that older adults are frequently excluded from routine screenings for diseases like cancer (Derby, 1991), that physicians often fail to treat pain in older adults effectively (Pasupathi & Lockenhoff, 2002), and that older adults are generally excluded from clinical drug trials. These are not strictly communicative issues, but they further reveal the ways in which older adults are systematically excluded from the medical mainstream. As noted by Pasupathi and Lockenhoff, the issue of pain management is an interesting one. On the one hand, inadequate management of older adults' pain by physicians might be seen as ageist—the physicians are treating pain as somehow "normal" for older people, which they should not. On the other hand, it's true that pain management with older people is more difficult because older adults have unusual side effects with some pain medications, and the pain medications may interact in unknown ways with other medications being taken by older people. Hence, the physician's job is somewhat harder with older adults. This reiterates the importance of older adults seeing physicians who are experienced in working with older patients and who are trained in geriatrics.

Support Groups for Caregivers

This book has emphasized the fact that most older adults live independent, healthy, productive lives for many years. However, for *some* older people there comes a time when they need the care and support of those around them. In these situations, care is typically provided by professionals in an institution or by friends and family. The latter type of support can be very beneficial, as it often allows the older person to live in their own house, or at least in a community setting rather than in an institution. Nevertheless, such care can prove to be problematic for both caregiver and care receiver (Edwards, 2001). Sometimes, the older recipient may receive care that is lower quality than they would receive from professionals in an institutional setting. Meanwhile, the caregiver is placed in a very stressful and demanding position. The caregiver is often the spouse of the older adult, and hence is probably also an older person. Hence caregiving becomes an important aspect of life for many older people.

While there are undoubtedly benefits that accrue to caregivers (e.g., the feeling of having helped, increased intimacy with a spouse), there are also many stresses and strains on these individuals. Considerable research shows that there are social problems from caregiving. For instance, time spent caring for an older person is time that may be taken away from friends or other family members who also want attention. Psychological problems may accrue—depression is more prevalent among caregivers than the general population (Toseland & Rossiter, 1989). Physical health problems are also apparent—caregivers are at risk for sleep problems, alcohol abuse, lack of exercise, weight gain, and increased smoking. All of these have direct health consequences, particularly for cardiovascular health. A recent study demonstrated that spousal illness can contribute directly to the death of the other spouse, presumably as a function of the stress a caregiver experiences during times of spousal illness (Christakis & Allison, 2006). Such findings make it clear that in addition to attending to the needs of care recipients, we also need to take good care of caregivers.

One means for such support that has received attention is the **support group**. It is now relatively common for caregivers to get together and talk about caregiving in a trusting and supportive context. When caregivers get together with one another, a number of benefits can accrue, as described by Garstka, McCallion, and Toseland (2001). First, caregivers gain information from these groups. Other caregivers may be aware of services, benefits, treatments, or other information that may be useful. Wright and Query (2004) note that this may be particularly common in online support groups, which have more diverse membership. In an online support group, you may get information from someone who lives on the other side of town (or in a different country!), who has unique information that you were not aware of.

Importantly, the groups don't just provide information but also give concrete models for using that information. For instance, you might have heard about a service in town that sounded helpful but been hesitant about using it. Hearing that somebody else in the support group used the service, and the precise steps they went through to get help, might provide the incentive you needed to get out there and actually use the service.

Second, support groups provide opportunities to learn **coping strategies**. Coping strategies can be divided into two types:

Emotion-focused coping: These strategies help people deal with stress by working on managing the feelings associated with caregiving. For instance, a support group might include a session on meditation, breathing, or relaxation techniques, all focused on reducing the *feeling* of stress. For people who are uncomfortable talking about feelings, or people who are having particularly embarrassing problems, online support groups can be particularly effective here: The relative anonymity of the medium means that people are able to share more openly, even about very personal issues (Wright & Query, 2004).

Problem-focused coping: These strategies focus on finding more concrete solutions to specific causes of stress. For instance, a support group might talk about time-management practices such as organizing the day so as to put less pressure on the "worst" periods. Toseland, Rossiter, Peak, and Hill (1990) demonstrated that support groups focused on specific problem-focused advice and led by professionals can lead to significant decreases in psychological problems among caregivers.

Third, support groups provide opportunities for **social comparison**. Finding other people who are in even worse shape than you are can be very valuable during difficult times, and support groups provide exactly this opportunity. By meeting other caregivers, people can understand that they are not alone, that their experiences are not strange, and that their level of stress and unhappiness is perhaps fairly normal given the situation that they are in. They might even find others who have even more to deal with, which could provide a sense of relief.

Fourth, support group participation has been shown to increase the size of social networks: People make new friendships and gain new allies through these groups. These friendships, of course, will serve all of the positive functions that were described in Chapter 5. By gaining new friends, especially new friends who share an important life experience, caregivers gain a new source of support—someone to call during bad times or to provide a break from caregiving. The combined effect of all of these benefits is to reduce the negative consequences of caregiving. People in support groups simply do better in terms of psychological and physical health, as well as social factors.

Of course, people don't have to be physically located together to participate in a support group. **Online support groups** are flourishing in recent years and serve particularly important functions for those who are geographically isolated (e.g., living in rural areas), or who have very specific problems (Wright & Query, 2004). For very unusual situations (a very rare disease, for instance), other people who understand your situation may be very widely dispersed. Online support groups include options that can facilitate the support process, including time shifting (you can log on in the middle of the night) and multimedia options like videoconferencing (Marziali & Donahue, 2006). They also have the advantage that you don't have to leave your home to seek and offer support—see, for instance, Hunt's (1997) description of an online support group for Alzheimer's caregivers.

In the context of all of this positive information about support groups, you should also think about some of the downsides. Some people may go to support groups only to discover that they are really a lot worse off than all of the other people in the group. Finding that you are suffering more than anyone else might be traumatizing for some people. Support groups might also provide information that is in some ways unwelcome, even if it is true. For instance, you might be told quite clearly that someone with your husband's disease is never going to get better and is going to die a long and painful death. While the information you've learned might be correct, you might not have the ability to cope with it and might have been better off not learning it, at least at this particular point in time (see Brashers et al., 2000, for more on this sort of event). Finally, support groups are almost universally voluntary activities. They do not help people who don't perceive themselves as needing help, or who actively resist help when it's offered. The complexities of why people refuse or avoid help go beyond the context of this book, but it is probably influenced by concerns with not being indebted to others and face management (see Chapter 4 and D. O. Braithwaite & Eckstein, 2003).

Support groups are not the only solution available for caregiving stress. Caregivers also need **respite help**—a person or service that will give them a break to have some personal time for themselves. Caregivers may also need more careful health monitoring, financial assistance, and easy access to social services that help with medical and financial paperwork and services. A strong support network for caregivers is important not just for the caregivers themselves, but also for their older wards. As described next, elder abuse often occurs as a result of caregiver isolation and stress, both of which can be ameliorated by more effective caregiver support networks.

Elder Abuse

Very little research has examined the communication phenomena surrounding the problem of **elder abuse**. Indeed, we know relatively little about any aspects of elder abuse. In part, this is undoubtedly a function of the inherent difficulties in addressing horrendous acts such as physical, verbal, and financial abuse of older people. It is also because older victims of abuse are often unable or unwilling to report it to authorities, and are frequently abused by the sole person on whom they rely for support. Finally, we may know little about this crime because some authorities may be unwilling or unable to recognize it, failing to differentiate age-related illness and disability from the consequences of abuse. Elder abuse can range from fairly extreme forms of physical abuse (hitting, restraining), to extreme forms of neglect (e.g., failing to provide food, bathing, or housekeeping), to verbal abuse (calling someone "useless"), to financial exploitation (e.g., using an older person's savings to buy a car for yourself) (National Center on Elder Abuse, 2004). Nationally, estimates appear to indicate about 8 reports of elder abuse for every 1000 older people, but it's hard to know how accurate those estimates are for reasons described later. It is clear that the majority of abuse occurs at the hands of family members, particularly adult children and spouses (National Center on Elder Abuse, 2004).

Elder abuse often occurs in situations where the older person is frail and dependent on another individual for caregiving. The individual on whom the older person relies for care has very significant levels of control over the older person in terms of having direct access to his or her money, as well as having control over with whom the older person communicates. Giles and Stoney (2005) argue that the combination of victim dependency and caregiver stress is a potent recipe for abuse. There are very clear health issues here, because it is often ill health that leads to the dependency experienced by most abuse victims. They are in poor health, so they need someone to take care of them, and that person ends up abusing them. There are also, of course, health consequences that may occur as a result of physical injury or malnutrition that may be a part of the abuse situation.

The *communicative* dimensions of elder abuse are complex and not well understood. Giles and Stoney (2005) have begun to explore these issues, developing a model of the communication pathways involved—who is talking to whom, and what is being said. Two of the pathways are presented here to illustrate the contributions that the model makes. First, communication between the older person and authorities is crucial. Giles and Stoney provide an example of an older abuse victim's 911 call in which the victim appears apologetic and anticipates not being believed (e.g., "I am sorry, but someone is trying to kill me and I don't know what to do . . . really, I'm not kidding . . . nobody is going to listen to me . . . they are going to think I'm crazy"). As with some other criminal contexts (e.g., rape, hate crimes), the victims of elder abuse may suffer from uncertainty that others will believe them, and their communication can reflect that uncertainty, resulting in talk that appears uncertain and probably lacking in credibility. Undoubtedly numerous other factors are important in determining communication between an older abuse victim and authorities (e.g., trust of police, encouragement from friends or other family members, fear of reprisals from the abuser, the abuser blocking such attempts). We need to know more about such communication.

A second crucial link is that between abuser and abusee. As noted earlier, abusers are often in positions of considerable power over their victims, and abusers are often family members. Hence, their interactions with the older victim may reflect the family history. If the family traditionally endorsed violent solutions to problems, then it is likely that such violence will extend to the caregiver–recipient relationship in older adulthood (e.g., M. J. Quinn & Tomita, 1997). There are undoubtedly links to our earlier discussions of ageist stereotypes and schemas that influence this relationship. Specifically, it seems likely that caregivers who endorse homogenized and negative views of aging (e.g., that older adulthood is a time of unmitigated and irreversible decline) might be more likely to engage in abuse. The less potential you see for positive change and development in older adulthood, the less respect you are likely to have for an older ward.

Communicatively, it is crucial to understand more about the dynamics that occur between caregiver and care recipient. Are there "warning signs" (e.g., baby talk or exceptionally rigid and controlling communication styles) that come prior to the first significant abuse episodes? Are there particular styles of talk from care *recipients* (e.g., excessively demanding communication; incoherent talk) that precipitate abuse? It is important to realize that many caregivers will not have sophisticated knowledge of how a disease like Alzheimer's influences communication. When they receive certain styles of talk, they may perceive the older adult as deliberately trying to annoy or hurt them (e.g., Alzheimer's patients will sometimes act aggressively or verbally abuse those around them). A caregiver who is not aware that this is normal and uncontrollable behavior might well act aggressively in response. Most important, of course, we need to examine how communication can be used to prevent abuse. For instance, there might be some relatively simple strategies that victims could use to forestall an abuse episode. Much of this section is speculative because the data simply don't exist, but Giles and Stoney's (2005) model at least provides a starting point for this incredibly important endeavor.

Additional Topics

In this chapter, I have only touched on some of the interesting issues pertaining to health. There are numerous fascinating communication phenomena surrounding Alzheimer's disease, including communication issues involving caregivers for people who have such dementias (e.g., Orange & Ryan, 2000). There are also important issues pertaining to communication training in medical schools, and the role of geriatricians in working with older people to ameliorate health issues. Industry and system issues (e.g., the "managed care" system and government Medicare organization) are crucial to understand (Nussbaum et al., 2001). These are great topics for organizational communication specialists to look at in the future. Finally, there are many important issues pertaining to institutional care (e.g., nursing homes). Grainger (2004), for instance, focuses on the simple absence of talk between caregivers and care receivers in institutions. She also notes that when talk does occur it is focused on task issues (getting the job done). You have already read some more about communication in institutions in Chapters 4 and 5. Hopefully this chapter has whetted your appetite to examine other issues relating to communication and aging in health care contexts.

Summary

This chapter has described some of the ways in which social and communicative processes are associated with health issues for older people. This can occur in relatively obvious ways (e.g., poor communication with a physician) as well as in a more subtle fashion (e.g., frailty and poor health leading to abuse, which itself influences health). The physician–patient context illustrated the role of both parties in contributing to a positive interactional context—physicians need to provide clear information, listen to their patients, and provide information in ways that is attuned to patients' needs (including their age) without being patronizing. Older patients need to carefully plan for medical visits, prioritize their needs, and discuss a companion's role carefully with that person. The support group context illustrated the importance of caregivers seeking help—positive support from such groups contributes to the mental and physical health of caregivers (many of whom are older adults), and indirectly contributes to the well-being of the older people for whom they are caring. The elder abuse context is one that needs considerably more attention, focused particularly on communication between caregiver and care receiver, as well as institutional and organizational communication factors that involve law enforcement and social services agencies. It is important to separate issues of aging from issues of health. There are lots of important areas of study for communication and aging scholars that have nothing to do with health. However, as this chapter has hopefully illustrated, this is also a vibrant area for people who are interested in how communication relates to physical health.

Keywords and Theories

Authoritarian model of care
Communication enhancement model
Communicatively disenfranchising
Continuity of care
Doctor–patient communication
Elder abuse
Emotion-focused vs. problem-
    focused coping strategies
Geriatrics
Managed care
Multiple chronic health problems
Multiple medications

Patient's agenda (written)
Personhood
Respite help
Social comparison
Support groups
Third party / triadic communication

Discussion Questions

- Why do older people often bring a companion to a physician's office?
- What can doctors and older patients do to improve communication in the medical encounter?
- What elements do you think would be most effective in a support group for older adult caregivers? How would you structure a support session for such individuals?
- How might online support groups differ from those occurring offline? What are some strengths and weaknesses of each format?
- What causes stress for caregivers? What specific strategies would you use to reduce stress if you were a caregiver? How might authorities be better able to recognize stress and reduce abuse?

Annotated Bibliography

Hummert, M. L., & Nussbaum, J. F. (Eds.). (2001). *Communication, aging, and health.* Mahwah, NJ: Lawrence Erlbaum. This edited book covers all of the key areas pertaining to communication, aging, and health in great detail. With chapters written by all of the experts in the field, this is the primary source for anybody interested in the intersection of the three concepts in the title.

Orange, J. B., & Ryan, E. B. (2000). Alzheimer's disease and other dementias. *Clinics in Geriatric Medicine, 16,* 153–173. This article examines in detail some of the communicative implications of Alzheimer's disease and other forms of age-related dementia. A hugely useful element is an Appendix that provides very concrete descriptions of effective communication behaviors that physicians (and others) can use with older adults who are cognitively impaired.

Thompson, T. L., Robinson, J. D., & Beisecker, A. E. (2004). The older patient–physician interaction. In J. F. Nussbaum & J. Coupland (Eds.), *Handbook of communication and aging research* (2nd ed., pp. 451–478). Mahwah, NJ: Lawrence Erlbaum. The most comprehensive current review of work on physician–patient interaction in older adulthood. The chapter addresses most of the issues covered in that section of this chapter, with more detailed references and examples. It is particularly strong in its coverage of the issues surrounding companions coming to the physician's office with the older patient.

TWELVE

Technology

This chapter focuses on specific ways in which older adults use (and don't use) new technologies. It addresses stereotypes associated with older adults' technology use and examines the ways in which seniors do use new technologies, focusing particularly on the functions that new communication technologies serve for older people in their personal lives and in the workplace. The chapter also discusses some issues of computer design that are challenging for older adults. By the end of this chapter you should be able to:

SOURCE: © Istockphoto.com

- Know what the digital divide is, and describe how much of a generational digital divide exists
- Provide explanations for why older adults use computers less than younger people
- Describe some of the design elements that make computer use particularly challenging for older people
- Describe some of the functions that computer use serves for older adults
- Talk about older adults' technology use in the workplace

I want to get in on things, find out stuff that's going on. I want to try some of this eBay stuff ... I don't think there's anything you can't do on the Internet anymore ... It's foolish not to get into it. Especially for older people ... Things you've always wondered about, and there it is.

—Margaret (age 70), quoted in Hilt & Lipschultz (2004)

While I was talking to a colleague recently, he mentioned visiting a friend's home. A grandmother and granddaughter were at the home—the grandmother was surfing the **Internet** and the granddaughter was knitting. The account is revealing in a couple of ways. First, it illustrates that older adults are "getting onboard" with new forms of technology. It also illustrates that generational stereotypes about technology use and habits are not always accurate. Activities come and go in popularity—suddenly knitting is back in fashion, at least among a certain demographic of younger women. And let's not forget that knitting needles are a form of technology too!

Discussions about technology in today's world tend to focus on computers and the Internet, and this chapter is no different. At the outset, though, it's worth remembering that technology covers a lot more than your 802.11g Wi-Fi network. The people who turned 65 years old in 2005 were:

- 7 years old when the transistor was invented (transistors are the basis for most of today's electronics—from our computers to our bedside alarm clocks)
- 11 when the first color television broadcast occurred (but they may not have owned a television at the time ... if they did, it almost certainly wasn't a color television!)
- 25 when it became possible to dial most long-distance numbers in the United States without the help of an operator
- 26 when the hand-held calculator was invented (can you imagine college without a calculator?)
- 27 when the first consumer microwave oven became available (how did they make popcorn?)

- 37 when personal computers became widely commercially available
- 40 when VHS became the standard format for home video recording (Betamax? Anyone?)
- 43 when audio CDs first hit the market
- 53 when the World Wide Web began its period of dramatic growth
- 55 when Amazon.com opened for business
- 61 when the iPod was first released

So while many younger people see technology as synonymous with computer technology, most older adults today have seen many rounds of technological change, and the Internet revolution is just the most recent. As you may recall from Chapter 9, older adults have been enthusiastic adopters of certain technologies (e.g., television). Wahl and Mollenkopf (2003) discuss the importance of other rather mundane technologies in improving older adults' life satisfaction (e.g., central heating).

Much discussion of new technologies has focused on the **digital divide**—this is the phenomenon whereby members of minority groups, women, and poor people have less competence and less access to computers and the Internet than wealthy white men. The divide is problematic because access to computers is such a fundamental resource in today's society, and so the digital divide makes disadvantaged people in our society even more disadvantaged. As will be described a little later, there also seems to be a digital divide in the generational sense—older adults have less access to digital technology and less knowledge. One of the most interesting comments on this front comes from Hagestad and Uhlenberg (2005) who note that SMS communication (the format used for text messaging on phones, among other things) is essentially a generational language, one in which older people typically have little competence. In other words, older people are actually *linguistically excluded* from certain areas of communication using new technology.

In this chapter, I'm going to first address some of the stereotypes of older adults' computer and technology literacy. Then I'll talk about the reality of older people's computer use, including some ways in which they use the Internet for **identity** functions. Finally, I'll talk about uses of technology in the workplace. Keep in mind that while many technologies are "communication" related (telephones, the Internet, etc.), some are not (e.g., digital clocks, microwave ovens). I'll focus on the communication technologies, but sometimes the research on non-communication technologies is informative on this issue as well.

Stereotypes of Older Adults' Technological Competence

The realm of computer use is one that is distinctly age-associated. As noted in Chapter 3, older adults suffer from more negative evaluations and expectations on **competence** dimensions than **warmth** evaluations. Computer use (and technological skills in general) are more associated with competence issues than warmth (hence, perhaps, the stereotype of the computer geek with poor social skills). Therefore, this is an arena in which negative expectations of older adults might be expected to have significant impacts. Indeed, perceptions of older people's computer competence tend to be very negative.

Ryan, Szechtman, and Bodkin (1992) provide some nice illustrations of these ageist **stereotypes** concerning technology. First, these authors show that older people who *are* learning to use computers are seen as less typical of their age group than younger computer users (by young research subjects). This finding relates nicely to some of the issues with contact theory described in Chapter 7. Remember that contact with an older person is only likely to influence a younger person's attitudes when the older person is seen as typical of that age group. So, a situation in which attitudes might be made more positive (encountering an older person in a computer class) is actually unlikely to influence attitudes because the older person is not seen as typical of older people in general. In addition to the perceived typicality effects, young research subjects also saw older people as less likely to successfully *complete* a computer course. Finally, when people failed at the computer task, their failure was framed in terms of lack of effort if they were young, but in terms of age if they were old. Hence, older people are seen as likely to fail, and when they do fail it is seen as inherently due to their age and therefore not something that can be fixed. In contrast, young people's failure is perceived to be due to less stable causes: If they'd only tried a little harder they would have done fine.

Stereotypes of older adults' abilities also influence attempts to inform them about technology. Thimm, Rademacher and Kruse (1998) demonstrated that younger people's instructions on how to use technology are influenced by stereotypes. When asked to explain the functioning of a digital alarm clock/radio to an old person, young subjects used more **patronizing speech** than when explaining the same thing to a young person. Hence, the issues described in Chapter 5 seem to apply to technological education as much as they do to other communication contexts.

These stereotypes are often internalized by older people—older adults "buy into" these stereotypes ("self-stereotyping": see Chapter 3). For instance, Charness and Holley (2004) found that about 20% of seniors who don't use a technology say that their lack of use is because they are "too old." These people have clearly bought into the stereotype, and the stereotype seems to be influencing them to not engage in computer activity. However, the stereotype doesn't harm only those older people who have come to believe it. The term **stereotype threat** is often used to describe situations where people *know about* a competence-related stereotype of their group, and they *don't* want to reinforce it. Mere knowledge of the stereotype is enough to induce anxiety that poor performance may occur, and that such performance will reflect negatively not just on the individual but also on the group as a whole. For instance, women are sometimes stereotyped as being bad at math and science; a woman who didn't believe this might experience anxiety when taking a math test as a result of not wanting to perform poorly and reinforce others' stereotypes (Steele, 1997). Indirect evidence for stereotype threat in older adults' computer use comes from studies demonstrating that older people experience more anxiety when using technology than younger people (Laguna & Babcock, 1997). Hence, the stereotype has the capacity to hurt computer performance of both older people who buy into it and those who reject it!

While there may be a kernel of truth to some of these stereotypes, the majority are inaccurate and unjustified, at least when applied in an undifferentiated manner to all older people. Numerous studies now demonstrate clearly that older people are interested in learning about computers (Hilt & Lipschultz, 2004) and are very competent at working with new technologies when given appropriate training and motivation (Cole, 2003; Sterns, 2005). Bill Gates will be 65 in 2020. Will we still think that older adults don't know anything about technology when that happens? The following sections examine older people's actual technology use in more detail.

The Reality of Older Adults' Computer Use

Older adults do lag the younger population in terms of computer and Internet use. As Figure 12.1 shows, older adults are much less likely to have a computer

| Exercise 12.1 | Variation in Older Adults' Reactions to Technology |

Obtain a copy of the Hilt and Lipschultz article cited below (it should be available via your local university library, from the publisher, or from your class instructor). If you are working with a group, divide up the personal stories on pages 61–69. Discuss the following questions, with each individual drawing on the information of that "character" to answer the questions. If you are the dramatic type, you might even role-play your character! Feel free to make up additional information. For example, from the individuals' ages, you know something about the sorts of technology they grew up with, and the sort that have come along during their lives. If you are working alone, try answering each question from each individual's perspective.

1. What do you use the computer for?

2. When did you first start using it?

3. What do you like most and least about the computer?

4. What sorts of activities have been replaced by your computer use?

5. Is there a "typical" experience that older people have in using computers?

SOURCE: Hilt, M. L., & Lipschultz, J. H. (2004). Elderly Americans and the Internet: E-mail, TV news, information and entertainment websites. *Educational Gerontology, 30,* 57–72.

in their homes, and much less likely to have Internet access than other age groups. There is clearly a digital divide across the generations as well as across, for instance, socioeconomic groups. This can be understood by examining some of the barriers to older people using computers.

Barriers

There are many barriers to becoming computer literate for older people. One **barrier** is simply experience. For most people under the age of 55, computer use has been a regular feature of their work lives, and many of those who are still working have high-speed Internet access in their workplaces. In contrast, for many of today's 65+ population, computers (particularly the Internet) were a late arrival in their workplace, perhaps arriving at a time when the individuals were already approaching retirement. These people may not have seen it as "worth their while" to learn the new technology, or their colleagues may have been influenced by stereotypes and decided that the older people would not be able to learn. Either scenario would reduce the probability of

Figure 12.1   Computer and Internet Access in the Home by Age Group in
2001 and 2003

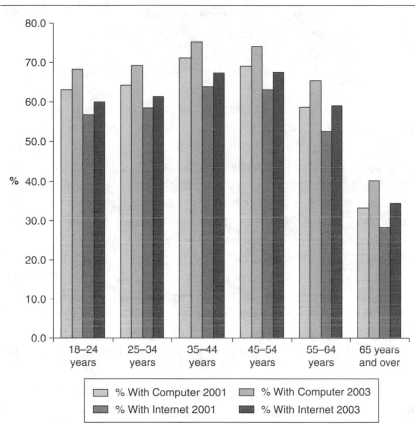

SOURCE: Table derived from data available from the U.S. Census Bureau (2001, 2005).

older adults becoming comfortable with technology through the work environment—the place where many of us first learned how to use computers
and the Internet. Further, if older people did use computers in their workplaces, they were probably using systems that by today's standards would be
very clunky and non-user-friendly—systems for things like financial record
keeping or inventory management. Experience with such systems is unlikely
to stimulate excitement about the idea of using a computer for leisure time
activities! These issues would explain current low levels of computer and
Internet use in the older generation as a **cohort effect** (see Chapter 1). As

younger generations get older, we would expect to see a substantial increase in computer use among older people. Charness and Holley (2004) present data suggesting that about twice as many 55- to 64-year-olds use the Internet regularly as compared to people over 65. Those 55- to 64-year-olds will be 65+ very soon!

Access to computers and the Internet is also an issue. Many younger working people have high-speed Internet access at work (and many of them use that access to buy their digital music, view their favorite viral videos, and pay their bills online). For the retired, access to computers has to be either in the home or in a public setting like a library. Hence, physically accessing a computer is somewhat more challenging and costly (e.g., a computer for the home has to be purchased). The access barrier might also be something of a cohort effect; decreasing computer prices and lower costs for high-speed Internet access in the future would reduce the impact of cost as a barrier, but the "churn" of constant **obsolescence** of equipment seems likely to continue (Selwyn, Gorard, Furlong, & Madden, 2003).

There are other barriers to computer and Internet use among older adults that are less cohort-specific. First, the stereotypes and attitudes described in the previous section undoubtedly reduce computer use. Also, a lot of older people who don't use computers have security or safety concerns (Eastman & Iyer, 2004), which have been magnified by the considerable attention paid to identity theft in recent years.

There are also issues with computer and **interface** design (**usability**). The mouse is central to much computer use, and using a mouse requires a certain degree of dexterity. For older people with arthritis, mouse use can be difficult, and perhaps painful, and "double-clicking" can be a particular problem for some older users (Czaja & Lee, 2003; Namazi & McClintic, 2003). Older adults who wear bifocal glasses also experience unique problems with computer use, because they have to hold their head up in order to "look down" at the screen. This can cause neck and back pain. Finally, many of the fonts and color choices of World Wide Web pages make life more difficult for older users. Small fonts and colors that do not contrast (e.g., yellow font on a pale blue background) make life very difficult for people with even minor visual impairments. The cursor is also hard to see for some older adults. A list of recommendations for accessible Web site design is available at http://www.nlm.nih.gov/pubs/check list.pdf.

Exercise 12.2	Web Site Design for Seniors

Visit: http://nihseniorhealth.gov/

This site was developed specifically using government guidelines for appropriate design for older adults. Find six elements of the site that you feel make it more accessible to older people. What would the effect of these elements be for individuals who are not suffering vision loss or other problems? Did any of the intended functions of the site not actually work for you? Can you imagine any problems that an older person might have using the site?

After you have visited the site and used it, read the Morrell, Dailey, and Rousseau (2003) chapter (cited below). They describe some of the design elements used by the site and the process of creating it, as well as a research study of how the site was evaluated. Re-visit the Web site and try to spot some of the elements mentioned in the chapter. Can you identify any further improvements to the Web site that may have occurred since the chapter was written?

SOURCE: Morrell, R. W., Dailey, S. R., & Rousseau, G. K. (2003). Applying research: The NIHSeniorHealth.gov project. In. N. Charness & K. W. Schaie (Eds.), *Impact of technology on successful aging* (pp. 134–161). New York: Springer.

Most of the problems experienced by older people reflect more broadly on sensible computer and interface design (**usability**: Laux, 2001; Rogers & Fisk, 2003). It is not just older people who have difficulties with some of the color choices made by amateur Web site designers! In fact, the problems that younger and older people have with a variety of technologies tend to be remarkably similar (Rogers & Fisk, 2003).

A final barrier for some older people is that they simply are not interested, or do not see the benefit in using computers. For many older people, if they want information they would rather go to the library. The library not only provides the information, but may also be a place where social networks are built and reinforced. A lack of computer use among seniors can, thus, be seen simply as a choice. Selwyn et al. (2003) point out that mobile phones have been adopted by older people in huge numbers and are very popular. When the technology is useful and fills a need, older people adopt it; when it doesn't, they don't. See Table 12.1 for a summary of barriers to older adults' computer and Internet use, as well as a description of some of the benefits.

Table 12.1   Benefits and Barriers to Older Adults' Computer and Internet Use

Benefits	Barriers
Immediate access to information, particularly health information	Technophobia (fear of computers and technology)
Access to goods and services from home (e.g., shopping, banking, access to public records)	Ageist stereotypes and attitudes (e.g., a feeling that older people can't, or shouldn't, deal with computers; messages from others saying so)
Family connections (e.g., ability to communicate with distant family members for little cost)	Poor support (e.g., instruction that is too fast or too slow; tech support unavailable)
Other social connections (e.g., participation in online discussions, including about aging issues)	Cost
	Churn (a fear that a computer, once bought, is immediately obsolete; constant updating of software needed)
Feeling "in touch" with contemporary society	Limited history with computers
Opportunities for distance learning	Poor interface design (e.g., bad color choices on Web pages, small fonts, mouse not suited for people with arthritis)
	Lack of interest/perceived benefits
	Security and safety concerns (e.g., identity theft, spyware, viruses)

Increasing Use

We are currently seeing substantial growth in older people's computer and Internet use. A recent report from the Pew Internet and American Life Project (2004) indicates a 47% jump in the number of seniors going online between 2000 and 2004. So while older people are among the least likely to use the Internet, they are also among the fastest growing groups of new users (Eastman & Iyer, 2004). Seniors who *are* online are actually among the most enthusiastic users, logging on more often than their younger peers (Pew, 2001). If you look back at Figure 12.1, you'll notice that there is very substantial growth in older people's use of computers and the Internet even in the relatively brief two-year span between 2001 and 2003. For instance, the percentage of older people with Internet access at home rises from 28.2 to 34.4%.

Equally important, over 60% of adults aged 50–58 have Internet access and use it regularly (Pew, 2004). It is unlikely that these people will suddenly give up using computers when they turn 65; hence substantial growth in the numbers of seniors online is inevitable. Unfortunately, seniors mirror the rest of the online population in that users tend to be more male than female, more white than minority, and more wealthy than poor. It appears that the digital divide discriminates equally across age groups.

Encouraging older adults to use computers and the Internet involves addressing a number of challenges. First, some of the "interface" barriers described above need to be addressed. Some of the technology needs to change to be more friendly to people with disabilities and normal age-related changes (e.g., a loss in visual acuity), while existing devices such as screen magnifiers need to be made more accessible and easy to use. This can often be achieved with usability studies: Observing people actually using technology and seeing where they experience problems helps improve individuals' technological skills; but such studies also tell you a lot about where the *tech nology* could be improved (Rogers & Fisk, 2003).

Older adults also simply need to be encouraged and trained to use computers. Repeated research has shown that trying a technology results in more positive attitudes toward it, and more use of it (Czaja & Sharit, 1998b). Even in challenging environments like long-term care settings for frail older people, training sessions on computer use result in excitement about the possibilities of the new technology (White et al., 2002). That said, the one constant in studies that train older adults in computer use appears to be **variation** in responses. Some participants end up as "silver surfers" (Cody, Dunn, Hoppin, & Wendt, 1999) who demonstrate great competence and notable skills. Others drop out rather quickly and appear uninterested (Namazi & McClintic, 2003). Some evidence suggests that this reflects a fairly stable orientation through life—people who embraced technology when young will continue to do so when they are older, and likewise for those who rejected technology when young (Wahl & Mollenkopf, 2003).

Other forms of new technology are also accessible to older people given the appropriate training. Sterns (2005) describes a program training older people to use a personal digital assistant (**PDA**: a handheld computer like a Palm Pilot). All of the older respondents managed to use the PDAs in some fashion, and a good number of them achieved mastery over the devices. The PDAs were programmed to do things like give people reminders about taking medication, so this research is offering some very practical uses of technology for older adults. Of course, such programming could also serve non-medical functions, reminding older people of their golf tee times, their yoga class, or to pick up their grandchildren from school.

A number of considerations are important when examining the quality of training given to older technology users. First, the pacing of the education is crucial. Individuals who feel totally out of their depth, or totally unchallenged, will probably not stick with the program, while those who feel challenged but are still able to achieve mastery will persevere (Cody et al., 1999). Second, older people prefer "hands on" and procedural (step-by-step) type training rather than "conceptual" training (Czaja and Lee, 2001). So if you were teaching an older person to use eBay, you might find something that they actually wanted to buy and direct them through the bidding and purchasing process on the computer. This would work better than printing out information and instructions on using eBay and telling the person to go home and read it. Third, quality training caters to people's *strengths* (e.g., life experience, verbal knowledge) and doesn't excessively strain areas of vulnerability (e.g., *speed* of cognitive processing). Fourth, good training incorporates assessment of basic skills that might be taken for granted. For instance, many older people will struggle if computer instruction assumes knowledge of how to use the mouse. Trainers should assess older adults' basic skills in mouse use, drag and drop, menu organization, etc., before beginning more specific training (Czaja & Lee, 2003).

There may be an important role for gerontology theory in understanding how and when older people adopt technology. For instance, remember the **selective optimization with compensation** model from Chapter 1. This is the model stating that people focus on some areas of their lives in which they can reap important rewards, while seeking help in areas where they need it, and abandoning areas of lesser importance. Technology can often provide tremendous compensation for losses experienced by older people. For instance, L. L. Liu and Park (2003) describe a situation in which an older woman (Mrs. X) was suffering vision loss that impaired her ability to drive. The woman's daughter purchased a cell phone for Mrs. X and programmed it with the number of a local cab company (as well as other numbers). Mrs. X learned to dial numbers on the cell phone by touch alone. The cab company agreed to keep a running tab of Mrs. X's trips. As a result, Mrs. X had easy access to transportation at any time. As technologies like voice recognition become more widespread, such compensatory functions of new technology will become even more powerful (L. L. Liu & Park, 2003).

What Do Older People *Do* on the Internet?

While the above discussion could apply to numerous technologies, I'll now focus particularly on the Internet. Currently, the Internet appears to present the most opportunities and interest with regard to new communication technologies, and it is an area where there is quite a bit of research concerning older adults. "Wired" seniors are as enthusiastic about the Internet and its various uses as younger users (Pew, 2004). The vast majority of seniors who are online use e-mail regularly and see this as the principal benefit of being online (Hilt & Lipschultz, 2004). For many, the Internet provides the opportunity for regular contact with friends and family that would otherwise be difficult. For instance, Climo (2001) describes the experience of family members living in different countries, who use e-mail to stay in touch. International phone calls can be prohibitively expensive, and time differences often make it difficult to talk on a regular basis. E-mail messages, in contrast, are virtually unconstrained by time differences or cost-per-message. Work by Holladay and Seipke (2003) has investigated e-mail contact specifically between grandparents and grandchildren. This research showed that grandparents and grandchildren are using e-mail very frequently—as frequently as the telephone and more frequently than face-to-face communication. However, e-mail communication didn't seem to contribute to positive feelings about the relationship as strongly as telephone or face-to-face communication in the research.

The benefits of maintaining social networks using technology should be relatively clear. One study provides at least suggestive evidence that training older people to use computers has positive consequences for things like loneliness (White et al., 2002; see also McConatha, McConatha, Deaner, & Dermigny, 1995; McMellon & Schiffman, 2002). Social interaction can also be achieved through participation in online "chat" or discussion sites, where older adults often find companionship (Wright, 2000). Indeed, in some cases, the computer itself can be seen as a type of social actor (Nass & Steuer, 1993). Blit-Cohen and Litwin (2004) describe how the computer may serve a symbolic function for some older adults. It is representative of a connection to a broader society, and to modern life, and hence gains importance over and above the specific activities that it is used for. The computer may even become like a relational partner—one of Blit-Cohen and Litwin's respondents commented: "I am having an affair with my computer . . . The computer pays attention to me . . . The computer says to me: Look at me!"

On a somewhat more mundane level, older adults also use the Internet for finding **medical information** (Eastman & Iyer, 2004; Kaiser Family Foundation, 2005). There are obviously concerns with some of the health-related information that is available online (Eysenbach, Powell, Kuss, & Sa, 2002; Pew, 2006), and therefore future research should examine older adults' abilities to critically examine such information. Nevertheless, plenty of extremely accurate and useful information is available through reputable sites (e.g., www.nihseniorhealth.gov; www.mayoclinic.com). Older people are also starting to get valuable health information from their doctors using new technology. **Telemedicine** programs have been growing in recent years. Telemedicine is the process of providing health care at a distance using electronic communication. Increasingly, the Internet is the medium for telemedicine, permitting patient interviews, testing, and diagnosis from a distance. Such techniques are very valuable when people live in inaccessible areas, or require regular monitoring (Whitten & Gregg, 2001).

Older people also use the Internet for doing product research, making travel reservations, finding government service information, tracking investments, dating, and purchasing products, although not in as large numbers as younger people. Most older people who use the Internet report informational purposes as very important, which parallels what was discussed about their use of television in Chapter 9. Smaller numbers of older people use the Internet for more recent innovations like online banking, but those uses are growing very rapidly. Given the large discretionary income commanded by older people, it seems likely that smart online businesses will start marketing and catering to this group in the near future (Eastman & Iyer, 2004). However, as noted in Chapter 8, this hasn't really happened in other media areas; it will be interesting to see if Internet marketers are any smarter!

Identity Functions of Internet Use

A key area of interest for communication and aging scholars is the way in which the Internet is used by seniors for identity functions. In one study, I looked at some features of personal Web sites created by older adults, with a particular focus on sites created by grandparents (Harwood, 2004). In those sites, I found a number of different identities being presented by the older people:

- Their **role as grandparents:** *Being* a grandparent is an important role in a family (see Chapter 6), and it's possible to mark this identity through online communication. One of my favorite ways in which this was demonstrated was when the grandparents referred to *themselves* as "grandma" or "grandpa" (e.g., "Grandma made this webpage just for you!"). If the grandchildren are beyond early childhood then some of these comments could be seen as having a slightly patronizing tone. However, they illustrate very clearly the ways in which grandparents are proud of their role and want to emphasize it.

- Their identification with other grandparents: Being a grandparent also brings with it numerous shared experiences, and hence a sense of identification with other grandparents. Comments on the Web pages sometimes began, "As all grandparents know . . . ," which emphasizes some of the commonality between grandparents. A couple of the sites even featured more explicit ways in which grandparents might act as a collective, for instance by advocating for visitation rights to their grandchildren (see also Holladay & Coombs, 2001).

- Their family identification: A number of the Web sites referenced family connections. References such as "he has his mother's looks" make clear the lineage within the family and the explicit connections between the individuals (e.g., by noting which of the grandchild's parents was the child of this grandparent). Sometimes the web of family relationship descriptions became quite convoluted as the same individual was referred to as "Bob's son" and "Margie's cousin" and "Jan's grandson," but again such referencing probably serves to reinforce the more general idea that "we are all connected."

- Their age identification: While references to age were not very common on these Web sites, those that did emerge were interesting. Most notably, individuals who were particularly *young* grandparents made note of this fact (e.g., "people are surprised that I'm a grandparent"). And one person explicitly addressed the ways in which being a grandparent invokes stereotypes of old age:

Gray hair and knitting in a rocking chair come to mind, and a certain complex societal demotion takes place; grandmothers are thought to lack worldliness and sex appeal, to have lost their snap and creativity, to no longer be major players. But isn't it the stereotyping about grandmas that's really passé? (Harwood, 2004, p. 311)

Thus, these grandparent Web sites illustrate some of the different ways in which older people are representing their family and relationship roles using new technology. Perhaps most important is the fact that these older adults were creating their own Web sites, something that flies in the face of many of our stereotypes of older people and technology.

Work by Lin, Hummert, and Harwood (2004) has examined a different context in which older adults explore their *age* identities online. Their work has examined older adults in online "successful aging" chat rooms, looking at the ways in which they represent their age and health. The older people in these chat rooms talked about taking a "mind over body" attitude toward aging, and emphasized their wisdom and maturity relative to their earlier years. One person wrote: "I carry the same heavy baggage, but I set it down quietly, and wait for a better moment" (p. 268). Others, however, adopted a somewhat more jaded view of old age: "Every time I hear that phrase 'Golden Age' I want to puke!" Interestingly, these older people's communication made extensive use of links between aging and health. The positive themes often related to "beating" age and staying healthy, while the negative themes concerned succumbing to age. As a result, both the positive and negative comments can be seen as generally reinforcing the idea that age is inevitably associated with health. This fits with forms of offline communication described earlier in the book—you may remember N. Coupland's "disjunctive" and "accounting" functions of age disclosure from Chapter 4.

Kanayama (2003) described some similar research on a Japanese senior chat group. Kanayama focused particularly on disclosures by the older participants, who develop a sense of community via sharing of childhood experiences and other personal information. This research provides some indications of older adults wanting to "colonize" the Web. By communicating online, these people expressed a desire to recapture the space from its current status as a youth-dominated sphere. One participant wrote:

> The Internet world is a youth-oriented culture. Most languages, expressions, and representations online are created for/by young people. The more senior adults use email and go online, the greater variety of languages and expressions online we have. It will be culturally richer and better. (Kanayama, 2003, p. 283)

So, while older adults are doing many of the things that all of us do online (looking for information, managing personal finances), they are also exploring their identities as older people, expressing and maintaining their important family roles, and examining their shared experiences with other seniors. These functions are likely to motivate more seniors to go online. Opportunities for social interaction and for sharing the experience of being older will be important for older people keen to understand who they are and where they stand in society. These processes are also likely to be central to new waves of research on older adults' behavior online. Once we stop asking questions about how *many* seniors are online, then we can start asking more sophisticated questions about what older people are doing once they get there.

Technology and the Workplace

Along with the personal use of technologies like the Internet, it is also important to consider professional uses of technology, particularly in the workplace. Given the stereotypes described earlier, it is reasonable to ask how older adults deal with technology in the work environment. Most of the relevant academic literature has focused on older adults' ability to learn new computer-based tasks (Czaja, 2001). In general, these studies indicate that older adults are slower at performing new tasks after the same amount of training as younger people. Most studies find that older people make similar numbers of errors as younger people do on these tasks. Research on how older people perform with "real" computer-based tasks in the workplace is less common, and the results less clear. One message, though, is that older people are generally pretty good at developing strategies for dealing with decline by compensating in creative ways. For instance, Czaja notes the ways in which older adults rely on their experience in real workplace tasks, applying unique knowledge in order to accomplish tasks effectively. Similarly, working slower but emphasizing accuracy is an important compensation device.

It is important to be aware that the focus of much of the research in this area is on **speed**—an area in which older adults often do not excel. Very few studies demonstrate age-based differences in **accuracy** of task performance, with those that do finding less differentiation between young and old (Czaja & Sharit, 1998a). Very little research has examined areas in which older adults might outperform younger workers—integration of decisions with past practice, incorporation of wisdom and experience into tasks, considering multiple points of view, clarity of written expression, and the like.

It's also important to mention that the kinds of computer interfaces used in this research are interfaces designed by younger people, and not necessarily designed with older users in mind. There are features of interface design that would enhance older adults' ability to deal with technology efficiently (e.g., the ability to increase font size, color contrasts designed for maximal visual discrimination). No studies have compared older and younger performance on an interface designed for the older user. Finally, as with much work on age differences, many of the differences emerging from this work are pretty small (Waldman & Avolio, 1986). Older adults are a tad slower at performing certain types of computer-based tasks, but the implications of this for actual performance in a real workplace are not very substantial. Frankly, it is rare that any of us work at our full capacity and maximum speed for very long, and so studies revealing that the maximum performance for older people is slightly slower than that for younger people don't necessarily reflect on actual productivity in the workplace. The real question is whether older workers take significantly longer to accomplish real tasks in a real work environment, and the jury is still out on that question.

ACHIEVEMENTS IN OLD AGE

I. M. Pei

SOURCE: © Jason Pratt, Pittsburgh, PA

Architect I. M. Pei was born in China in 1917. During a distinguished career he has designed a large number of very significant buildings, including the Louvre pyramid in Paris, the Bank of China Tower in Hong Kong, the John Hancock tower in Boston, and the East Building of the National Gallery of Art in Washington, DC. In 1995, Pei received acclaim for his design for the Rock and Roll Hall of Fame in Cleveland, Ohio (see picture). The museum opened when Pei was 78 years old, and his architectural design work has continued into his 80s. He received the Pritzker Prize (architecture's most prestigious award) in 1983, with the citation noting that he "has given this century some of its most beautiful interior spaces and exterior forms."

Summary

It is worth revisiting some comments from earlier in the book about variability among older people. There are older adults who are true Luddites—they have little interest in technology, and even when given training they quickly drop out. Then there are older people who embrace all forms of technology and learn to use them quickly and effectively. And there are older people who fall in every place in between those two extremes. All older people, however, are increasingly required to deal with technology. This chapter has shown that many older adults can deal effectively with technology given the appropriate training and effective interface design. However, a digital divide still exists such that older people are at the back end of the computer revolution. This is due to some cohort effects but also to some aspects of current computer design that create barriers for older people. Nevertheless, as the chapter shows, older adults are using computers in growing numbers. They are not only shopping and looking for information online but also communicating with one another about aging issues. In the workplace, older adults are successfully adopting computers. As noted, some studies show that older adults are a little slower to learn and slower in using new technologies in the workplace, but they are often more accurate once they have mastered the technology.

Future technology designers should pay more attention to the needs of older people and design technologies that allow more universal access, even for individuals with visual impairments or arthritis. Typically, things that are easier to read for people with visual impairments are also easier to read for everyone else. There are many other aging and technology issues that you might want to explore. For some older people, assistive technologies are very important (the most basic being a hearing aid). You could explore the role of assistive technologies in older people's lives, and whether there are differences between assistive technologies for older adults and other people (e.g., are hearing aids for older people with hearing problems any different from hearing aids for younger people with hearing problems). The study of technology in older adulthood has a name (**gerotechnology:** Gutman, 2003) and it is likely to be a growth area in the next few years. Additional online resources related to this topic are listed in Box 12.1.

Box 12.1   Online Resources With Information About Older Adults'
                 Computer and Internet Use

www.seniornet.org
www.pewinternet.org
www.aarp.org/learntech/computers/
www.nlm.nih.gov/pubs/checklist.pdf
www.generationsonline.com/
www.agingtech.org
http://www.aarp.org/research/ageline/
http://www.npr.org/templates/story/story.php?storyId=5443317
The last link is a radio news story about using technology as a surveillance
mechanism for older people. You may want to listen to the story, and then
think about the implications of technology in this instance for elder care,
privacy, and family relationships.

Keywords and Theories

Barriers to computer use
Cohort effect
Competence vs. warmth
Digital divide
Gerotechnology
Grandparent role
Identity
Interface
Internet
Obsolescence

Patronizing speech
PDA
Selective optimization
   with compensation
Speed vs. accuracy
Stereotypes of technology use
Stereotype threat
Telemedicine
Usability
Variation in response to training

Discussion Questions

- Why do we think older adults can't use technology? Where do you think this stereo-
  type comes from?
- What are some ways in which older people build community with one another online?
  How are these distinct from or similar to their offline communication?
- How might technology influence older adults' health and health care in the coming
  years?
- Is the Internet a space primarily for young people?

- What kinds of new technology do you anticipate being important for older adults 20 years from now?

Annotated Bibliography

Charness, N., & Schaie, K. W. (Eds.). (2003). *Impact of technology on successful aging.* New York: Springer. This edited book covers a huge variety of issues relating to technology's role in older people's lives. It includes coverage of assistive technologies like hearing aids, and technologies to make it possible for frail older people to live at home longer ("aging in place"). The book includes work by scholars in a very wide variety of academic disciplines. A number of the authors have extensive practical experience in working with older people and technology.

Czaja, S. J. (2001) Technological change and the older worker. In J. E. Birren & K. W. Schaie (Eds.), *Handbook of the psychology of aging* (5th ed., pp. 547–569). San Diego: Academic Press. Focusing particularly on the business context, this chapter provides a nice review of the research on older adults' employment patterns, work performance, and ability to deal with new technologies. The chapter balances nicely between coverage of skills deficits in old age and a broader perspective on the origin and size of those deficits.

Pew Internet and American Life Project. (2001). *Wired seniors: A fervent few inspired by family ties.* Retrieved May 10, 2006, from http://www.pewinternet.org/reports.asp A seminal research report concerning older adults' use of the Internet. In 2001, the results were quite shocking for people who thought that older adults never go near a computer. Even today, some of the findings take people by surprise!

PART V

Conclusion

⊰ THIRTEEN ⊱

Conclusion

This final chapter returns to some of the themes presented earlier in the book. It provides a schematic model that includes individual and societal factors influencing how people understand their own aging. I take this opportunity to briefly discuss some issues that have not been addressed

SOURCE: © Istockphoto.com

earlier in the book (e.g., retirement). The chapter then presents an agenda for how individuals can address problematic aspects of communication and aging in their own lives—different ways in which we can think and communicate about older adulthood for the benefit of us all. By the end of this chapter you should be able to:

- Distinguish between individual (micro) and societal (macro) communication factors that influence how we perceive our age
- Discuss age segregation
- Describe some factors influencing retirement trends
- Discuss how individuals can challenge ageism in their lives
- Discuss connections between individual and societal processes in maintaining ageism—how might individual actions challenge broader social structures?

*I'm 74, and I ski, swim and stand on my head in yoga, and I'm
frustrated by society's attitude of putting the word 'still' in front
of these activities.*

—De Vee Lange of San Diego, CA, quoted
in *Parade Magazine* (March 19, 2006)

N ow that you're approaching the end of this book, take a couple of minutes to do Exercise 13.1. It's the same thing you did in Chapter 1 (but don't look back at Chapter 1 until you're done this time around). In comparing your two responses, think about how you felt when you first did the exercise and how you feel at this point. It's my hope that you have developed a more detailed picture of your own aging, that perhaps your expectations are a little more positive, and that you see *options* for your older adulthood that you weren't aware of before. The goal of this final chapter is to return to a broad picture of how we understand our own aging and our position in the life span from a communication perspective, and then to discuss some concrete ways in which you can make a difference to how we all experience getting old.

A Model of Aging in Individual and Societal Context

Figure 13.1 provides one way to think about the material that's been covered in the previous chapters by outlining three key factors that contribute to how we understand our own age and aging. The model distinguishes **chronological age** from **individual (micro) level** and **societal (macro) level** factors. The goal of the model is to illustrate how our actual age, our individual experiences, and the society we live in all work together to shape how we think about age.

Chronological Age

The top of the figure indicates chronological age. Here is the undeniable, irreversible, and inevitable progression of getting older. This is aging in the sense

| Exercise 13.1 | Perceptions and Expectations of My Own Aging |

Birth ——————————————————▶ Death

1. Draw a line (like a temperature chart) across the page to depict the peaks and troughs that you have experienced and that you expect to experience in your life.

2. Use vertical lines to divide your lifeline up into important life periods, with as many or as few stages as you like.

3. Give each stage a name and indicate the approximate age at which it starts and ends.

4. Above each stage mark ++, +, 0, –, or – –, depending upon how you feel about that stage.

5. Answer the following questions:
   - What is the shape of the line, and what does that tell you about your experiences and expectations? What does a peak indicate? Happiness? Wealth? Control over your life?
   - Are the peaks and troughs major or minor?
   - Is there more volatility (ups and downs) during certain periods of the life span?
   - How could you decrease the troughs, increase the peaks? What changes could you have made in the past (or might you make in the future) to make life better?
   - Might some positive results have emerged from the troughs, or negative results from the peaks?
   - Where are the divisions closest together? Further apart?
   - What are the important events/issues marking boundaries between stages?
   - Why did transitions occur at the time that they did? Are these transitions that lots of other people might experience at about the same time, or are they unique to you?

6. Revisit your responses to this exercise in Chapter 1. What has changed? What has stayed the same?

7. If you are working as a class, consider sharing your (anonymous) responses and discussing some of the differences between your individual responses, as well as whether any of the changes you've experienced since Chapter 1 also occurred in other people's drawings.

SOURCE: This exercise is derived from Whitbourne and Dannefer (1985) and Harwood and Giles (1994).

Figure 13.1   Aging in Individual and Societal Context

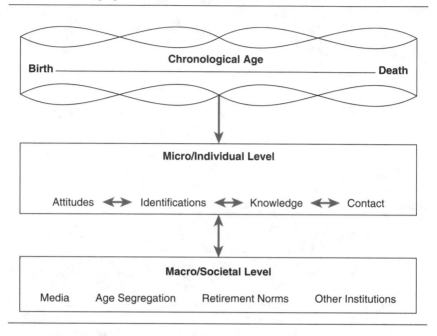

of having a birthday each year, and not being able to purchase a time machine. As has been discussed throughout this book, aging means many other things to us as individuals and as a society, but to talk about aging we have to first return to the very basic point that chronological aging is continuous, normal, and inevitable. The undulating lines represent the **variation** that is apparent in people at all ages: At any point in the life span, there are individuals who are thriving and individuals who are struggling. The undulating lines also illustrate the fact that characteristics and competencies change with age in positive *and* negative ways—as one area is improving (e.g., vocabulary), another may be declining (e.g., short-term memory). In other words, those lines are meant to remind you of the dynamic nature of development at all points in the life span.

Societal Forces

The bottom of the figure indicates the influence that societal/cultural forces play. We are all influenced by our societies in terms of how we think and feel about everything, and that includes our own aging. The **mass media** are an important part of North American and European culture, and so Chapters 7 and 8 were devoted to those as key societal *communication* forces. Media representations of aging and intergenerational relations clearly influence how we think and feel about getting old. The media also profoundly shape the experience of getting older. An older person who watches 5 hours of television in a day might be spending more time with the TV than with friends or family. For that person, media messages not only affect attitudes and beliefs. The television may also be the most important force structuring daily activities. If *Power Lunch* is on CNBC, then it must be time to make a sandwich!

Other macro-societal factors not discussed earlier in the book are also important, and some of these are mentioned in Figure 13.1. **Age segregation** practices keep the generations apart and allow for misconceptions to develop. Numerous institutions in society work explicitly or implicitly to keep the generations apart. Nursing homes, retirement communities, schools, colleges, some athletic leagues, and senior centers are just a few examples of segregating forces. Table 13.1 shows that people have very little intergenerational contact outside of the family. For young and old alike, fewer than 10% of key social contacts outside the family are with people from a substantially different age group. (As noted in Chapter 6, the family is one of the few sources for regular intergenerational contact for many people, something that Table 13.1 reinforces.) The fact that age groups are so often segregated by broad structural factors reduces the opportunity to learn about aging directly from older people. Merton and Kitt (1950) first used the phrase **anticipatory socialization** to describe the idea of getting information about an upcoming role before you actually take on that role. If you had older siblings, you probably learned something about being in high school from them: That's anticipatory socialization. The same kind of socialization occurs with bigger life phases— as we approach old age, we want to learn more about what it's like to be older. The less contact we have with older generations, the less anticipatory socialization we get concerning life stages we are yet to experience, and hence we are less well equipped to deal with those life stages when we reach them.

Retirement is also a macro-level phenomenon that needs to be considered here. Retirement practices influence older adults' experiences of aging and the scope and nature of contact between younger and older people in the workplace. The 1980s and 1990s saw substantial changes in retirement

Table 13.1   Age Segregation in Family and Non-Family Relationships

Respondent's age	Partner's age			
	Non-kin		Kin (excl. spouses)	
	< 36	> 53	< 36	> 53
19–30 years	83%	3%	32%	28%
61+ years	6%	72%	24%	42%

SOURCE: From "The Social Separation of Old and Young: A Root of Ageism," by G. O. Hagestad and P. Uhlenberg, 2005, *Journal of Social Issues, 61,* 343–360. Data were derived from the 1985 General Social Survey.

NOTE: Numbers represent "age distribution of 'core discussion partners' by respondent's age group."

Figure 13.2   Age Segregation Occurs in Many Ways

practices. Fewer older adults were retiring permanently at age 65, and more were retiring early (Czaja, 2006). In the past few years, however, the trend toward early retirement has shifted. People are retiring later, and people who call themselves "retired" are continuing to work in various capacities—they retired from their lifetime career, but are continuing with less intense part-time work, self-employment, consulting, or seasonal work. In some cases, older adults cannot afford to retire at age 55. **Life expectancy** is creeping into the 80s, and **health care costs** are increasing, so it is very difficult to retire at 55 and retain a high quality of life for perhaps 30 or more years (Korczyk, 2004). In addition, older people are recognizing that they value the social and intellectual stimulation of work. Further, employers are encouraging older workers to stay at work because of a feared **labor short-age** when the baby boomers retire in large numbers. Employers also recognize the unique skills and experience that older workers have. Hence, some people are deciding to work longer, and some early retirees are returning to the workforce (Korczyk, 2004). These changes have implications for how we view retirement and how we understand older people's roles in organizations. They will also lead to changes in the social environment of the workplace and the prospects for intergenerational contact at work. Of course, changes in retirement also have implications for relationships at home—if you're at work, you're not at home! See the June 12, 2006, issue of *U.S. News and World Report* magazine for a number of stories on current retirement trends (the cover story is "Seven Reasons NOT to Retire"). There are fascinating *communication* issues associated with retirement that remain relatively unstudied (Bernard & Phillipson, 2004). For example, we don't know much about how retirement programs are marketed to workers, or the effects of how saving plans are framed. When I get a statement of my retirement savings, it includes estimates of my income when I'm 65 (Social Security benefits statements do the same thing). It's interesting to hypothesize how this framing might influence behavior: "Gee, for all these years I've been putting into my retirement account based on retiring at age 65, now I'm 65 so I guess I should retire!" There are also interesting ways in which terms like "retirees" (or "pensioners") are used as a substitute for "older adults." As discussed in Chapter 5, retirement can also bring relocation (e.g., to a retirement community or "home"), which has huge implications for more micro-level interpersonal communication phenomena (A. Williams & Guendouzi, 2000).

The model also indicates that other institutions might be important. Preachers, rabbis, or imams might be the authorities who establish local views of aging among some groups. Social institutions such as pubs, theaters, community festivals, or luaus might be the key places where knowledge and beliefs about aging are shared and reinforced among other groups.

Micro Factors

The middle of Figure 13.1 represents some of the individual (micro) factors that bear on our perceived life-position. The phenomena in the previous section were big societal-level stuff; this portion of the model is devoted to small stuff happening between or within individuals. As described extensively in Chapters 3–6, our **attitudes** and expectations about aging will influence our understanding of our age. If you don't like old people, then as you age you may begin to experience uncertainty or despair about where you are in the life span. If I expect to be sick in old age, then my understanding of illness in my later years will differ from someone expecting a vibrant and healthy old age. Age **identifications** will also influence this process— if you love being a teenager, then as you enter your 20s you may feel disoriented and unwilling to adopt the new responsibilities and factors that come into play at that age. Alternatively, you may continue to view yourself as a teenager (which could at times be problematic!). **Knowledge** of aging will also be influential. If you are aware that less than 5% of over-65s live in nursing homes, then you will probably not expect to end up in an institution. If you don't have that knowledge, you're left to rely on guesswork or what your cultural environment is telling you. Finally, of course, **intergenerational contact** is crucial. We learn through personal experience, and sometimes our personal experience with people of other age groups tells us something about what it's like to be that age. Hence, I spent quite a lot of time in Chapter 7 discussing how our understanding of the life span is shaped by intergenerational relations, both within and outside of the family (e.g., contact theory). Of course, intergenerational contact is, again, a fundamentally *communicative* process.

Overall, then, Figure 13.1 indicates that chronological age and macro-societal forces influence our individual behaviors, thoughts, and feelings about our own position in the life span. It also points out that individual-level phenomena can influence macro-level phenomena (note that the arrow in the bottom portion of the model is bidirectional). For example, individuals who all identify strongly with their group may work together to make changes at a broader societal level—search the Web for references to the "raging grannies" for an example of such a group. In addition to summarizing some important themes from earlier in the book, Figure 13.1 also provides a communication structure for addressing *change* in how we consider aging. What can we do to decrease ageism in society, including our own ageism? In the next section, I describe how the model can be applied in making positive changes in the aging experience for all of us.

What Can You Do Now?

Cultural Change

At the cultural level, there are some obvious messages that we receive from the media and other social institutions about age. We have choices about how we receive and respond to such messages. No matter how entertaining they may be on the surface, we can boycott birthday cards that send negative messages about aging. The next time you see a card that tells someone that they're "over the hill," or that teases them because they're decaying, leave it on the shelf. While the card might be quite entertaining, it probably does not provide a positive message for you or the person to whom you're sending it. More important, buying the card just encourages Hallmark to make more in the same vein. When you see TV shows or commercials that make fun of older people, change the channel or don't buy the product. We all need to make more careful decisions concerning what messages about age are acceptable. In the same way that we turn away from racist or sexist images and messages, we need to turn away from ageism.

Advertisements for **cosmetics** are particularly powerful in reinforcing negative images of aging, and encouraging fear of aging. It is unlikely that everyone will be able to resist the latest anti-wrinkle cream or potion, but the fewer people that buy them, the more likely it is that they will disappear. This is not merely about appreciating people's "inner beauty." It is also about coming to realize that outer beauty is possible with a few wrinkles. Those wrinkles might even add a little character that makes you more attractive. The effect of age on physical attractiveness has traditionally been a women's

issue—most cosmetics (and cosmetic surgeries) are targeted at and con-
sumed by women. Men have benefited from the impression of "maturity"
that wrinkles grant them for many years. However, as a society we are still
unwilling to grant that same recognition to women. Indeed, men are increasingly targeted for cosmetics, with messages being sent that their sexuality
and attractiveness will be compromised by signs of age. For example, a
recent ad for a L'Oreal moisturizer aimed at men says, "Pick-up lines are one
thing. Age lines are another." The messages that accompany many cosmetics
are diagnostic of the degree to which we desire to conceal and deny our own
aging—many of you probably own products similar to those pictured in
Figure 13.3. Men are also openly using **cosmetic surgery** and products such
as botox. "Voice lifts" are also gaining popularity—these are surgeries to
make the *voice* sound younger. Full respect and acknowledgment of old age
will only occur when we stop trying to conceal it, and that involves making
individual decisions about personal appearance. If nothing else, choosing to
purchase the product that is advertised in a non-ageist fashion would send a
message to manufacturers and advertisers that the anti-aging message is the
wrong one.

Changing culture is not something that happens quickly or easily, and
one individual's actions are unlikely to have an effect. However, social change
has to begin somewhere. Perhaps if you are reading this book as part of a large
class, you could consider a boycott of a specific product or service that is marketed based on pejorative stereotypes of older adults. That sort of group effort
might get some publicity—tell your student newspaper what you're doing
and why!

Individual Change

The center of the model presents options for individual action. In communication with older people, we can all work harder to gauge our partners'
individual characteristics and competencies, and to shape our communication based on those individual features—remember the communication
enhancement model from Chapter 7? If you are changing the way you talk
based on an older person's disability (e.g., talking louder, talking slower),
ask yourself whether you're sure that the person really has a disability! If
you feel that there is a topic that you cannot talk about with an older person,

Figure 13.3   Cosmetics Products Are Often Marketed on the Basis That They
Somehow Conceal or Reverse the Signs of Aging

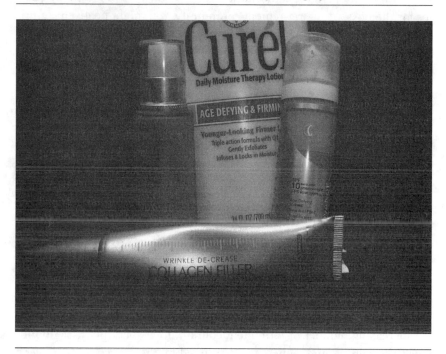

consider the worst that could happen if you brought it up—are you reluctant to talk about the topic because of a stereotype of older people? This is
not just advice for younger people—as was discussed earlier in the book,
older people quite often stereotype other older adults, and even themselves.
Therefore, it is important for people of all ages to become more aware of
how their stereotyped expectations might be influencing their talk in negative ways.

Of course, in our culture it can be a challenge for people to have
any intergenerational contact at all due to the age segregation mentioned
earlier in the chapter. However, as an individual, you can seek out ways to
challenge that. If you are a younger person considering an internship or
selecting a career, think about settings in which older adults are present.

Consider an internship at a local retirement community rather than the local radio station. At the radio station you'll be lucky if you're making coffee for the boss. At the retirement community, you might be given significant responsibility, and you'll certainly gain by the social interaction. Older adults can also challenge age segregation by involving themselves in new contexts. A class at a local community college will provide more cross-generational contact than a class at the local senior center. Indeed, continuing education for older people is a crucial aspect of successful aging. Seniors who continue learning in the formal as well as the informal sense tend to do better on numerous measures of well-being (Glendenning, 2004). More broadly, a society with an educated and actively learning older population is simply a healthier place in which to live. The potential contributions of older people to our society are enhanced by continuing education into older adulthood (Glendenning, 2004)—perhaps this group can even act as society's conscience and defenders of our civil liberties (Tallis, 2006). Of course, a mandate for encouraging older adults to enter the classroom carries with it a mandate for instructors to teach in ways that are inclusive of this population (Baringer, Kundrat, & Nussbaum, 2004). Evidence that older people are seeking out this environment is provided by the increasing number of retirement communities operating close to university campuses, and sometimes developed by the university (e.g., Penn State University, Indiana University, University of Florida, University of Virginia).

Box 13.1   Webliography

Chapter 12 presented a list of Web sites specifically oriented to older adults and technology issues. This webliography considers topics other than technology. It may be useful to provide a stimulus for papers, group discussions, or further research. If you want to be able to click on these links, they are all available in "clickable" form at www.u.arizona.edu/~jharwood/aging.htm

Topic/URL	Description
Demographics	
www.census.gov	U.S. Census Bureau
http://www.ac.wwu.edu/~stephan/ Animation/pyramid.html	Features cool animations of population change over time
Aging, health, and health care	
http://www.nia.nih.gov/	National Institute on Aging (research and health information)
http://www.healthandage.com/	Commercial site providing some useful information on links between age and health
http://www.azgec.arizona.edu/	Arizona Geriatrics Education Center—links to information on geriatric care
http://www.agingresearch.org/	The Alliance for Aging Research—a nonprofit that funds research on aging and health issues
http://www.azgec.arizona.edu/scripts/ ggrShowV2.asp	Features video presentations on aging and health, including one by your trusty author
http://www.alz.org/	Homepage for the Alzheimer's Association. Great information on Alzheimer's, including stages of the disease, and myths about the disease
http://www.npr.org/templates/story/ story.php?storyId=1788967	Radio news story about shortage of geriatricians
Aging and legal issues	
http://www.abanet.org/aging/	American Bar Association resources relating to aging
http://www.nsclc.org	A non-profit group focusing on legal issues related to aging
http://www.elder-law.com/	A private law firm that focuses exclusively on aging issues
Ageism	
http://www.fair.org	Search for "ageism" within the site to find commentary on media portrayals of age
http://en.wikipedia.org/wiki/Ageism	Wikipedia coverage of ageism

(Continued)

(Continued)

Topic/URL	Description
Retirement	
http://www.dontretirerewire.com	Commercial site promoting a book that argues against retirement
http://www.npr.org/templates/story/ story.php?storyId=5330348	News story about alternatives to traditional retirement
http://www.ahca.org/	National association for long-term care centers
Organizations and government agencies	
http://www.aarp.org	The AARP
http://www.aoa.gov/	The federal government's Administration on Aging
http://www.seniors.gov	The portion of the main government portal designed for seniors
http://www.graypanthers.org/	Home page for one of the more "radical" organizations fighting for older people's rights
http://www.ifa-fiv.org/en/	The International Federation on Aging is an organization with similar goals to the AARP, but on a global scale
U.S. university graduate programs specializing in aging/communication	
http://www.usc.edu/dept/gero/	University of Southern California (Gerontology)
http://www.comm.arizona.edu	University of Arizona (Communication)
http://cas.la.psu.edu/	Penn State University (Communication)
http://www.comm.ucsb.edu/	University of California, Santa Barbara (Communication)
http://www.ku.edu/~kugeron/	University of Kansas (Communication)
http://www.lsu.edu/cmst	Louisiana State University (Communication)
http://communication.gsu.edu	Georgia State University (Communication)

Topic/URL	Description
Information about careers in aging	
http://www.usc.edu/dept/gero/pages/ careersinagingPS.shtml	Information from the University of Southern California
http://www.aging.unc.edu/infocenter/ tutorials/careers.html	Information from the University of North Carolina
Miscellaneous sites of interest	
http://www.elderwisdomcircle.org/	Ask a question, have an old person answer it!
http://www.topix.net/family/elderly	Current news relating to aging issues
http://www.npr.org/templates/story/story .php?storyId=4583142	News discussion and call-in show about aging issues in general
http://www.npr.org/templates/story/story .php?storyId=1034568	Radio news story about aging in China
http://www.timegoesby.net/	A great blog addressing issues relating to aging
http://www.writeseniors.com/	A place for over 55s to find a penpal—over 55s only!
http://www.aarp.org/research/academic/	The AARP office of academic affairs: A variety of great resources for students and teachers
http://www.seniorcorps.org/	A federal government program similar to the Peace Corps, designed to involve older adults in volunteer activities in their communities

However it occurs, communication across social boundaries is often challenging and frequently enriching and stimulating. As described in Chapter 6, some of the best intergenerational contact occurs in the family, and nurturing those relationships is crucial. If you are a parent, you can work directly on encouraging positive contact between your children and their grandparents. In the context of the model, it is worth noting that individual acts of seeking out intergenerational contact serve to challenge the norms of age segregation that are common in society—hence we are now talking about ways of linking the "micro" and "macro" portions of the model.

As discussed in detail in Chapters 3 and 4, there are lots of ways in which our casual communication can reinforce negative attitudes about aging. One example here is the use of **senior moment** to explain a memory lapse (Bonnesen & Burgess, 2004). Using this phrase (whether you're young or old) is easy and perhaps funny, but serves to reinforce stereotypical and negative perceptions of aging. Similarly, think about the quotation at the start of this chapter. Saying that an older person is "*still* fit and active" rolls off the tongue very easily, and might be seen as a compliment. However, the underlying message of the "still" is that this person has beaten the odds, and that an end to his or her fitness and activity is probably not far away. We need to be more sensitive to how we use language in describing aging, and how we invoke age as a way of explaining things. Sherry Holladay has examined "memorable messages" that people receive about aging: What are the everyday "nuggets" that we receive about aging, and how do they help us make sense of the life-span development process. Holladay describes a number of interesting types of memorable message, ranging from the negative ("your mind is the first thing to go") to the positive ("growing old is an honor"). Her work draws attention to the ways in which we shape perceptions of aging with the ways in which we talk about it, some of which "stick with us" over our lives and become guiding scripts for understanding how we age. Some more potentially memorable messages about aging are provided in Exercise 13.2—see which ones you can relate to.

The top part of Figure 13.1 presents relatively few opportunities for direct action. However, it does remind us of some of the key messages of this book. The model encourages us to remember the **diversity** inherent in the older population (and indeed people at any age). On any dimension you care to pick, you will find older adults across the full range (healthy–unhealthy, funny–serious, optimistic–pessimistic, etc.). When we forget this, we begin to stereotype. Also, consider positive experiences that are unique to older adulthood. Not everyone can afford a comfortable retirement spent engaging in leisure activities and giving back to the community by volunteering; but large numbers of people can—what a deal! Older adults also have unique firsthand knowledge of events in the past, and they have an ability to understand current events in a unique fashion as a result of that. Many have a high degree of social confidence as a result of a lifetime's experience in social situations.

Exercise 13.2   Positive and Negative Themes in Messages About Aging

As a group or an individual, try to decide which particular quotation seems to capture the most positive attitude toward aging and which the most negative attitude toward aging. What is the basis for your decision? As you do this, see whether there are themes in these quotations that reflect some of the research findings you've read about in this book (or that are refuted by the research). Do any of these statements address core theories that you have learned in the book?

1. Such to me is the new image of aging: Growth in self and service for all mankind.

2. I'm not interested in age. People who tell me their age are silly. You're as old as you feel. (Elizabeth Arden)

3. We grow neither better nor worse as we get old, but more like ourselves. (Mary Lamberton Becker)

4. You may search my time worn face, You'll find a merry eye that twinkles, I am NOT an old lady, Just a little girl with wrinkles! (Edythe E. Bregnard)

5. Women are not forgiven for aging. Robert Redford's lines of distinction are my old-age wrinkles. (Jane Fonda)

6. When I was young, I was poor; when old, I became rich; but in each condition I found disappointment. When I had the faculties for enjoyment, I had not the means; when the means came, the faculties were gone.

7. I enjoy my wrinkles and regard them as badges of distinction—I've worked hard for them!

8. Once I looked into the mirror and saw my father's tired eyes look back at me; reaching to smooth a vagrant hair, Mother's wrinkled hand. Age came upon me unaware.

9. I have everything I had twenty years ago, only it's a little bit lower. (Gypsy Rose Lee)

10. Age is totally unimportant. The years are really irrelevant. It's how you cope with them.

11. There is a fountain of youth; it is your mind, your talents, the creativity you bring to your life and the lives of people you love. When you learn to tap this source, you will truly have defeated age. (Sophia Loren)

12. Being seventy is not a sin. (Golda Meir)

13. Age doesn't protect you from love. But love, to some extent, protects you from age. (Jeanne Moreau)

14. Thank God I have the "seeing eye." That is to say, as I lie in bed I can walk step by step on the fells and rough land seeing every stone and flower and patch of box and cotton pass where my old legs will never again take me. (Beatrix Potter)

15. We can go into a quiet retirement, which is the traditional stereotype of a 65-year-old, or we can take a risk and put ourselves out where the action is.

16. When men reach their sixties and retire they go to pieces. Women just go right on cooking. (Gail Sheehy)

17. So much has been said and sung of beautiful young girls, why doesn't somebody wake up to the beauty of old women? (Harriet Beecher Stowe)

18. He who would pass his declining years with honor and comfort, should, when young, consider that he might one day become old, and remember when he is old, that he had once been young. (Joseph Addison)

19. Age is an issue of mind over matter. If you don't mind, it doesn't matter. (Mark Twain)

20. Youth is a wonderful thing. What a crime to waste it on children. (George Bernard Shaw)

21. We do not grow absolutely, chronologically. We grow sometimes in one dimension, and not in another; unevenly. We grow partially. We are relative. We are mature in one realm, childish in another. The past, present, and future mingle and pull us backward, forward, or fix us in the present. We are made up of layers, cells, constellations. (Anais Nin)

22. What I liked most about Miu was that she didn't try to hide her age. According to Sumire, she must be thirty-eight or thirty-nine. And indeed she looked that age. With her slim, tight figure, a little makeup and she'd easily pass for late twenties. But she didn't make the effort. Miu let age naturally rise to the surface, accepted it for what it was, and made her peace with it. (Haruki Murakami)

When we get hung up on the negative aspects of old age, it can be useful to recall the positive. When we talk about health declines in old age and worry about a grey hair or two, recall the benefits that accrue from more years on the planet. Long before you personally get old, it is useful to begin questioning messages that deny older people respect, dignity, and equal opportunity or that fail to recognize positive aspects of old age. One day it will be you who is on the receiving end of those messages.

Summary

We cannot understand everything about aging through a communication lens. There is much that we need to learn from the health sciences, from psychology, sociology, economics, and anthropology, and increasingly from the discipline of gerontology, which has grown hugely in the past 40 years. Nevertheless, there are aspects to a communication perspective that are invaluable. The model and discussion in this chapter should stimulate your thinking about the messages we all send and receive about aging, and how we might change those for our individual benefit, as well as the broader benefit of society. Remember Chapter 3: Levy's work demonstrates that people who hold negative attitudes about aging die considerably younger than those who don't. So, changing your attitudes about aging isn't just about being nice to old people. It's about ensuring that you approach your own aging with the right attitude, that you appreciate the incredibly diverse opportunities available to you for your entire life span, and that you get the most out of *all* of the years of your life. Enjoy the journey . . .

Keywords and Theories

Age segregation

Anticipatory socialization

Attitudes

Cosmetics and cosmetic surgery

Health care costs

Identifications

Individual (micro) factors

Intergenerational contact

Knowledge about aging

Labor shortage

Life expectancy

Mass media

Retirement

Societal (macro) factors

Variation/diversity

Discussion Questions

- How are societal/cultural norms of aging transmitted to individuals?
- What single recommendation would you make to a 50-year-old wanting to proactively prepare for his or her own older adulthood? What steps can younger people take now to make this world a better place in which to grow old?
- What is age segregation, and why does it happen?
- What factors might play into a decision to retire from full-time work?
- Discuss the various connections in Figure 13.1. Try to come up with examples of how each area influences others, both within the broad regions of the model and between them.

Annotated Bibliography

Bernard, M., & Phillipson, C. (2004). Retirement and leisure. In J. F. Nussbaum & J. Coupland (Eds.), *Handbook of communication and aging research* (2nd ed., pp. 353–378). Mahwah, NJ: Lawrence Erlbaum. Provides in-depth coverage on retirement processes, including discussion of sex differences in career planning and retirement. Describes some of the North American and European trends in retirement in recent years, including patterns of leisure activities in retirement.

Bonnesen, J. L., & Burgess, E. O. (2004). Senior moments: The acceptability of an ageist phrase. *Journal of Aging Studies, 18,* 123–142. This study provides an example of a specific ageist phrase ("senior moment") and examines the different contexts in which it is used. While it focuses on media uses of the term, you should think about interpersonal uses in everyday talk while reading the article. The article is a nice example of how communication scientists can examine and *question* ageist communication practices.

Hagestad, G. O., & Uhlenberg, P. (2005). The social separation of old and young: A root of ageism. *Journal of Social Issues, 61,* 343–360. An article that describes some of the ways in which our society segregates and separates young and old. Provides a good introduction to a more sociological approach to aging and society.

References

AARP. (2005). *Reimagining America: AARP's blueprint for the future*. Washington, DC: Author.

Aartsen, M. J., van Tilburg, T., Smits, C. H. M., & Knipscheer, K. C. R. M. (2004). A longitudinal study of the impact of physical and cognitive decline on the personal network in old age. *Journal of Social & Personal Relationships, 21*, 249–266.

Adams, R. G. (1986). Emotional closeness and physical distance between friends: Implications for elderly women living in age-segregated and age-integrated settings. *International Journal of Aging and Human Development, 22*, 55–76.

Adelman, R. D., Greene, M. G., & Charon, R. (1987). The physician-elderly patient-companion triad in the medical encounter: The development of a conceptual framework and research agenda. *The Gerontologist, 27*, 729–734.

Adelman, R. D., Greene, M. G., & Charon, R. (1991). Issues in physician-elderly patient interaction. *Aging and Society, 11*, 127–148.

Allan, G. (1977). Sibling solidarity. *Journal of Marriage and the Family, 39*, 177–184.

Allman, J., Ragan, S. L., Newsome, C., Soufos, L., & Nussbaum, J. F. (1999). Elderly women speak about their interactions with health care providers. In H. Hamilton (Eds.), *Language and communication in old age: Multidisciplinary perspectives* (pp. 319–350). New York: Garland.

Allport, G. W. (1954). *The nature of prejudice*. Reading, MA: Addison-Wesley.

Almerico, G. M., & Fillmer, H. T. (1988). Portrayal of older characters in children's magazines. *Educational Gerontology, 14*, 15–31.

Analects of Confucius (J. Legge, Trans.). (1893). Retrieved June 2, 2006, from http://www.ishwar.com/confucianism/holy_confucian_analects/part_01.html

Anderson, K., Harwood, J., & Hummert, M. L. (2005). The grandparent-grandchild relationship: Implications for models of intergenerational communication. *Human Communication Research, 31*, 268–294.

Antonucci, T. C. (1985). Personal characteristics, social support, and social behavior. In R. H. Binstock & E. Shanas (Eds.), *Handbook of aging and social sciences* (2nd ed., pp. 94–128). New York: Van Nostrand Reinhold.

Antonucci, T. C. (2001). Social relations: An examination of social networks, social support, and sense of control. In J. E. Birren & K. W. Schaie (Eds.), *Handbook of the psychology of aging* (5th ed., pp. 427–453). San Diego, CA: Academic Press.

Antonucci, T. C., & Akiyama, H. (1995). Convoys of social relations: Family and friendships within a life span context. In R. Blieszner & V. H. Bedford (Eds.), *Handbook of aging and the family* (pp. 355–372). Westport, CT: Greenwood Press.

Arnoff, C. (1974). Old age in prime time. *Journal of Communication, 24*(4), 86–87.

Aronsson, K., Sätterlund Larsson, U., & Säljö, R. (1995). Clinical diagnosis and the joint construction of a medical voice. In I. Marková & R. M. Farr (Eds.), *Representations of health, illness and handicap* (pp. 131–144). Langhorne, PA: Harwood Academic Publishers.

Arp, D., & Arp, C. (1996). *The second half of marriage.* New York: Zondervan.

Association of American Medical Colleges. (2003, October). *Analysis in brief* [Vol. 3(2)]. Washington, DC: Author.

Atkins, T. V., Jenkins, M. C., & Perkins, M. H. (1991). Portrayal of persons in television commercials age 50 and older. *Psychology: A Journal of Human Behavior, 28,* 30–37.

Atkinson, J. L., & Ragab, S. (2004, November). *Grandparents, ghosts, or genies: Portrayals of older characters in films.* Paper presented at the annual meeting of the Gerontological Society of America, Washington, DC.

Baltes, M. M., & Wahl, H. (1996). Patterns of communication in old age: The dependence-support and independence-ignore script. *Health Communication, 8,* 217–232.

Baltes, P. B. (1987). Theoretical propositions of lifespan developmental psychology: On the dynamics between growth and decline. *Developmental Psychology, 23*(5), 611–626.

Baltes, P. B. (1997). On the incomplete architecture of human ontogeny: Selection, optimization and compensation as foundation of developmental theory. *American Psychologist, 52,* 366–380.

Baltes P. B., & Baltes, M. M. (1990). Psychological perspectives on successful aging: The model of selective optimization with compensation. In P. B. Baltes & M. M. Baltes (Eds.), *Successful aging: Perspectives from the behavioral sciences* (pp. 1–34). New York: Cambridge University Press.

Baltes, P. B., & Smith, J. (2003). New frontiers in the future of aging: From successful aging of the young old to the dilemmas of the fourth age. *Gerontology, 49,* 123–135.

Baringer, D. K., Kundrat, A. L., & Nussbaum, J. F. (2004). Instructional communication and older adults. In J. F. Nussbaum & J. Coupland (Eds.), *Handbook of communication and aging research* (2nd ed., pp. 543–562). Mahwah, NJ: Lawrence Erlbaum.

Barker, V., & Giles, H. (2003). Integrating the communicative predicament and enhancement of aging models: The case of older Native Americans. *Health Communication, 15,* 255–275.

Barusch, A. S., & Steen, P. (1996). Keepers of community in a changing world. *Generations, 20,* 49–52.

Bastida, E., & Gonzalez, G. (1993). Ethnic variations in measurement of physical health status: Implications for long-term care. In C. Barresi & D. Stull (Eds.), *Ethnic elderly in long-term care* (pp. 22–35). New York: Springer.

Baxter, L. (1990). Dialectical contradictions in relationship development. *Journal of Social and Personal Relationships, 7,* 69–88.

Beisecker, A. E. (1989). The influence of a companion on the doctor-elderly patient interaction. *Health Communication, 1,* 55–70.

Beisecker, A. E., & Beisecker, T. D. (1993). Using metaphors to characterize doctor-patient relationships: Paternalism versus consumerism. *Health Communication, 5,* 41–58.

Bell, J. (1992). In search of a discourse on aging: The elderly on television. *The Gerontologist, 32*(3), 305–311.

Bengtson, V. L., & Roberts, R. E. (1991). Intergenerational solidarity in aging families: An example of formal theory construction. *Journal of Marriage and the Family, 53,* 856–870.

Berg, C. R. (2002). *Latino images in film: Stereotypes, subversion, and resistance.* Austin: University of Texas Press.

Bernard, M., & Phillipson, C. (2004). Retirement and leisure. In J. F. Nussbaum & J. Coupland (Eds.), *Handbook of communication and aging research* (2nd ed., pp. 353–378). Mahwah, NJ: Lawrence Erlbaum.

Best and worst by numbers. (1989, July). *TV Guide, 8,* 12–13.

Bhat, A. K., & Dhruvarajan, R. (2001). Ageing in India: Drifting intergenerational relations, challenges and options. *Aging and Society, 21,* 621–640.

Bielby, D. D., & Bielby, W. T. (2001). Audience segmentation and age stratification among television writers. *Journal of Broadcasting and Electronic Media, 45,* 391–412.

Bleise, N. W. (1979). Media in the rocking chair: Media uses and functions among the elderly. In G. Gumpert & R. Cathcart (Eds.), *Inter/media: Interpersonal communication in a media world* (pp. 624–634). New York: Oxford University Press.

Blieszner, R. (2000). Close relationships in old age. In C. Hendrick S. S. Hendrick (Eds.), *Close relationships: A sourcebook* (pp. 85–96). Thousand Oaks, CA: Sage.

Blit Cohen, E., & Litwin, H. (2004). Elder participation in cyberspace: A qualitative analysis of Israeli retirees. *Journal of Aging Studies, 18,* 385–398.

Bonnesen, J. L., & Burgess, E. O. (2004). Senior moments: The acceptability of an ageist phrase. *Journal of Aging Studies, 18,* 123–142.

Braithwaite, D. O., & Eckstein, N. J. (2003). How people with disabilities communicatively manage assistance: Helping as instrumental social support. *Journal of Applied Communication Research, 31,* 1–26.

Braithwaite, V., Lynd-Stevenson, R., & Pigram, D. (1993). An empirical study of ageism: From polemics to scientific utility. *Australian Psychologist, 28,* 9–15.

Brashers, D. E., Neidig, J. L., Haas, S. M., Dobbs, L. K., Cardillo, L. W., & Russell, J. A. (2000). Communication in the management of uncertainty: The case of persons living with HIV or AIDS. *Communication Monographs, 67,* 63–84.

Briller, B. R. (2000). TV's distorted and missing images of women and the elderly. *Television Quarterly, 31,* 69–74.

Brown, P., & Levinson, S. C. (1987). *Politeness: Some universals in language use.* Cambridge, UK: Cambridge University Press.

Brown, S. L., Bulanda, J. R., & Lee, G. R. (2005). The significance of nonmarital cohabitation: Marital status and mental health benefits among middle-aged and older adults. *Journals of Gerontology, 60B,* S21–S29.

Brussoni, M. J., & Boon, S. D. (1998). Grandparental impact in young adults' relationships with their closest grandparents: The role of relationship strength and emotional closeness. *International Journal of Aging and Human Development, 46,* 267–286.

Buchanan, K., & Middleton, D. J. (1993). Discursively formulating the significance of reminiscence in later life. In N. Coupland & J. F. Nussbaum (Eds.), *Discourse and lifespan identity* (pp. 55–80). Newbury Park, CA: Sage.

Buchholz, M., & Bynum, J. E. (1982). Newspaper presentation of America's aged: A content analysis of image and role. *The Gerontologist, 22,* 83–87.

Burholt, V., & Wenger, G. C. (1998). Differences over time in older people's relationships with children and siblings. *Ageing and Society, 18,* 537–562.

Burleson, B. R., Delia, J. G., & Applegate, J. L. (1995). The socialization of person-centered communication: Parental contributions to the social-cognitive and communication skills of their children. In M. A. Fitzpatrick and A. L. Vangelisti (Eds.), *Explaining family interactions* (pp. 34–76). Thousand Oaks, CA: Sage.

Burnett, J. J. (1991). Examining the media habits of the affluent elderly. *Journal of Advertising Research, 31*(5), 33–41.

Burr, J. A., & Mutchler, J. E. (1999). Race and ethnic variation in norms of filial responsibility among older persons. *Journal of Marriage & the Family, 61*(3), 674–687.

Burton, L. M., & Bengtson, V. L. (1985). Black grandmothers: Timing and continuity of roles. In V. L. Bengtson & J. F. Robertson (Eds.), *Grandparenthood* (pp. 61–78). Beverly Hills, CA: Sage.

Caporael, L. R. (1981). The paralanguage of caregiving: Baby talk to the institutionalized aged. *Journal of Personality and Social Psychology, 40,* 876–884.

Carstensen, L. L. (1992). Social and emotional patterns in adulthood: Support for socioemotional selectivity theory. *Psychology and Aging, 7,* 331–338.

Carstensen, L. L., Gottman, J. M., & Levenson, R. W. (1995). Emotional behavior in long-term marriage. *Psychology and Aging, 10,* 140–149.

Caspari, R., & Lee, S. (2004). Older age becomes common late in human evolution. *Proceedings of the National Academy of Sciences of the United States of America, 101*(30), 10895–10900.

Cassata, M., Anderson, P., & Skill, T. (1980). The older adult in daytime serial drama. *Journal of Communication, 30,* 48–49.

Cassata, M., & Irwin, B. J. (1997). Young by day: The older person on daytime serial drama. In H. S. Noor al-Deen (Ed.), *Cross cultural communication and aging in the United States* (pp. 215–231). Mahwah, NJ: Lawrence Erlbaum.

Charness, N., & Holley, P. (2004). The new media and older adults: Usable and useful? *American Behavioral Scientist, 48,* 416–433.

Charness, N., & Schaie, K. W. (Eds.). (2003). *Impact of technology on successful aging.* New York: Springer.

Chen, Y., & King, B. E. (2002). Intra- and intergenerational communication satisfaction as a function of an individual's age and age stereotypes. *International Journal of Behavioral Development, 26,* 562–570.

Cherlin, A. J., & Furstenberg, F. F., Jr. (1986). *The new American grandparent: A place in the family, a life apart.* New York: Basic Books.

Christakis, N. A., & Allison, P. D. (2006). Mortality after the hospitalization of a spouse. *New England Journal of Medicine, 354*(7), 719–30.

Cicirelli, V. (1991). Attachment theory in old age: Protection of the attached figure. In K. Pillemer & K. McCartney (Eds.), *Parent–child relationships throughout life* (pp. 2–42). Hillsdale, NJ: Lawrence Erlbaum.

Cicirelli, V. (1993). Intergenerational communication in the mother–daughter dyad regarding caregiving decisions. In N. Coupland & J. F. Nussbaum (Eds.), *Discourse and lifespan identity* (pp. 215–236). Newbury Park, CA: Sage.

Cliggett, L. (2001). Survival strategies of the elderly in Gwembe Valley, Zambia: Gender, residence and kin networks. *Journal of Cross-Cultural Gerontology, 16,* 309–333.

Climo, J. (2001). Images of aging in virtual reality: The Internet and the community of affect. *Generations, 25,* 64–68.

Cockerham, W. C. (1997). *This aging society.* Upper Saddle River, NJ: Prentice Hall.

Cody, M. J., Dunn, D., Hoppin, S., & Wendt, P. (1999). Silver surfers: Training and evaluating Internet use among older adult learners. *Communication Education, 48,* 269–286.

Cogswell, C., & Henry, C. (1995). Grandchildren's perceptions of grandparental support in divorced and intact families. *Journal of Divorce & Remarriage, 23,* 127–150.

Cohen, G. (1994). Age-related problems in the use of proper names in communication. In M. L., Hummert, J. M. Wiemann, & J. F. Nussbaum (Eds.), *Interpersonal communication in older adulthood: Interdisciplinary perspectives* (pp. 40–57). Thousand Oaks, CA: Sage.

Cohen, G., & Faulkner, D. (1986). Memory for proper names: Age differences in retrieval. *British Journal of Developmental Psychology, 4,* 187–197.

Cole, J. I. (2003). *The UCLA Internet report: Surveying the digital future, year three.* Los Angeles, CA: UCLA Center for Communication Policy.

Colonia-Willner, R. (1998). Practical intelligence at work. Relationship between aging and cognitive efficiency among managers in a bank environment. *Psychology & Aging, 13,* 45–58.

Coupland, J. (2003). Ageist ideology and discourses of control in skincare product marketing. In J. Coupland & R. Gwyn (Eds.), *Discourse, the body, and identity* (pp. 127–150). New York: Palgrave-Macmillan.

Coupland, J., & Coupland, N. (2001). Roles, responsibilities, and alignments: Multiparty talk in geriatric care. In M. L. Hummert & J. F. Nussbaum (Eds.), *Aging, communication, and health: Linking research and practice for successful aging* (pp. 121–156). Mahwah, NJ: Lawrence Erlbaum.

Coupland, J., Coupland, N., Giles, H., & Wiemann, J. M. (1988). My life in your hands: Processes of self-disclosure in intergenerational talk. In N. Coupland (Ed.), *Styles of discourse* (pp. 201–253). London: Croom Helm.

Coupland, N., & Coupland, J. (1995). Discourse, identity, and aging. In J. F. Nussbaum & J. Coupland (Eds.), *Handbook of communication and aging research* (pp. 79–104). Mahwah, NJ: Lawrence Erlbaum.

Coupland, N., & Coupland, J. (1999). Ageing, ageism, and anti-ageism: Moral stance in geriatric medical discourse. In H. Hamilton (Ed.), *Language and communication in old age: Multidisciplinary perspectives* (pp. 177–208). New York: Garland.

Coupland, N., & Coupland, J. (2001). Language, ageing and ageism. In W. P. Robinson & H. Giles (Eds.), *The new handbook of language and social psychology* (pp. 451–468). New York: John Wiley.

Coupland, N., Coupland, J., & Giles, H. (1989). Telling age in later life: Identity and face implications. *Text, 9,* 129–151.

Creasey, G., & Koblewski, P. (1991). Adolescent grandchildren's relationships with maternal and paternal grandmothers and grandfathers. *Journal of Adolescence, 14,* 373–387.

Cuddy, A. J. C., & Fiske, S. J. (2002). Doddering but dear: Process, content and function in stereotyping of older persons. In T. D. Nelson (Ed.), *Ageism : Stereotyping and prejudice against older persons* (pp. 3–27). Cambridge, MA: MIT Press.

Czaja, S. J. (2001). Technological change and the older worker. In J. E. Birren & K. W. Schaie (Eds.), *Handbook of the psychology of aging* (5th ed., pp. 547–569). San Diego: Academic Press.

Czaja, S. J. (2006). Employment and the baby boomers: What can we expect in the future? In S. K. Whitbourne & S. L. Willis (Eds.), *The baby boomers grow up: Contemporary perspectives on midlife* (pp. 283–298). Mahwah, NJ: Lawrence Erlbaum.

Czaja, S. J., & Lee, C. C. (2001). The Internet and older adults: Design challenges and opportunities. In N. Charness, D. C. Parks, & B. A. Sabel (Eds.), *Communication, technology and aging: Opportunities and challenges for the future* (pp. 60–78). New York: Springer.

Czaja, S. J., & Lee, C. C. (2003). The impact of the internet on older adults. In N. Charness & K. W. Schaie (Eds.), *Impact of technology on successful aging* (pp. 113–133). New York: Springer.

Czaja, S. J., & Sharit, J. (1998a). Ability-performance relationships as a function of age and task experience for a data entry task. *Journal of Experimental Psychology: Applied, 4,* 332–351.

Czaja, S. J., & Sharit, J. (1998b). Age differences in attitudes toward computers. *Journals of Gerontology, 53,* 329–340.

Dannefer, D., & Perlmutter, M. (1990). Development as a multidimensional process: Individual and social constraints. *Human Development, 22,* 108–137.

Davis, L. (2002). *In black and white: A matter of gray. How media portray aging in the US and the UK, 1996–2001.* Paper presented at the world NGO forum on aging, 2002. Retrieved September 25, 2005, from http://assets.aarp.org/www.aarp.org_/build/templates/international/Media.pdf

Davis, R. H., & Westbrook, G. J. (1985). Television in the lives of the elderly: Attitudes and opinions. *Journal of Broadcasting and Electronic Media, 29,* 209–214.

Derby, S. E. (1991). Ageism in cancer care of the elderly. *Oncology Nursing Forum, 18,* 921–926.

Dickson, F. C., Christian, A., & Remmo, C. J. (2004). An exploration of the marital and family issues of the later-life adult. In A. L. Vangelisti (Ed.), *Handbook of family communication* (pp. 153–174). Mahwah, NJ: Lawrence Erlbaum.

Dillon, K. M., & Jones, B. S. (1981). Attitudes toward aging portrayed by birthday cards. *International Journal of Aging and Human Development, 13,* 79–84.

Donlon, M. M., Ashman, O., & Levy, B. R. (2005). Re-vision of older television characters: A stereotype-awareness intervention. *Journal of Social Issues, 61,* 307–319.

Downs, V. C. (1989). The grandparent-grandchild relationship. In J. F. Nussbaum (Ed.), *Lifespan communication: Normative processes* (pp. 257–281). Hillsdale, NJ: Lawrence Erlbaum.

Doyle, A. B., & Aboud, F. E. (1995). A longitudinal study of white children's racial prejudice as a social-cognitive development. *Merrill-Palmer Quarterly, 41,* 209–228.

Dreher, B. B. (2001). *Communication skills for working with elders.* New York: Springer.

Dressel, P. L., & Barnhill, S. K. (1994). Reframing gerontological thought and practice: The case of grandmothers with daughters in prison. *The Gerontologist, 34,* 685–691.

Drew, L. M., & Smith, P. K. (2002). Implications for grandparents when they lose contact with their grandchildren: Divorce, family feud, and geographical separation. *Journal of Mental Health & Aging, 8*(2), 95–119.

Eastman, J. K., & Iyer, R. (2004). The elderly's uses and attitudes towards the Internet. *Journal of Consumer Marketing, 21,* 208–220.

Edwards, H. (2001). Family caregiving, communication, and the health of care receivers. In M. L. Hummert & J. F. Nussbaum (Eds.), *Aging, communication, and health: Linking research and practice for successful aging* (pp. 203–224). Mahwah, NJ: Lawrence Erlbaum.

Edwards, H., & Noller, P. (1998). Factors influencing caregiver-care receiver communication and its impact on the well-being of older care receivers. *Journal of Social and Personal Relationships, 10,* 355–370.

Eggebeen, D. J., & Hogan, D. P. (1990). Giving between generations in American families. *Human Nature, 1,* 211–232.

Elliott, J. A. (1984). The daytime television drama portrayal of older adults. *The Gerontologist, 24*(6), 628–633.

Erber, J. T., & Prager, I. G. (2000). Age and excuses for forgetting: Self-handicapping versus damage-control strategies. *International Journal of Aging and Human Development, 50,* 201–214.

Erikson, E. H. (1968). *Identity: Youth and crisis.* New York: Norton.

Estes, C. (Ed.). (2001). *Social policy and aging: A critical perspective.* Thousand Oaks, CA: Sage.

Estes, C. L., & Binney, E. A. (1989). The biomedicalization of aging: Dangers and dilemmas. *The Gerontologist, 29,* 587–596.

Eysenbach, G., Powell, J., Kuss, O., & Sa, E. R. (2002). Empirical studies assessing the quality of health information for consumers of the World Wide Web. *Journal of the American Medical Association, 287,* 2691–2702.

Falk, U. A., & Falk, G. (2002). *Grandparents: A new look at the supporting generation.* Amherst, NY: Prometheus.

Fallowfield, L., Jenkins, V., Farewell, V., Saul, J., Duffy, A., & Eves, R. (2002). Efficacy of a Cancer Research UK communication skills training model for oncologists: A randomised controlled trial. *The Lancet, 359,* 650–656.

Fingerman, K., Chen, P.-C., Hay, E., Cichy, K. E., & Lefkowitz, E. S. (2006). Ambivalent reactions in the parent and offspring relationship. *Journal of Gerontology: Psychological Sciences, 61B,* P152–P160.

Folwell, A. L., Chung, L. C., Nussbaum, J. F., Bethea, L. S., & Grant, J. A. (1997). Differential accounts of closeness in older adult sibling relationships. *Journal of Social and Personal Relationships, 14,* 843–849.

Fox, S., & Giles, H. (1993). Accommodating intergenerational contact: A critique and theoretical model. *Journal of Aging Studies, 7,* 423–451.

Fryberg, S. A. (2003). Really? You don't look like an American Indian: Social representations and social group identities. *Dissertation Abstracts International: Section B: The Sciences and Engineering, 64*(3-B), 1549.

Gallois, C., Giles, H., Ota, H., Pierson, H. D., Ng, S. H., Lim, T. S., et al. (1999). Intergenerational communication across the Pacific Rim: The impact of filial piety. In J. C. Lasry, J. Adair, & K. Dion (Eds.), *Latest contributions to cross-cultural psychology* (pp. 192–211). Lisse, Netherlands: Swets & Zeitlinger.

Ganje, L. (2004). Elderly [Encyclopedia entry]. In C. A. Barrett & B. J. Markowitz (Eds.), *American Indian Culture* (Vol. 1, pp. 260–262). Pasadena, CA: Salem Press.

Gantz, W., Gartenberg, H., & Rainbow, C. (1980). Approaching invisibility: The portrayal of the elderly in magazine advertisements. *Journal of Communication, 30,* 56–60.

Garstka, T. A., McCallion, P., & Toseland, R. W. (2001). Using support groups to improve caregiving health. In M. L. Hummert & J. F. Nussbaum (Eds.), *Aging, communication, and health: Linking research and practice for successful aging* (pp. 75–100). Mahwah, NJ: Lawrence Erlbaum.

Gattuso, S., & Shadbolt, A. (2002). Attitudes toward aging among Pacific Islander health students in Fiji. *Educational Gerontology, 28*(2), 99–106.

General Social Survey. (2006). *General social survey* (Machine-readable data file). Retrieved January 2006 from http://www.norc.uchicago.edu/projects/gensoc.asp

Gerard, J. M., Landry-Meyer, L., & Guzell Roe, J. (2006). Grandparents raising grandchildren: The role of social support in coping with caregiving challenges. *International Journal of Aging & Human Development, 62,* 359–383.

Gerbner, G., Gross, L., Signorielli, N., & Morgan, M. (1980). Aging with television: Images on television drama and conceptions of social reality. *Journal of Communication, 30*(1), 37–48.

Giarrusso, R., Silverstein, M., & Bengtson, V. (1996, Spring). Family complexity and the grandparent role. *Generations,* 17–23.

Gibb, H., & O'Brien, B. (1990). Jokes and reassurance are not enough: Ways in which nurses relate through conversation with elderly clients. *Journal of Advanced Nursing, 15,* 1389–1401.

Giles, H. (1999). Managing dilemmas in the "silent revolution": A call to arms! *Journal of Communication, 49,* 170–182.

Giles, H., Dailey, R. M., Makoni, S., & Sarkar, J. M. (2006). *Intergenerational communication beliefs across the lifespan: Comparative data from India.* Unpublished manuscript, University of California, Santa Barbara.

Giles, H., Noels, K. A., Williams, A., Ota, H., Lim, T.-S., Ng, S. H., et al. (2003). Intergenerational communication across cultures: Young people's perceptions of conversations with family elders, non-family elders and same-age peers. *Journal of Cross-Cultural Gerontology, 18,* 1–32.

Giles, H., & Stoney, T. (2005, November). *The darkest side of intergenerational communication: Elder abuse.* Paper presented at the annual meeting of the National Communication Association, Boston, MA.

Glascock, J., & Ruggiero, T. E. (2004). Representations of class and gender on primetime Spanish language television in the United States. *Communication Quarterly, 52,* 390–402.

Glendenning, F. (2004). Education for older adults: Lifelong learning, empowerment, and social change. In J. F. Nussbaum & J. Coupland (Eds.), *Handbook of communication and aging research* (2nd ed., pp. 543–562). Mahwah, NJ: Lawrence Erlbaum.

Glenn, N. D. (1990). Quantitative research in marital quality in the 1980s: A critical review. *Journal of Marriage and the family, 52,* 818–831.

Goetting, A. (1986). The developmental tasks of siblingship over the life cycle. *Journal of Marriage and the Family, 48,* 703–714.

Goffman, E. (1967). *Interaction ritual: Essays on face-to-face behavior.* New York: Pantheon.

Gold, D. P., & Arbuckle, T. Y. (1995). A longitudinal study of off-target verbosity. *Journal of Gerontology: Psychological Sciences, 50B,* P307–P315.

Gold, D. P., Arbuckle, T. Y., & Andres, D. (1994). Verbosity in older adults. In M. L. Hummert, J. M. Wiemann, & J. F. Nussbaum (Eds.), *Interpersonal communication in older adulthood: Interdisciplinary perspectives* (pp. 107–129). Thousand Oaks, CA: Sage.

Golish, T. (2000). Changes in closeness between adult children and their parents. *Communication Reports, 13,* 79–97.

Grainger, K. (2004). Communication and the institutionalized elderly. In J. F. Nussbaum & J. Coupland (Eds.), *Handbook of communication and aging research* (2nd ed., pp. 479–498). Mahwah, NJ: Lawrence Erlbaum.

Granny lifts baby Jesus from Nativity scene. (2005, December 14). *Arizona Daily Star,* p. A2.

Gravell, R. (1988). *Communication problems in elderly people: Practical approaches to management.* London: Croom Helm.

Graves, K., & Shavings, L. (2005). Our view of dignified aging: Listening to the voices of our elders. *Journal of Native Aging and Health, 1,* 29–40.

Greenberg, B. S., Korzenny, F., & Atkin, C. K. (1980). Trends in the portrayal of the elderly. In B. S. Greenberg (Ed.), *Life on television: Content analysis of U. S. TV drama* (pp. 23–33). Norwood, NJ: Ablex.

Greene, M. G., & Adelman, R. D. (2001). Building the physician–older patient relationship. In M. L. Hummert & J. F. Nussbaum (Eds.), *Aging, communication, and health: Linking research and practice for successful aging* (pp. 101–120). Mahwah, NJ: Lawrence Erlbaum.

Gutman, G. M. (2003). Commentary: Gerotechnology and the home environment. In N. Charness & K. W. Schaie (Eds.), *Impact of technology on successful aging* (pp. 251–261). New York: Springer.

Hagestad, G. O., & Uhlenberg, P. (2005). The social separation of old and young: A root of ageism. *Journal of Social Issues, 61,* 343–360.

Hanley, P., & Webster, K. (2000). *Age in the frame: Television and the over-50s: A study of portrayal, representation, and viewing.* London: Age Concern England and the Independent Television Commission.

Hansson, R. O., & Carpenter, B. N. (1994). *Relationships in old age: Coping with the challenge of transition.* New York: Guilford.

Harris, A., & Feinberg, J. (1977). Television and aging: Is what you see what you get? *Gerontologist, 17*(5), 464–468.

Harwood, J. (1997). Viewing age: Lifespan identity and television viewing choices. *Journal of Broadcasting and Electronic Media, 41,* 203–213.

Harwood, J. (2000a). Communication media use in the grandparent–grandchild relationship. *Journal of Communication, 50*(4), 56–78.

Harwood, J. (2000b). Communicative predictors of solidarity in the grandparent–grandchild relationship. *Journal of Social and Personal Relationships, 17,* 743–766.

Harwood, J. (2004). Relational, role, and social identity as expressed in grandparents' personal web sites. *Communication Studies, 55,* 300–318.

Harwood, J., & Anderson, K. (2002). The presence and portrayal of social groups on prime-time television. *Communication Reports, 15,* 81–98.

Harwood, J., & Giles, H. (1992). "Don't make me laugh": Age representations in a humorous context. *Discourse and Society, 3,* 403–436.

Harwood, J., & Giles, H. (1994, February). *Cognitive representations of the life-span.* Presented at the annual meeting of the Western Speech Communication Association, San Jose, CA.

Harwood, J., Giles, H., McCann, R. M., Cai, D., Somera, L. P., Ng, S. H., et al. (2001). Older adults' trait ratings of three age-groups around the Pacific rim. *Journal of Cross-Cultural Gerontology, 16,* 157–171.

Harwood, J., Giles, H., Ota, H., Pierson, H. D., Gallois, C., Ng, S. H., et al. (1996). College students' trait ratings of three age groups around the Pacific Rim. *Journal of Cross-Cultural Gerontology, 11,* 307–317.

Harwood, J., Giles, H., & Ryan, E. B. (1995). Aging, communication, and intergroup theory: Social identity and intergenerational communication. In J. F. Nussbaum & J. Coupland (Eds.), *Handbook of communication and aging research* (pp. 133–159). Mahwah, NJ: Lawrence Erlbaum.

Harwood, J., Hewstone, M., Paolini, S., & Voci, A. (2005). Grandparent–grandchild contact and attitudes towards older adults: Moderator and mediator effects. *Personality and Social Psychology Bulletin, 31,* 393–406.

Harwood, J., & Lin, M.-C. (2000). Affiliation, pride, exchange, and distance: Grandparents' accounts of relationships with their college-aged grandchildren. *Journal of Communication, 50,* 31–47.

Harwood, J., Raman, P., & Hewstone, M. (2006). Communicative dynamics of age salience. *Journal of Family Communication, 6,* 181–200.

Harwood, J., & Roy, A. (1999). Portrayals of older adults in magazine advertisements in India and the United States. *Howard Journal of Communications, 10,* 269–280.

Hasher, L., & Zacks, R. T. (1988). Working memory, comprehension, and aging: A review and a new view. In G. H. Bower (Ed.), *The psychology of learning and motivation* (Vol. 22, pp. 193–226). New York: Academic Press.

Hatch, L. R., & Bulcroft, K. (2004). Does long term marriage bring less frequent disagreements? Five explanatory frameworks. *Journal of Family Issues, 25,* 465–495.

Haug, M. R., & Ory, M. G. (1987). Issues in elderly patient–provider interactions. *Research in Aging, 9,* 3–44.

Hawkes, K. (2003). Grandmothers and the evolution of human longevity. *American Journal of Human Biology, 15,* 380–400.

Hayslip, B., & Kaminski, P. L. (2005). Grandparents raising their grandchildren: A review of the literature and suggestions for practice. *The Gerontologist, 45,* 262–269.

He, W., Sengupta, M., Velkoff, V. A., & DeBarros, K. A. (2005). 65+ in the United States: 2005. Washington, DC: U.S. Department of Health and Human Services, U.S. Census Bureau.

Healey, T., & Ross, K. (2002). Growing old invisibly: Older viewers talk television. *Media, Culture, & Society, 24,* 105–120.

Hedlund, A. L. (1999). Give-and-take: Navajo grandmothers and the role of craftswomen. In M. M. Schweitzer (Ed.), *American Indian Grandmothers: Traditions and transitions* (pp. 53–78). Albuquerque: University of New Mexico Press.

Henwood, K. (1993). The discursive construction of identities within family relationships. *Journal of Ageing Studies, 7,* 303–319.

Henwood, K., Giles, H., Coupland, J., & Coupland, N. (1993). Stereotyping and affect in discourse: Interpreting the meaning of elderly painful self-disclosure. In D. M. Mackie & D. L. Hamilton (Eds.), *Affect, cognition, and stereotyping* (pp. 269–296). San Diego, CA: Academic Press.

Hilt, M. L., & Lipschultz, J. H. (2004). Elderly Americans and the Internet: E-mail, TV news, information and entertainment websites. *Educational Gerontology, 30,* 57–72.

Himes, C. L. (1994). Parental caregiving by adult women. *Research on Aging, 16,* 191–211.

Hodgson, L. G. (1995). Adult grandchildren and their grandparents: The enduring bond. In J. Hendricks (Ed.), *The ties of later life* (pp. 155–170). Amityville, NY: Baywood.

Hofstede, G. (1980). *Culture's consequences.* Newbury Park, CA: Sage.

Hofstede, G. (1984). Cultural dimensions in management and planning. *Asia Pacific Journal of Management, 1,* 81–98.

Holladay, S. J., & Coombs, W. T. (2001, November). *Media portrayals of the intergenerational battle over "grandparents' rights": An examination of the* Troxell v Granville *case.* Paper presented at the annual meeting of the National Communication Association, Atlanta.

Holladay, S. J., & Coombs, W. T. (2004). The political power of seniors. In J. F. Nussbaum and J. Coupland (Eds.), *Handbook of communication and aging research* (2nd ed., pp. 383–406). Mahwah, NJ: Lawrence Erlbaum.

Holladay, S. J., & Kerns, K. S. (1999). Do age differences matter in close and casual friendships?: A comparison of age discrepant and age peer friendships. *Communication Reports, 12,* 101–115.

Holladay, S. J., Lackovich, R., & Lee, M. (1998). (Re)constructing relationships with grandparents: A turning point analysis of granddaughters' relational development with maternal grandmothers. *International Journal of Aging and Human Development, 46,* 287–303.

Holladay, S. J., & Seipke, H. L. (2003, November). *Communication between grandparents and grandchildren in geographically dispersed relationships.* Paper presented at the annual meeting of the National Communication Association, Miami.

Hoyert, D. L., Kung, H. C., & Smith, B. L. (2005). Deaths: Preliminary data for 2003. *National Vital Statistics Reports, 53*(15). Hyattsville, MD: National Center for Health Statistics.

Hummert, M. L. (1994). Stereotypes of the elderly and patronizing speech. In M. L. Hummert, J. M. Wiemann, & J. F. Nussbaum (Eds.), *Interpersonal communication in older adulthood: Interdisciplinary theory and research* (2nd ed., pp. 162–184). Newbury Park, CA: Sage.

Hummert, M. L., Garstka, T. A., O'Brien, L. T., Greenwald, A. G., & Mellott, D. S. (2002). Using the implicit association test to measure age differences in implicit social cognitions. *Psychology and Aging, 17,* 482–495

Hummert, M. L., Garstka, T. A., Ryan, E. B., & Bonnesen, J. L. (2004). The role of age stereotypes in interpersonal communication. In J. F. Nussbaum and J. Coupland (Eds.), *Handbook of communication and aging research* (2nd ed., pp. 91–121). Mahwah, NJ: Lawrence Erlbaum.

Hummert, M. L., Garstka, T. A., Shaner, J. L., & Strahm, S. (1994). Stereotypes of the elderly held by young, middle-aged and elderly adults. *Journal of Gerontology: Psychological Sciences, 49,* 240–249.

Hummert, M. L., & Nussbaum, J. F. (2001). *Communication, aging, and health.* Mahwah, NJ: Lawrence Erlbaum.

Hummert, M. L., & Ryan, E. B. (2001). Patronizing. In W. P. Robinson & H. Giles (Eds.), *The new handbook of language and social psychology* (pp. 253–270). Chichester, England: John Wiley.

Hunt, G. G. (1997). Cleveland Free-Net Alzheimer's forum. *Generations, 21*(3), 37.

Ikels, C. (2004). The impact of housing policy on China's urban elderly. *Urban Anthropology & Studies of Cultural Systems & World Economic Development, 33,* 321–355.

Ingersoll-Dayton, B., & Saengtienchai, C. (1999). Respect for the elderly in Asia: Stability and change. *International Journal of Aging and Human Development, 48,* 113–130.

Ishikawa, H., Roter, D. L., Yamazaki, Y., & Takayama, T. (2005). Physician–elder patient–companion communication and roles of companions in Japanese geriatric encounters. *Social Science and Medicine, 60,* 2307–2320.

Jackson, D. D., & Chapleski, E. E. (2000). Not traditional, not assimilated: Elderly American Indians and the notion of "cohort." *Journal of Cross-Cultural Gerontology, 15,* 229–259.

James, L. E. (2006). Specific effects of aging on proper name retrieval: Now you see them, now you don't. *Journals of Gerontology: Psychological Sciences, 61B,* P180–P183.

Jendrek, M. P. (1993). Grandparents who parent their grandchildren: Effects on lifestyle. *Journal of Marriage and the Family, 55,* 609–621.

Kaiser Family Foundation. (2005). *E-health and the elderly: How seniors use the Internet for health information.* Menlo Park, CA: Author.

Kanayama, T. (2003). Ethnographic research on the experience of Japanese elderly people online. *New Media & Society, 5,* 267–288.

Kehl, D. G. (1985). Thalia meets Tithonus: Gerontological wit and humor in literature. *The Gerontologist, 25,* 539–544.

Kemper, S. (1994). Elderspeak: Speech accommodations to older adults. *Aging and Cognition, 1,* 17–28.

Kemper, S., & Harden, T. (1999). Experimentally disentangling what's beneficial about elderspeak from what's not. *Psychology and Aging, 14,* 656–670.

Kemper, S., Kynette, D., & Norman, S. (1992). Age differences in spoken language. In R. West & J. Sinnot (Eds.), *Everyday memory and aging* (pp. 138–154). New York: Springer-Verlag.

Kemper, S., Kynette, D., Rash, S., O'Brien, K., & Sprott, R. (1989). Lifespan changes to adults' language: Effects of memory and genre. *Applied Psycholinguistics, 10,* 49–66.

Kemper, S., & Mitzner, T. L. (2001). Language production and comprehension. In J. E. Birren & K. W. Schaie (Eds.), *Handbook of the psychology of aging* (5th ed., pp. 378–398). San Diego: Academic Press.

Kemper, S., Rash, S. R., Kynette, D., & Norman, S. (1990). Telling stories: The structure of adults' narratives. *European Journal of Cognitive Psychology, 2,* 205–228.

Kemper, S., & Sumner, A. (2001). The structure of verbal abilities in young and older adults. *Psychology and Aging, 16,* 312–322.

Kessler, E.-M., Rekoczy, K., & Staudinger, U. M. (2004). The portrayal of older people in prime time television series: The match with gerontological evidence. *Ageing and Society, 24,* 531–552.

King, V., & Elder, G. H., Jr. (1997). The legacy of grandparenting: Childhood experiences with grandparents and current involvement with grandchildren. *Journal of Marriage and the Family, 59,* 848–859.

King, V., Elder, G. H., & Conger, R. D. (2000). Church, family, and friends. In G. H. Elder & R. D. Conger (Eds.), *Children of the land: Adversity and success in rural America* (pp. 151–163). Chicago: University of Chicago Press.

King, V., Russell, S. T., & Elder, G. H. (1998). Grandparenting in family systems: An ecological perspective. In M. E. Szinovacz (Ed.), *Handbook on grandparenthood* (pp. 53–69). Westport, CT: Greenwood Press.

Kite, M. E., & Johnson, B. T. (1988). Attitudes toward older and younger adults: A meta-analysis. *Psychology and Aging, 3,* 233–244.

Kite, M. E., Stockdale, G. D., Whitley, B. E., & Johnson, B. T. (2005). Attitudes towards younger and older adults: An updated meta-analytic review. *Journal of Social Issues, 61,* 241–266.

Knox, V. J., Gekoski, W. L., & Johnson, E. A. (1986). Contact with and perceptions of the elderly. *The Gerontologist, 26,* 309–313.

Kogan, N., & Mills, M. (1992). Gender influences on age cognitions and preferences: Sociocultural or sociobiological? *Psychology and Aging, 7,* 98–106.

Kojima, H. (2000). Japan: Hyper-aging and its policy implications. In V. L. Bengtson, K.-D. Kim, G. C. Myers, & K.-S. Eun (Eds.), *Aging in East and West: Families, states and the elderly* (pp. 95–120). New York: Springer.

Korczyk, S. M. (2004). *Is early retirement ending?* Washington, DC: AARP. Retrieved May 23, 2006, from http://assets.aarp.org/rgcenter/post-import/2004_10_retire.pdf

Kornhaber, A. (1996). *Contemporary grandparenting*. Thousand Oaks, CA: Sage.

Kornhaber, A., & Woodward, K. L. (1981). *Grandparents/grandchildren: The vital connection*. Garden City, NY: Anchor Press/Doubleday.

Korzenny, F., & Neuendorf, K. (1980). Television viewing and the self concept of the elderly. *Journal of Communication, 30,* 71–80.

Krause, N. (1997). Received support, anticipated support, social class, and mortality. *Research on Aging, 19,* 387–422.

Kruk, E., & Hall, B. L. (1995). The disengagement of paternal grandparents subsequent to divorce. *Journal of Divorce and Remarriage, 23,* 131–147.

Kwak, J., & Haley, W. E. (2005). Current research findings on end-of-life decision making among racially or ethnically diverse groups. *The Gerontologist, 45,* 634–641.

Kynette, D., & Kemper, S. (1986). Aging and the loss of grammatical forms. *Language and Communication, 6,* 65–72.

Laguna, K., & Babcock, R. (1997). Computer anxiety in young and older adults: Implications for human computer interactions in older populations. *Computers in Human Behavior, 13*(3), 317–326.

Landry, L. (1999). Research into action: Recommended intervention strategies for grandparent caregivers. *Family Relations, 48*(4), 381–390.

Langer, E. J., & Rodin, J. (1976). The effects of choice and enhanced personal responsibility for the aged.: A field experiment in an institutional setting. *Journal of Personality and Social Psychology, 34,* 191–198.

Laux, L. F. (2001). Aging, communication, and interface design. In N. Charness, D. C. Parks, & B. A. Sabel (Eds.), *Communication, technology, and aging: Opportunities and challenges for the future* (pp. 153–168). New York: Springer.

Lauzen, M. M., & Dozier, D. M. (2005). Maintaining the double standard: Portrayals of age and gender in popular films. *Sex Roles, 52,* 437–446.

Leitner, M. J. (1983). The representation of aging in pop/rock music of the 1960s and '70s. *Activities, Adaptation, and Aging, 4,* 49–53.

Levenson, R. W., Carstensen, L. L., & Gottman, J. M. (1993). Long-term marriage: Age, gender, and satisfaction. *Psychology & Aging, 8,* 301–313.

Levenson, R. W., Carstensen, L. L., & Gottman, J. M. (1994). The influence of age and gender on affect, physiology, and their interrelations: A study of long-term marriage. *Journal of Personality and Social Psychology, 67,* 56–68.

Levinson, R. (1973). From Olive Oyle to Sweet Poly Purebread: Sex role stereotypes and televised cartoons. *Journal of Popular Culture, 9,* 561–572.

Levitt, S. D. (2004). Testing theories of discrimination: Evidence from "The Weakest Link." *Journal of Law and Economics, 17,* 431–452.

Levy, B., & Langer, E. (1994). Aging free from negative stereotypes: Successful memory in China and among the American deaf. *Journal of Personality and Social Psychology, 66,* 989–997.

Levy, B. R. (1996). Improving memory in old-age through implicit self-stereotyping. *Journal of Personality and Social Psychology, 71,* 1092–1107.

Levy, B. R., Slade, M. D., Kunkel, S. R., & Kasl, S. V. (2002). Longevity increased by positive self-perceptions of aging. *Journal of Personality and Social Psychology, 83,* 261–270.

Lin, C. (2001). Cultural values reflected in Chinese and American television advertising. *Journal of Advertising, 30,* 83–94.

Lin, M.-C., & Harwood, J. (2003). Predictors of grandparent–grandchild relational solidarity in Taiwan. *Journal of Social and Personal Relationships, 20,* 537–563.

Lin, M.-C., Harwood, J., & Bonnesen, J. L. (2002). Topics of conversation in the grandparent–grandchild relationship. *Journal of Language and Social Psychology, 21,* 302–323.

Lin, M.-C., Harwood, J., & Hummert, M. L. (2006). *Young adults' intergenerational communication schemas in the Taiwan and the US.* Unpublished manuscript, Kent State University.

Lin, M.-C., Hummert, M. L., & Harwood, J. (2004). Representation of age identities in on-line discourse. *Journal of Aging Studies, 18,* 261–274.

Lin, M.-C., Zhang, Y. B., & Harwood, J. (2004). Taiwanese younger adults' intergenerational communication schemas. *Journal of Cross-Cultural Gerontology, 19,* 321–342.

Liu, L.-F., & Tinker, A. (2001, August). Factors associated with nursing home entry for older people in Taiwan, Republic of China. *Journal of Interprofessional Care, 15,* 245–255.

Liu, L. L., & Park, D. C. (2003). Technology and the promise of independent living for adults: A cognitive perspective. In N. Charness & K. W. Schaie (Eds.), *Impact of technology on successful aging* (pp. 262–289). New York: Springer.

Lund, R., Avlund, K., Modvig, J., Due, P., & Holstein, B. E. (2004). Development in self rated health among older people as determinant of social relations. *Scandinavian Journal of Public Health, 32,* 419–425.

Lye, D. N. (1996). Adult child–parent relationships. *Annual Review of Sociology, 22,* 79–102.

Lyyra, T.-M., & Heikkinen, R.-L. (2006). Perceived social support and mortality in older people. *Journal of Gerontology: Social Sciences, 61B,* S147–S152.

Mancini, J., & Blieszner, R. (1989). Aging parents and adult children. *Journal of Marriage and Family, 51,* 275–290.

Mares, M. L., & Cantor, J. (1992). Elderly viewers' responses to televised portrayals of old age: Empathy and mood management versus social comparison, *Communication Research, 19,* 459–478.

Mares, M. L., & Woodard, E. (2006). Desperately seeking the elderly audience: Adult age differences in television viewing. *Journal of Broadcasting and Electronic Media.*

Markides, K. S., Martin, H. W., & Gomez, E. (1983). *Older Mexican Americans: A study in an urban barrio.* Austin: Center for Mexican American Studies, University of Texas at Austin.

Marks, R., Newman, S., & Onawola, R. (1985). Latency-aged children's views of aging. *Educational Gerontology, 11,* 89–99.

Martens, A., Greenberg, J., Schimel, J., & Landau, M. J. (2004). Ageism and death: Effects of mortality salience and perceived similarity to elders on reactions to elderly people. *Personality and Social Psychology Bulletin, 30,* 1524–1536.

Marziali, E., & Donahue, P. (2006). Caring for others: Internet video-conferencing group intervention for family caregivers of older adults with neurodegenerative disease. *The Gerontologist, 46,* 398–403.

Mastro, D., & Ortiz, M. (in press). *A content analysis of social groups in primetime Spanish language television.* Paper presented in the Mass Communication Division, International Communication Association, Dresden, Germany.

Mastro, D. E., & Stern, S. R. (2003). Representations of race in television commercials: A content analysis of prime-time advertising. *Journal of Broadcasting & Electronic Media, 47,* 638–647.

Matsumoto, Y. (in press). 'We'll be dead by then!'—*Comical self-disclosure by elderly Japanese women.* To appear in the Proceedings of the 30th Annual Meeting of the Berkeley Linguistics Society, February 2004 meeting.

Matthews, S. H. (1996). *Friendships through the life course: Oral biographies in old age.* Beverly Hills, CA: Sage.

Matthews, S. H. (2005). Reaching beyond the dyad: Research on adult siblings. In V. L. Bengtson, A. C. Acock, K. R. Allen, P. Dilworth-Anderson, & D. M. Klein (Eds.), *Sourcebook of family theory and research* (pp. 181–184). Thousand Oaks, CA: Sage.

McConatha, J. T., McConatha, D., Deaner, S., & Dermigny, R. (1995). A computer-based intervention for the education and therapy of institutionalized older adults. *Educational Gerontology, 21,* 129–138.

McGoldrick, J. P., Pearce, J., & Giordana, N. (1982). *Ethnicity and family therapy.* New York: Guilford.

McKay, V. C. (1999). Grandmothers and granddaughters in African American families: Imparting cultural tradition and womanhood between generations of women. In H. Hamilton (Eds.), *Language and communication in old age: Multidisciplinary perspectives* (pp. 351–374). New York: Garland.

McKay, V. C., & Caverly, R. S. (2004). The nature of family relationships between and within generations: Relations between grandparents, grandchildren, and siblings in later life. In J. F. Nussbaum & J. Coupland (Eds.), *Handbook of communication and aging research* (2nd ed., pp. 251–272). Mahwah, NJ: Lawrence Erlbaum.

McMellon, C., & Schiffman, L. (2002). Cybersenior empowerment: How some older individuals are taking control of their lives. *Journal of Applied Gerontology, 21,* 157–175,

Merton, R. K., & Kitt, A. (1950). *Contributions to the theory of reference group behavior.* Glencoe, IL: Free Press.

Mikkelson, A. C. (2006). Communication among peers: Adult sibling relationships. In K. Floyd & M. T. Mormon (Eds.), *Widening the family circle: New research on family communication* (pp. 21–36). Thousand Oaks, CA: Sage.

Miller, D. W., Leyell, T. S., & Mazachek, J. (2004). Stereotypes of the elderly in U.S. television commercials from the 1950s to the 1990s. *International Journal of Aging and Human Development, 58,* 315–340.

Miller-Day, M. A. (2004). *Communication among grandmothers, mothers, and adult daughters: A qualitative study of maternal relationships.* Mahwah, NJ: Lawrence Erlbaum.

Montepare, J. M., Steinberg, J., & Rosenberg, B. (1992). Characteristics of vocal communication between young adults and their parents and grandparents. *Communication Research, 19,* 479–492.

Morrell, R. W., Dailey, S. R., & Rousseau, G. K. (2003). Applying research: The NIHSeniorHealth.gov project. In N. Charness & K. W. Schaie (Eds.), *Impact of technology on successful aging* (pp. 134–161). New York: Springer.

Mundorf, N., & Brownell, W. (1990). Media preferences of older and younger adults. *The Gerontologist, 30*(5), 685–692.

Murphy, B., Schofield, H., Nankervis, J., Bloch, S., Herrman, H., & Singh, B. (1997). Women with multiple roles: The emotional impact of caring for ageing parents. *Ageing and Society, 17,* 277–291.

Musick, K. (2005). Does marriage make people happier? Marriage, cohabitation and trajectories in well-being. In V. L. Bengtson, A. C. Acock, K. R. Allen, P. Dilworth-Anderson, & D. M. Klein (Eds.), *Sourcebook of family theory and research* (pp. 103–107). Thousand Oaks, CA: Sage.

Namazi, K. H., & McClintic, M. (2003). Computer use among elderly persons in long term care facilities. *Educational Gerontology, 29,* 535–550.

Nass, C., & Steuer, J. S. (1993). Voices, boxes, and sources of messages: Computers and social actors. *Human Communication Research, 19,* 504–527.

National Center on Elder Abuse. (2004). *The 2004 survey of state adult protective services.* Retrieved June 21, 2006, from http://www.elderabusecenter.org/pdf/2-14-06%2060FACT%20SHEET.pdf

National Center for Health Statistics. (2005). *Data Warehouse on Trends in Health and Aging, Prevalence of Selected Conditions by Age and Sex: United States, 1984-1995.* NHIS (NHIC95). Retrieved June, 2005 from http://www.cdc.gov/nchs/agingact.htm

National Center for Health Statistics (2005). *Health, United States, 2005 with chartbook on trends in the health of Americans.* Centers for Disease Control: Hyattsville, MD.

Nelson, T. D. (Ed.). (2004). *Ageism: Stereotyping and prejudice against older persons.* Cambridge, MA: MIT Press.

Neussel, F. (1992). *The image of older adults in the media: An annotated bibliography.* Westport, CT: Greenwood Press.

Ng, S. H., & He, A. (2004). Code-switching in tri-generational family conversations among Chinese immigrants in New Zealand. *Journal of Language and Social Psychology, 23,* 28–48.

Noller, P., Feeney, J., & Peterson, C. C. (2001). *Personal relationships across the lifespan.* Philadelphia: Psychology Press.

Norman, S., Kemper, S., Kynette, D., Cheung, H., & Anagnopoulos, C. (1991). Syntactic complexity and adults' running memory span. *Journal of Gerontology: Psychological Sciences, 46,* 346–351.

Normann, H. K., Norberg, A., & Asplund, K. (2002). Confirmation and lucidity during conversations with a woman with severe dementia. *Journal of Advanced Nursing, 39,* 370–376.

Nussbaum, J. F. (1983). Relationship closeness of elderly interaction: Implications for life satisfaction. *The Western Journal of Speech Communication, 47,* 229–243.

Nussbaum, J. F. (1991). Communication, language, and the institutionalized elderly. *Ageing and Society, 11,* 149–166.

Nussbaum, J. F., & Bettini, L. (1994). Shared stories of the grandparent–grandchild relationship. *International Journal of Aging and Human Development, 39,* 67–80.

Nussbaum, J. F., & Coupland, J. (Eds.). (2004). *Handbook of communication and aging research* (2nd ed.). Mahwah, NJ: Lawrence Erlbaum.

Nussbaum, J. F., Hummert, M. L., Williams, A., & Harwood, J. (1996). Communication and older adults. In B. R. Burleson (Ed.), *Communication Yearbook 19* (pp. 1–48). Newbury Park, CA: Sage.

Nussbaum, J. F., Pecchioni, L. L., & Crowell, T. (2001). The older patient–health care provider relationship in a managed care environment. In M. L. Hummert & J. F. Nussbaum (Eds.), *Aging, communication, and health: Linking research and practice for successful aging* (pp. 23–42). Mahwah, NJ: Lawrence Erlbaum.

Nussbaum, J. F., Pecchioni, L. L., Robinson, J. D., & Thompson, T. L. (2000). *Communication and aging* (2nd ed.). Mahwah, NJ: Lawrence Erlbaum.

O'Connor, B. P., & Rigby, H. (1996). Perceptions of baby talk, frequency of receiving baby talk, and self-esteem among community and nursing home residents. *Psychology and Aging, 11,* 147–154.

Orange, J. B., & Ryan, E. B. (2000). Alzheimer's disease and other dementias. *Clinics in Geriatric Medicine, 16,* 153–173.

Ory, M. G., Abeles, R. P., & Lipman, P. (1992). *Aging, health, and behavior.* Newbury Park, CA: Sage.

Parameswaran, R. E. (2004). Spectacles of gender and globalization: Mapping Miss World's media event space in the news. *Communication Review, 7*(4), 371–407.

Park, D. C., Lautenschlager, G., Hedden, T., Davidson, N., Smith, A. D., & Smith, P. (2002). Models of visuospatial and verbal memory across the adult lifespan. *Psychology and Aging, 17,* 299–320.

Parrott, T. M., & Bengtson, V. L. (1999). The effects of earlier intergenerational affection, normative expectations, and family conflict on contemporary exchanges of help and support. *Research on Aging, 21,* 73–106.

Passuth, P. M., & Cook, F. L. (1985). Effects of television viewing on knowledge and attitudes about older adults: A critical reexamination. *The Gerontologist, 25,* 69–77.

Pasupathi, M., & Lockenhoff, C. E. (2002). Ageist behavior. In T. D. Nelson (Ed.), *Ageism: Stereotyping and prejudice against older persons* (pp. 201–246). Cambridge, MA: MIT Press.

Pecchioni, L. L., Ota, H., & Sparks, L. (2004). Cultural issues in communication and aging. In J. F. Nussbaum & J. Coupland (Eds.), *Handbook of communication and aging research* (2nd ed., pp. 167–213). Mahwah, NJ: Lawrence Erlbaum.

Perloff, R. M., & Krevans, J. (1987). Tracking the psychosocial predictors of older individuals' television uses. *The Journal of Psychology, 121*, 365–372.

Petersen, M. (1973). The visibility and image of old people on television. *Journalism Quarterly, 50*, 569–573.

Petrecca, L. (1999). Fox Sports baseball ads take a swing at elderly. *Advertising Age, 70*(19), 8.

Pettigrew, T. (1998). Intergroup contact theory. *Annual Review of Psychology, 49*, 65–85.

Pew Internet and American Life Project. (2001). *Wired seniors: A fervent few inspired by family ties.* Retrieved May 10, 2006, from http://www.pewinternet.org/reports.asp

Pew Internet and American Life Project. (2004). *Older Americans and the Internet.* Retrieved May 12, 2006, from http://www.pewinternet.org/reports.asp

Pew Internet and American Life Project. (2006). *Finding answers online in sickness and in health.* Retrieved May 12, 2006, from http://www.pewinternet.org/reports.asp

Phillips, L. H., MacPherson, S. E. S., & Sala, S. D. (2002). Age, cognition and emotion: The role of anatomical segregation in the frontal lobes. In J. Grafman (Ed.), *Handbook of neuropsychology* (2nd ed., Vol. 7, pp. 73–97). New York: Elsevier.

Polacca, M. (2001). American Indian and Alaska Native elderly. In L. K. Olson (Ed.), *Age through ethnic lenses: Caring for the elderly in a multicultural society* (pp. 113–122). New York: Rowman Littlefield.

Polivka, J. S. (1988). Is America aging? A message from media cartoons. *Communication and Cognition, 21*(1), 97–106.

Polyak, I. (2000). The center of attention. *American Demographics, 22*(11), 30–33.

Potter, W. J. (2004). *Theory of media literacy: A cognitive approach.* Thousand Oaks, CA: Sage.

Quinn, M. J., & Tomita, S. K. (1997). *Elder abuse and neglect: Causes, diagnosis, and intervention strategies.* New York: Springer.

Quinn, W. H. (1983). Personal and family adjustment in later life. *Journal of Marriage and the Family, 45*, 57–73.

Radecki, S. E., Kane, R. L., Solomon, D. H., Mendenhall, R. C., & Beck, J. C. (1988). Do physicians spend less time with older patients? *Journal of the American Geriatrics Society, 36*, 713–718.

Raman, P., Harwood, J., Weis, D., Anderson, J., & Miller, G. (2006). *Portrayals of age groups in U.S. and Indian magazine advertisements: A cross-cultural comparison.* Unpublished manuscript, University of Arizona.

Raphael, E. I. (1989). Grandparents: A study of their role in Hispanic families. *Physical and Occupational Therapy in Geriatrics, 6*, 31–62.

Rasulo, D., Christensen, K., & Tomassini, C. (2005). The influence of social relations on mortality in later life: A study on elderly Danish twins. *Gerontologist, 45*, 601–608.

Rawlins, W. K. (1982). Cross-sex friendship and the communicative management of sex-role expectations. *Communication Quarterly, 30*, 343–352.

Rawlins, W. K. (2004). Friendships in later life. In J. F. Nussbaum & J. Coupland (Eds.), *Handbook of communication and aging research* (2nd ed., pp. 273–304). Mahwah, NJ: Lawrence Erlbaum.

Rexroat, C., & Shehan, C. (1987). The family life cycle and spouses' time in housework. *Journal of Marriage and the Family, 49,* 737–750.

Richman, J. (1977). The foolishness and wisdom of age: Attitudes toward the elderly as reflected in jokes. *The Gerontologist, 17,* 210–219.

Riggs, K. (1996). Television use in a retirement community. *Journal of Communication, 46,* 144–156.

Riggs, K. (1998). *Mature audiences.* Piscataway, NJ: Rutgers University Press.

Roberto, K. A., & Scott, I. P. (1986). Equity consideration in the friendships of older adults. *Journal of Gerontology, 41,* 241–247.

Robin, E. P. (1977). Old age in elementary school readers. *Educational Gerontology, 2,* 275–292.

Robinson, J. D., & Skill, T. (1995a). The invisible generation: Portrayals of the elderly on prime-time television. *Communication Reports, 8*(2), 111–119.

Robinson, J. D., & Skill, T. (1995b). Media usage patterns and portrayals of the elderly. In J. F. Nussbaum & J. Coupland (Eds.), *Handbook of communication and aging research* (pp. 359–391). Mahwah, NJ: Lawrence Erlbaum.

Robinson, J. D., Skill, T., & Turner, J. W. (2004). Media usage patterns and portrayals of seniors. In J. F. Nussbaum & J. Coupland (Eds.), *Handbook of communication and aging research* (2nd ed., pp. 423–450). Mahwah, NJ: Lawrence Erlbaum.

Robinson, T., & Anderson, C. (2006). Older characters in children's animated television programs: A context analysis of their portrayal. *Journal of Broadcasting and Electronic Media, 50,* 287–304.

Robinson, T., Popvich, M., Gustafson, R., & Fraser, C. (2003). Older adults' perceptions of offensive senior stereotypes in magazine advertisements: Results of a Q-method analysis. *Educational Gerontology, 29,* 503–519.

Rodin, J., & Langer, E. J. (1977). Long-term effects of a control-relevant intervention with the institutionalized aged. *Journal of Personality and Social Psychology, 35,* 897–902.

Rodrigue, J. R., & Park, T. L. (1996). General and illness-specific adjustment to cancer: Relationship to marital status and marital quality. *Journal of Psychosomatic Research, 40,* 29–36.

Rogers, W. A., & Fisk, A. D. (2003). Technology design, usability, and aging: Human factors techniques and considerations. In N. Charness & K. W. Schaie (Eds.), *Impact of technology on successful aging* (pp. 1–14). New York: Springer.

Rollins, B. C., & Feldman, H. H. (1970). Marital satisfaction over the family life cycle. *Journal of Marriage and the Family, 32,* 20–28.

Rosenkranz, M. A., Jackson, D. C., Dalton, K. M., Dolski, I., Ryff, C. D., Singer, B. H., et al. (2003). Affective style and in vivo immune response: Neurobehavioral mechanisms. *Proceedings of the National Academy of Sciences of the United States of America, 100,* 11148–11153.

Ross, C. (1995). Reconceptualizing marital status as a continuum of attachment. *Journal of Marriage and the Family, 57,* 129–140.

Rowe, J. W., & Kahn, R. L. (1998). *Successful aging.* New York: Random House.

Roy, A., & Harwood, J. (1997). Underrepresented, positively portrayed: Older adults in television commercials. *Journal of Applied Communication Research, 25,* 39–56.

Rubin, A. M. (1986). Television, aging and information seeking. *Language & Communication, 6,* 125–137.

Ryan, E. B. (1991). Normal aging and language. In R. Lubinski (Ed.), *Dementia and communication: Clinical and research issues* (pp. 84–97). Toronto: B. C. Decker.

Ryan, E. B., Bajorek, S., Beaman, A., & Anas, A. (2005). "I just want you to know that 'them' is me": Intergroup perspectives on communication and disability. In J. Harwood & H. Giles (Eds.), *Intergroup communication: Multiple perspectives* (pp. 117–137). New York: Peter Lang.

Ryan, E. B., Bourhis, R. Y., & Knops, U. (1991). Evaluative perceptions of patronizing speech addressed to elders. *Psychology and Aging, 6,* 442–450.

Ryan, E. B., Giles, H., Bartolucci, G., & Henwood, K. (1986). Psycholinguistic and social psychological components of communication by and with the elderly. *Language and Communication, 6,* 1–24.

Ryan, E. B., Jin, Y., Anas, A. P., & Luh, J. J. (2004). Communication beliefs about youth and old age in Asia and Canada. *Journal of Cross-Cultural Gerontology, 19,* 343–360.

Ryan, E. B., Kennaley, D. E., Pratt, M. W., & Shumovich, M. A. (2000). Evaluations by staff, residents, and community seniors of patronizing speech in the nursing home: Impact of passive, assertive, or humorous responses. *Psychology and Aging, 15,* 272–285.

Ryan, E. B., Kwong See, S., Meneer, W. B., & Trovato, D. (1994). Age-based perceptions of conversational skills among younger and older adults. In M. T. Hummert, J. M. Wiemann, & J. F. Nussbaum (Eds.), *Interpersonal communication in older adulthood: Interdisciplinary perspectives* (pp. 15–39). Thousand Oaks, CA: Sage.

Ryan, E. B., Meredith, S. D., MacLean, M. J., & Orange, J. B. (1995). Changing the way we talk with elders: Promoting health using the communication enhancement model. *International Journal of Aging and Human Development, 41,* 87–105.

Ryan, E. B., Szechtman, B., & Bodkin, J. (1992). Attitudes toward younger and older adults learning to use computers. *Journal of Gerontology, 47,* P96–101.

Sabat, S. R. (1999). Facilitating conversation with an Alzheimer's disease sufferer. In H. Hamilton (Eds.), *Language and communication in old age: Multidisciplinary perspectives* (pp. 115–131). New York: Garland.

Salari, S. (2002). Invisible in aging research: Arab Americans, Middle Eastern immigrants, and Muslims in the United States. *The Gerontologist, 42,* 580–589.

Salthouse, T. A. (1988). Effects of aging on verbal abilities. In L. L. Light & D. M. Burke (Eds.), *Language, memory and aging* (pp. 17–35). New York: Cambridge University Press.

Sarkisian, C. A., Prohaska, T. R., Wong, M. D., Hirsch, S., & Mangione, C. M. (2005). The relationship between expectations for aging and physical activity among older adults. *Journal of General Internal Medicine, 20,* 911–915.

Scharlach, A. E., Fuller-Thomson, E., & Kramer, B. J. (1994). *Curriculum modules on aging and ethnicity.* Berkeley: University of California, School of Social Welfare.

Schecter, S. R., & Bayley, R. (1997). Language socialization practices and cultural identity: Case studies of Mexican-descent families in California and Texas. *TESOL Quarterly, 31,* 513–541.

Schneider, B. A., Pichora-Fuller, M. K., Kowalchuk, D., & Lamb, M. (1994). Gap detection and the precedence effect in young and old adults. *Journal of the Acoustical Society of America, 95,* 980–991.

Seefeldt, C., & Ahn, U. R. (1990). Children's attitudes toward the elderly in Korea and the United States. *International Journal of Comparative Sociology, 31,* 248–256.

Segerstrom, S. C., Taylor, S. E., & Kemeny, M. E. (1996). Causal attributions predict rate of immune decline in HIV-seropositive gay men. *Health Psychology, 15,* 485–493.

Segrin, C., & Flora, J. (2000). Poor social skills are a vulnerability factor in the development of psychosocial problems. *Human Communication Research, 26,* 489–514.

Segrin, C., & Flora, J. (2005). *Family communication.* Mahwah, NJ: Lawrence Erlbaum.

Selwyn, N., Gorard, S., Furlong, J., & Madden, L. (2003). Older adults' use of information and communications technology in everyday life. *Ageing and Society, 23,* 561–582.

Sharma, R. N. (1980). *Ancient India according to Manu.* New Delhi: Nag Publishers.

Shaver, L. D. (1997). The dilemma of Oklahoma Native American women elders: Traditional roles and sociocultural roles. In H. S. Noor Al-Deen (Ed.), *Cross-cultural communication and aging in the United States* (pp. 161–178). Mahwah, NJ: Lawrence Erlbaum.

Shenk, D., & Fullmer, E. (1996). Significant relationships among older women: Cultural and personal constructions of lesbianism. *Journal of Women and Aging, 8*(3/4), 75–90.

Signorielli, N. (2004). Aging on television: Messages relating to gender, race, and occupation in prime time. *Journal of Broadcasting and Electronic Media, 48,* 279–301.

Sillars, A. L., Burggraf, C. S., Yost, S., & Zietlow, P. H. (1992). Conversational themes and marital relationship definitions: Quantitative and qualitative investigations. *Human Communication Research, 19,* 124–154.

Sillars, A. L., & Zietlow, P. H. (1993). Investigations of marital communication and lifespan development. In N. Coupland & J. F. Nussbaum (Eds.), *Discourse and lifespan identity* (pp. 237–261). Newbury Park, CA: Sage.

Silverstein, M., & Parrott, T. M. (1997). Attitudes toward public support of the elderly: Does early involvement with grandparents moderate generational tensions? *Research on Aging, 19,* 108–132.

Slevin, K. F. (2005). Intergenerational and community responsibility: Race uplift work in the retirement activities of professional African American women. *Journal of Aging Studies, 19,* 309–326.

Snowdon, D. A., Kemper, S. J., Mortimer, J. A., Greiner, L. H., Wekstein, D. R., & Markesbery, W. R. (1996). Linguistic ability in early life and cognitive function and Alzheimer's disease in late life: Findings from the nun study. *Journal of the American Medical Association, 275,* 528–532.

Soliz, J. (in press). Communicative predictors of a shared family identity: Comparison of grandchildren's perceptions of family-of-origin grandparents and stepgrandparents. *Journal of Family Communication.*

Soliz, J., & Harwood, J. (2003). Perceptions of communication in a family relationship and the reduction of intergroup prejudice. *Journal of Applied Communication Research, 31,* 320–345.

Soliz, J., & Harwood, J. (2006). Shared family identity, age salience, and intergroup contact: Investigation of the grandparent–grandchild relationship. *Communication Monographs, 73,* 87–107.

Soliz, J., Lin, M.-C., Anderson, K., & Harwood, J. (2006). Friends and allies: Communication in grandparent–grandchild relationships. In K. Floyd & M. Mormon (Eds.), *Widening the family circle: New research on family communication* (pp. 65–79). Thousand Oaks, CA: Sage.

Steele, C. M. (1997). A threat in the air: How stereotypes shape the intellectual identities and performance of women and African Americans. *American Psychologist, 52,* 613–629.

Stern, S. R., & Mastro, D. (2004). Gender portrayals across the life span: A content analytic look at broadcast commercials. *Mass Communication and Society, 7,* 215–236.

Sternberg, R. J., & Lubart, T. I. (2001). Wisdom and creativity. In J. E. Birren & K. W. Schaie (Eds.), *Handbook of the psychology of aging* (5th ed., pp. 500–522). San Diego: Academic Press.

Sterns, A. A. (2005). Curriculum design and program to train older adults to use personal digital assistants. *The Gerontologist, 45,* 828–834.

Stine, E. L., & Wingfield, A. (1987). Process and strategy in memory for speech among younger and older adults. *Psychology and Aging, 2,* 272–279.

Stine-Morrow, E. L., Loveless, M. K., & Soederberg, L. M. (1996). Resource allocation in on-line reading by younger and older adults. *Psychology and Aging, 11,* 475–486.

Swayne, L. E., & Greco, A. J. (1987). The portrayal of older Americans in television commercials. *Journal of Advertising, 16,* 47–54.

Szinovacz, M. E. (Ed.). (1998). *Handbook on grandparenthood.* Westport, CT: Greenwood Press.

Tajfel, H., & Turner, J. C. (1986). The social identity theory of intergroup behavior. In S. Worchel & W. Austin (Eds.), *Psychology of intergroup relations* (pp. 7–24). Chicago: Nelson-Hall.

Tallis, R. (2006). To the barricades, old codgers: You're the last bastions of threatened liberty. *The Times of London,* July 31.

Thimm, C., Rademacher, U., & Kruse, L. (1998). Age stereotypes and patronizing messages: Features of age-adapted speech in technical instructions to the elderly. *Journal of Applied Communication Research, 26,* 66–82.

Thompson, L., & Walker, A. J. (1989). Gender and families in marriage, work, and parenthood. *Journal of Marriage and the Family, 52,* 845–871.

Thompson, T. L., Robinson, J. D., & Beisecker, A. E. (2004). The older patient–physician interaction. In J. F. Nussbaum & J. Coupland (Eds.), *Handbook of communication and aging research* (2nd ed., pp. 451–478). Mahwah, NJ: Lawrence Erlbaum.

Toseland, R., & Rossiter, C. (1989). Group interventions to support family caregivers: A review and analysis. *Gerontologist, 29,* 438–448.

Toseland, R., Rossiter, C., Peak, T., & Hill, P. (1990). Therapeutic processes in support groups for caregivers. *International Journal of Group Psychotherapy, 40,* 297–303.

Troxell v. Granville, 99–138 S. Ct. (2000).

Uchino, B. N., Cacioppo, J. T., & Kiecolt-Glaser, J. K. (1996). The relationship between social support and physiological processes: A review with emphasis on underlying mechanisms and implications for health. *Psychological Bulletin, 119,* 488–531.

Uhlenberg, P., & Hammill, B. G. (1998). Frequency of grandparent contact with grandchild sets: Six factors that make a difference. *The Gerontologist, 38,* 276–285.

Uhlenberg, P., & Kirby, J. B. (1998). Grandparenthood over time: Historical and demographic trends. In M. E. Szinovacz (Ed.), *Handbook on Grandparenthood* (pp. 23–39). Westport, CT: Greenwood Press.

United Nations Department of Economic and Social Affairs. (2005). *World population prospects: The 2004 Revision Population Database.* Retrieved June 3, 2005, from http://esa.un.org/unpp/

U.S. Census Bureau. (2001). *Current population survey report on computer use and ownership* (Table 2B: Presence of a Computer and the Internet at Home for People 18 Years and Over, by Selected Characteristics). Retrieved May 24, 2005, from http://www.census.gov/population/www/socdemo/computer.html

U.S. Census Bureau. (2005). *Computer and Internet use in the United States.* Washington, DC: Author.

Van der Goot, M., Beentjes, J. W. J., & van Selm, M. (2006). Older adults' television viewing from a lifespan perspective: Past research and future challenges. In C. Beck (Ed.), *Communication Yearbook 30* (pp. 431–469). Mahwah, NJ: Lawrence Erlbaum.

Vandeputte, D. D., Kemper, S., Hummert, M. L., Kemtes, K. A., Shaner, J., & Segrin, C. (1999). Social skills of older people: Conversations in same- and mixed-age dyads. *Discourse Processes, 27,* 55–79.

VanLaningham, J., Johnson, D. R., & Amato, P. (2001). Marital happiness, marital duration, and the U-shaped curve: Evidence from a five-wave panel study. *Social Forces, 78,* 1313–1341.

Vernon, J. A., Williams, J. A., Phillips, T., & Wilson, J. (1990). Media stereotyping: A comparison of the way elderly women and men are portrayed on prime-time television. *Journal of Women & Aging, 2,* 55–68.

Vidal, C. (1988). Godparenting among Hispanic Americans. *Child Welfare, 67,* 453–459.

Wahl, H., & Mollenkopf, H. (2003). Impact of everyday technology in the home environment on older adults' quality of life. In N. Charness & K. W. Schaie (Eds.), *Impact of technology on successful aging* (pp. 215–241). New York: Springer.

Waldman, D. A., & Avolio, B. J. (1986). Meta-analysis of age differences in job performance. *Journal of Applied Psychology, 71,* 33–38.

Waldron, V. R., Gitelson, R., & Kelley, D. L. (2005). Gender differences in social adaptation to a retirement community: Longitudinal changes and the role of mediated communication. *Journal of Applied Gerontology, 24,* 283–298.

Waldrop, D. P., & Weber, J. A. (2001). From grandparent to caregiver: The stress and satisfaction of raising grandchildren. *Journal of Contemporary Human Services, 82,* 461–472.

Walker, A. J., Allen, K. R., & Connidis, I. A. (2005). Theorizing and studying sibling ties in adulthood. In V. L. Bengtson, A. C. Acock, K. R. Allen, P. Dilworth-Anderson, & D. M. Klein (Eds.), *Sourcebook of family theory and research* (pp. 167–172). Thousand Oaks, CA: Sage.

Walker, A. J., Manoogian-O'Dell, M., McGraw, L. A., & White, D. L. G. (2001). *Families in later life: Connections and transitions.* Thousand Oaks, CA: Pine Forge Press.

Walker, A. J., Pratt, C. C., & Eddy, L. (1995). Informal caregiving to aging family members: A critical review. *Family Relations, 44,* 402–411.

Weishaus, S., & Field, D. (1988). A half century of marriage: Continuity or change? *Journal of Marriage and the Family, 50,* 763–774.

Whitbourne, S. K., & Dannefer, W. D. (1985). The "life drawing" as a measure of time perspective in adulthood. *International Journal of Aging & Human Development, 22*(2), 147–155.

White, H., McConnell, F., Clipp, E., Branch, L. G., Sloane, R., Pieper, C., et al. (2002). A randomized controlled trial of the psychosocial impact of providing Internet training and access to older adults. *Aging and Mental Health, 6,* 213–221.

Whitten, P., & Gregg, J. L. (2001). Telemedicine: Using telecommunication technologies to deliver health services to older adults. In M. L. Hummert & J. F. Nussbaum (Eds.), *Aging, communication, and health: Linking research and practice for successful aging* (pp. 3–22). Mahwah, NJ: Lawrence Erlbaum.

Williams, A., & Giles, H. (1996). Intergenerational conversations: Young adults' retrospective accounts. *Human Communication Research, 23,* 220–250.

Williams, A., & Guendouzi, J. (2000). Adjusting to "the home": Dialectical dilemmas and personal relationships in a retirement community. *Journal of Communication, 50,* 65–83.

Williams, A., & Harwood, J. (2004). Intergenerational communication: Intergroup, accommodation and family perspectives. In J. F. Nussbaum & J. Coupland (Eds.), *Handbook of communication and aging research* (2nd ed., pp. 115–138). Mahwah, NJ: Lawrence Erlbaum.

Williams, A., & Nussbaum, J. F. (2001). *Intergenerational communication across the lifespan.* Mahwah, NJ: Lawrence Erlbaum.

Williams, K., Kemper, S., & Hummert, M. L. (2003). Improving nursing home communication: An intervention to reduce elderspeak. *The Gerontologist, 43,* 242–246.

Williams, N., & Torrez, D. J. (1998). Grandparenthood among Hispanics. In M. E. Szinovacz (Ed.), *Handbook on Grandparenthood* (pp. 87–96). Westport, CT: Greenwood Press.

Wiscott, R., & Kopera-Frye, K. (2000). Sharing the culture: Adult grandchildren's perceptions of intergenerational relations. *International Journal of Aging & Human Development, 51*(3), 199–215.

Woodward, K. (1991). *Aging and its discontents: Freud and other fictions.* Bloomington: Indiana University Press.

Wright, K. (2000). Computer-mediated social support, older adults, and coping. *Journal of Communication, 50*(3), 100–118.

Wright, K., & Query, J. L. (2004). Online support and older adults: A theoretical examination of benefits and limitations of computer-mediated support networks for older adults and possible health outcomes. In J. F. Nussbaum & J. Coupland (Eds.), *Handbook of communication and aging research* (2nd ed., pp. 499–522). Mahwah, NJ: Lawrence Erlbaum.

Ylänne-McEwen, V., & Williams, A. (2003). *New lifestyles, new cultures, new challenges? Changing images of older people in British magazine advertisements.* Paper presented at the 4th International Symposium on Cultural Gerontology, University of Tampere, Finland.

Zhang, Y. B. (2004). Initiating factors of Chinese intergenerational conflict: Young adults' written accounts. *Journal of Cross-Cultural Gerontology, 19,* 299–319.

Zhang, Y. B., Harwood, J., & Hummert, M. L. (2005). Perceptions of conflict management styles in Chinese intergenerational dyads. *Communication Monographs, 72,* 71–91.

Zhang, Y. B., & Hummert, M. L. (2001). Harmonies and tensions in Chinese intergenerational communication. *Journal of Asian Pacific Communication, 11,* 203–230.

Index

About the Author

Jake Harwood (Ph.D., University of California, Santa Barbara) is Professor of Communication and former director of the Graduate Program in Gerontology at the University of Arizona. His research focuses on communication and aging. He is interested in the ways in which cognitive (e.g., stereotypes) and societal (e.g., mass media) representations of age groups relate to communication processes. His research draws on theories of social identity, intergroup behavior, and communication accommodation. He is the coeditor of *Intergroup Communication: Multiple Perspectives* (2005) and has published over 50 articles in professional journals. His recent publications have appeared in *Personality and Social Psychology Bulletin, Journal of Communication, Communication Monographs,* and *Human Communication Research.* He currently serves as the editor of *Human Communication Research* and is book review editor for the *Journal of Language and Social Psychology.* In 2004 he was the recipient of the National Communication Association's Giles/Nussbaum Distinguished Scholar Award for outstanding teaching, scholarship, and service to the field of communication and aging. Dr. Harwood taught at the University of Kansas before moving to the University of Arizona.